BEGINNING
IOS APPLICATION DEVELOPMENT
WITH HTML AND JAVASCRIPT®

APR   2012

BEGINNING

iOS Application Development with HTML and JavaScript®

BEGINNING

iOS Application Development
with HTML and JavaScript®

Richard Wagner

WILEY

John Wiley & Sons, Inc.

Beginning iOS Application Development with HTML and JavaScript®

Published by
John Wiley & Sons, Inc.
10475 Crosspoint Boulevard
Indianapolis, IN 46256
www.wiley.com

Copyright © 2012 by John Wiley & Sons, Inc., Indianapolis, Indiana

Published simultaneously in Canada

ISBN: 978-1-118-15900-2
ISBN: 978-1-118-22607-0 (ebk)
ISBN: 978-1-118-23751-9 (ebk)
ISBN: 978-1-118-26405-8 (ebk)

Manufactured in the United States of America

10 9 8 7 6 5 4 3 2 1

For general information on our other products and services please contact our Customer Care Department within the United States at (877) 762-2974, outside the United States at (317) 572-3993 or fax (317) 572-4002.

Wiley publishes in a variety of print and electronic formats and by print-on-demand. Some material included with standard print versions of this book may not be included in e-books or in print-on-demand. If this book refers to media such as a CD or DVD that is not included in the version you purchased, you may download this material at http://booksupport.wiley.com. For more information about Wiley products, visit www.wiley.com.

Library of Congress Control Number: 2011945668

To KimmyWags and the J-Team

ABOUT THE AUTHOR

RICHARD WAGNER is Lead Product Architect of Mobile/Web at Maark, LLC. Previously, he was the head of engineering for the Web scripting company Nombas and VP of Product Development for NetObjects, where he was the chief architect of a CNET award-winning JavaScript tool named NetObjects ScriptBuilder. He is an experienced web designer and developer and the author of several Web-related books on the underlying technologies of the iOS application platform.

CREDITS

EXECUTIVE EDITOR
Carol Long

PROJECT EDITOR
Kelly Talbot

TECHNICAL EDITOR
Michael Gilbert

PRODUCTION EDITOR
Kathleen Wisor

COPY EDITOR
Charlotte Kughen

EDITORIAL MANAGER
Mary Beth Wakefield

FREELANCER EDITORIAL MANAGER
Rosemarie Graham

ASSOCIATE DIRECTOR OF MARKETING
David Mayhew

MARKETING MANAGER
Ashley Zurcher

BUSINESS MANAGER
Amy Knies

PRODUCTION MANAGER
Tim Tate

VICE PRESIDENT AND EXECUTIVE GROUP PUBLISHER
Richard Swadley

VICE PRESIDENT AND EXECUTIVE PUBLISHER
Neil Edde

ASSOCIATE PUBLISHER
Jim Minatel

PROJECT COORDINATOR, COVER
Katie Crocker

PROOFREADER
Sheilah Ledwidge, Word One

INDEXER
Robert Swanson

COVER DESIGNER
Ryan Sneed

COVER IMAGE
© Sam Burt Photography / iStockPhoto

ACKNOWLEDGMENTS

THE IPHONE AND IPAD HAVE EMERGED as my favorite pieces of technology I have ever owned. As such, the topic of iOS application development has been a joy to write about. However, the book was also a joy because of the stellar team I had working with me on this book. First and foremost, I'd like to thank Kelly Talbot for his masterful role as project editor. He kept the project on track and running smoothly from start to finish. I'd also like to thank Michael Gilbert for his insights and ever-watchful eye that ensured technical accuracy in this book. Further, thanks also to Charlotte Kughen for her editing prowess.

CONTENTS

INTRODUCTION

THE AMAZING SUCCESS OF THE IPHONE and iPad over the past four years has proven that application developers are now smack deep in a brave new world of sophisticated, multifunctional mobile applications. No longer do applications and various media need to live in separate silos. Instead, mobile web-based applications can bring together elements of web apps, native apps, multimedia video and audio, and the mobile device.

This book covers the various aspects of developing web-based applications for iOS. Specifically, you will discover how to create a mobile application from the ground up, utilize existing open source frameworks to speed up your development times, emulate the look and feel of built-in Apple applications, capture finger touch interactions, and optimize applications for Wi-Fi and wireless networks.

WHO THIS BOOK IS FOR

This book is aimed primarily for beginning and intermediate web developers who want to build new applications for iOS or migrate existing web apps to this platform. In general, readers will find it helpful to have a working knowledge of the following technologies:

- ➤ HTML/XHTML
- ➤ CSS
- ➤ JavaScript
- ➤ Ajax

However, if you are a less experienced working with these technologies, be sure to take advantage of the early chapters at the start of the book.

WHAT THIS BOOK COVERS

This book introduces readers to the web application platform for iOS. It guides readers through the process of building new applications from scratch and migrating existing web applications to this new mobile platform. As it does so, it helps readers design a user interface that is optimized for iOS touch-screen displays and integrate their applications with iPhone services, including Phone, Mail, Google Maps, and GPS.

HOW THIS BOOK IS STRUCTURED

The chapter-level breakdown is as follows:

1. **Introducing iOS Development Using Web Technologies.** Explores the Safari development platform and walks you through different ways you can develop apps for iOS.

2. **Working with Core Technologies.** Provides an overview of some of the key technologies you'll be working with as you develop iOS web apps.

3. **The Document Object Model.** Explores how you can work with an HTML page as a tree in order to navigate and control various parts in your app.

4. **Writing Your First Hello World Application.** Guides you through the steps needed to create your first iOS app.

5. **Enabling and Optimizing Web Sites for iPhone and iPad.** Covers how to make an existing website compatible with mobile versions of Safari and then how to optimize the site for use as a full-fledged web application.

6. **Designing the iPhone UI.** Gives an overview of the key design concepts and principles you need to use when developing a highly usable interface for Safari on iPhone and iPod touch devices.

7. **Designing for iPad.** Looks at how to design UI's for the iPad and how they differ from iPhone designs.

8. **Styling with CSS.** Discusses specific Safari-specific styles that are useful for developing web apps for iOS.

9. **Programming the Interface.** Provides a code-level look at developing an iPhone and iPad web application interface.

10. **Handling Touch Interactions and Events.** The heart of an iOS device is its touch screen interface. This chapter explores how to handle touch interactions and capture JavaScript events.

11. **Special Effects and Animation.** The Safari canvas provides an ideal environment for advanced graphic techniques, including gradients and masks

12. **Integrating with iOS Services.** Discusses how a web application can integrate with core services, including Phone, Mail, Google Maps, and GPS.

13. **Packaging Apps as Bookmarks: Bookmarklets and Data URLs.** This chapter explains how you can use two little used web technologies to support limited offline support.

14. **Programming the Canvas.** The mobile version of Safari provides full support for canvas drawing and painting, opening up opportunities for developers. This chapter dives into these advanced techniques.

15. **Offline Applications.** Covers how you can use HTML 5 offline cache to create local web apps that don't need a live server connection.

16. **Building with Web App Frameworks.** Highlights the major open source iPhone web app frameworks and shows you how to be productive quickly with each of them.

17. **Bandwidth and Performance Optimizations.** Deals with the all-important issue of performance of web-based applications and what techniques developers can do to minimize constraints and maximize bandwidth and app execution performance.

18. **Debug and Deploy.** Discusses various methods of debugging Safari web applications.

19. **Preparing for Native iOS Development.** Walks you through all of the steps needed to join the Apple Developer Program and obtaining necessary credentials for publishing to the App Store.

20. **PhoneGap: Native Apps from Your HTML, CSS, and JavaScript.** How do you know when you need to move your web app to a native iPhone? This chapters explores migration strategies and shows you how you can take your Web app and wrap it inside of a native iOS shell.

21. **Submitting Your App to the App Store.** This final chapter wraps up the discussion by showing you how to take your app and submit it to the App Store for public distribution.

WHAT YOU NEED TO USE THIS BOOK

In order to work with the examples of the book, you will need:

- ➤ iPhone, iPad, or iPod touch
- ➤ Safari for Mac or Windows

The complete source code for the examples is available for download from our website at www.wrox.com.

CONVENTIONS

To help you get the most from the text and keep track of what's happening, we've used a number of conventions throughout the book.

TRY IT OUT

The *Try It Out* is an exercise you should work through, following the text in the book.

1. They usually consist of a set of steps.

2. Each step has a number.

3. Follow the steps through with your copy of the database.

How It Works

After each *Try It Out*, the code you've typed will be explained in detail.

 WARNING *Boxes with a warning icon like this one hold important, not-to-be-forgotten information that is directly relevant to the surrounding text.*

 NOTE *The pencil icon indicates notes, tips, hints, tricks, or asides to the current discussion.*

As for styles in the text:

➤ We *highlight* new terms and important words when we introduce them.

➤ We show keyboard strokes like this: Ctrl+A.

➤ We show file names, URLs, and code within the text like so: `persistence.properties`.

➤ We present code in two different ways:

```
We use a monofont type with no highlighting for most code examples.
We use bold to emphasize code that is particularly important in the present
context or to show changes from a previous code snippet.
```

SOURCE CODE

As you work through the examples in this book, you may choose either to type in all the code manually, or to use the source code files that accompany the book. All the source code used in this book is available for download at `http://www.wrox.com`. When at the site, simply locate the book's title (use the Search box or one of the title lists) and click the Download Code link on the book's detail page to obtain all the source code for the book. Code that is included on the website is highlighted by the following icon:

**Available for
download on
Wrox.com**

Listings include the filename in the title. If it is just a code snippet, you'll find the filename in a code note such as this:

Code snippet filename

 NOTE *Because many books have similar titles, you may find it easiest to search by ISBN; this book's ISBN is 978-1-118-15900-2.*

Once you download the code, just decompress it with your favorite compression tool. Alternately, you can go to the main Wrox code download page at `http://www.wrox.com/dynamic/books/download.aspx` to see the code available for this book and all other Wrox books.

ERRATA

The editors and I worked hard to ensure that the contents of this book are accurate and that there are no errors either in the text or in the code examples. However, in cases future iOS releases impact what's been said here, I recommend making a visit to `www.wrox.com` and checking out the book's

Errata link. You will be taken to a page which lists all errata that has been submitted for the book and posted by Wrox editors.

If you discover an issue that is not found on the Errata page, I would be grateful for you to let us know about it. To do so, go to www.wrox.com/contact/techsupport.shtml and provide this information in the online form. The Wrox team will double check your information and, as appropriate, post it on the Errata page as well as correct the problem in future versions of the book.

P2P.WROX.COM

For author and peer discussion, join the P2P forums at p2p.wrox.com. The forums are a web-based system for you to post messages relating to Wrox books and related technologies and interact with other readers and technology users. The forums offer a subscription feature to e-mail you topics of interest of your choosing when new posts are made to the forums. Wrox authors, editors, other industry experts, and your fellow readers are present on these forums.

At http://p2p.wrox.com, you will find a number of different forums that will help you, not only as you read this book, but also as you develop your own applications. To join the forums, just follow these steps:

1. Go to p2p.wrox.com and click the Register link.

2. Read the terms of use and click Agree.

3. Complete the required information to join, as well as any optional information you wish to provide, and click Submit.

4. You will receive an e-mail with information describing how to verify your account and complete the joining process.

 NOTE You can read messages in the forums without joining P2P, but in order to post your own messages, you must join.

Once you join, you can post new messages and respond to messages other users post. You can read messages at any time on the Web. If you would like to have new messages from a particular forum e-mailed to you, click the Subscribe to this Forum icon by the forum name in the forum listing.

For more information about how to use the Wrox P2P, be sure to read the P2P FAQs for answers to questions about how the forum software works, as well as many common questions specific to P2P and Wrox books. To read the FAQs, click the FAQ link on any P2P page.

BEGINNING

iOS Application Development with HTML and JavaScript®

PART I
Getting Started

1

Introducing iOS Development Using Web Technologies

WHAT YOU WILL LEARN IN THIS CHAPTER:

➤ Using Safari on iOS as a development environment

➤ Developing touch-oriented apps

➤ Setting up your development environment

The introduction of the iPhone, and the subsequent unveilings of the iPod touch and iPad, revolutionized the way people interacted with hand-held devices. No longer did users have to use a keypad for screen navigation or browse the Web through "dumbed down" pages. These mobile devices brought touch screen input, a revolutionary interface design, and a fully functional web browser right into the palms of people's hands.

Seeing the platform's potential, the developer community jumped on board. Although native applications may receive most of the attention, you can still create apps for iOS devices without writing a single line of Objective-C. In fact, the Safari on iOS browser provides a compelling application development platform for web developers who want to create custom apps for iOS using familiar web technologies.

DISCOVERING THE SAFARI ON IOS PLATFORM

An iOS web application runs inside the built-in Safari browser that is based on web standards, including the following:

➤ HTML/XHTML (HTML 4.01 and XHTML 1.9, XHTML mobile profile document types)

➤ CSS (CSS 2.1 and partial CSS3)

➤ JavaScript (ECMAScript 3 (ECMA 262), JavaScript 1.4)

➤ AJAX (for example, XMLHTTPRequest)

➤ SVG (Scalable Vector Graphics) 1.1

➤ HTML5 media tags

➤ Ancillary technologies (video and audio media, PDF, and so on)

Safari on iOS (which I refer to throughout the book interchangeably as *Safari* or *Safari on iOS*) becomes the platform upon which you develop applications and becomes the shell in which your apps must operate (see Figure 1-1).

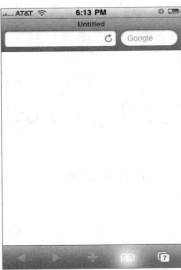

Safari is built with the same open source WebKit browser engine as Safari for OS X and Safari for Windows. However, although the Safari family of browsers is built on a common framework, you'll find it helpful to think of Safari on iOS as a close sibling to its Mac and Windows counterparts rather than as an identical twin to either of them. Safari on iOS, for example, does not provide the full extent of CSS or JavaScript functionality that its desktop counterpart does.

In addition, Safari on iOS provides only a limited number of settings that users can configure. As Figure 1-2 shows, users can turn off and on support for JavaScript, plug-ins, and a pop-up blocker. Users can also choose whether they want to always accept cookies, accept cookies only from sites they visit, or never accept cookies. A user can also manually clear the history, cookies, and cache from this screen.

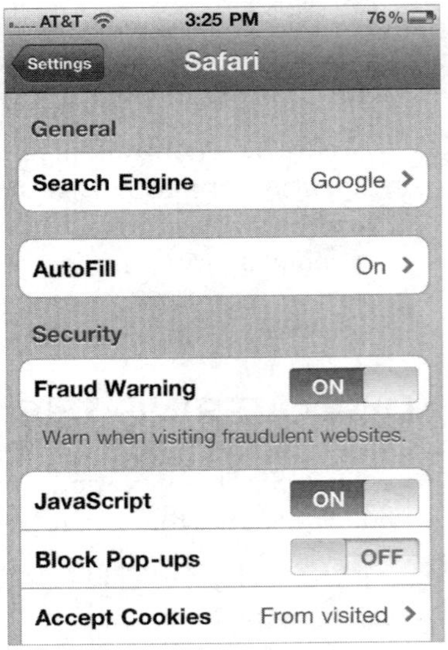

FIGURE 1-1

Quite obviously, native apps and Web apps are not identical to each other — both from developer and end-user standpoints. From a developer standpoint, the major difference is the programming language — utilizing Web technologies rather than Objective-C. However, there are also key end-user implications, including the following:

➤ **Performance:** The performance of a Safari-based web application is not going to be as responsive as a native compiled application, both because of the interpretive nature of the programming languages as well as the fact that the application operates over Wi-Fi and 3G networks. (Remember, some iPad models and all models of the iPod touch support Wi-Fi access only.) However, in spite of the technological constraints, you can perform many optimizations to achieve acceptable performance.

FIGURE 1-2

Table 1-1 shows the bandwidth performance of Wi-Fi, 3G, and the older EDGE networks.

TABLE 1-1: Network Performance

NETWORK	BANDWIDTH
Wi-Fi	54 Mbps
3G	Up to 7.2 Mbps
EDGE	70–135 Kbps, 200 Kbps burst

➤ **Launching:** Native applications are all launched from the main Home screen of the iOS device (see Figure 1-3). In the original iPhone OS release, Apple provided no way for web apps to be launched from here, which meant that web apps to be accessed from the Safari Bookmarks list. Fortunately, the most recent iOS enables users to add "Web Clip" icons for their web app (such as the Color Mail web app shown in Figure 1-4) so that they can appear on the Home screen, too.

FIGURE 1-3

FIGURE 1-4

➤ **User interface (UI):** Native iOS applications often adhere to Apple UI design guidelines. When you design a web app, you should never feel compelled to try to perfectly re-create a native-looking UI. At the same time, you should create a UI that is ideally suited for a mobile, touch device. Fortunately, using open source frameworks and standard web technologies, you can do so using a combination of HTML, CSS, and JavaScript. Figures 1-5 and 1-6 compare the UI design of a native application and a Safari-based web app.

What's more, recent upgrades to the iOS now enable you to hide all Safari browser UI elements through meta tags, so you can essentially emulate the look and feel of a native app. (See Figure 1-7.)

FIGURE 1-5

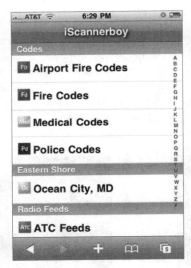

FIGURE 1-6

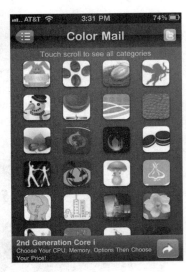

FIGURE 1-7

KEY SAFARI FEATURES FOR WEB DEVELOPERS

There are several capabilities available to web app developers with the recent releases of iOS. These are highlighted in the following list.

➤ **Geolocation:** Safari on iOS supports HTML5 geolocation capabilities, which enables JavaScript to interact with the iPhone or iPad's GPS service to retrieve the current location of the device (see Figures 1-8 and 1-9). As a result, you can create apps that can broadcast the location of a GPS-enabled iOS device.

FIGURE 1-8

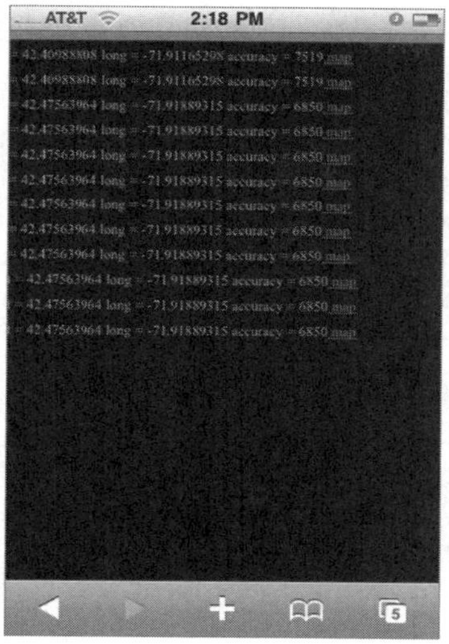

FIGURE 1-9

Google, for example, uses this capability with its Web-based Latitude service for sharing your location with your friends.

➤ **HTML5 Media Tags:** Safari on iOS supports HTML5 `video` and `audio` elements for embedding video and audio content in Web pages. These new elements eliminate the need for complicated `embed` and `object` tags for embedding multimedia elements and enable you to utilize a powerful JavaScript API. What's more, because iOS devices don't support Flash, you can use the `video` tag to embed QuickTime `.mov` files. Because Safari is the first major browser to provide full support for HTML5 media tags, you have to be careful in their usage on standard websites because other browsers may not support it yet. However, because you are creating an app specifically for iOS, you can make full use of these tags.

➤ **CSS animation and effects:** The new release of Safari supports *CSS animation*, which enables you to manipulate elements in various ways, such as scaling, rotating, fading, and skewing. Safari on iOS also supports *CSS effects*, which enable you to create gradients, masks, and reflections entirely through CSS.

➤ **SVG:** SVG (Scalable Vector Graphics) is an XML-based format for creating static and animated vector graphics. With SVG support, Safari on iOS not only provides a way to work with scalable graphics, but actually provides a technology that could replace the need for Flash to create animated media.

FOUR WAYS TO DEVELOP WEB APPS FOR IOS

A web application that you can run in any browser and an iOS web application are certainly made using the same common ingredients — HTML, CSS, JavaScript, and AJAX — but they are not identical. In fact, there are four approaches to consider when developing for iOS devices:

➤ **Level 1 — Fully compatible website or application:** The ground level approach is to develop a website or app that is "iOS friendly" and is fully compatible with the Apple mobile devices (see Figure 1-10). These sites avoid using technologies that the Apple mobile devices do not support, including Flash, Java, and other plug-ins. The basic structure of the presentation layer also maximizes use of blocks and columns to make it easy for users to navigate and zoom within the site. This basic approach does not do anything specific for iOS users, but makes sure that there are no barriers to a satisfactory browsing experience.

➤ **Level 2 — Website or application optimized for Safari on iOS:** The second level of support for iOS is to not only provide a basic level of experience for the user of Safari on iOS but also to provide an optimized user experience for users who use Safari browsers, such as utilizing some of the enhanced WebKit CSS properties supported by Safari.

➤ **Level 3 — Dedicated mobile website or application:** A third level of support is to provide a website or app tailored to the viewport dimensions of iPhone and/or iPad and provide a strong web browsing experience for all mobile device users (see Figures 1-11 and 1-12). However, although these sites are tailored for mobile viewing, they are not designed to take full advantage of iOS capabilities. And, in many cases, these are often stripped-down versions of a more complete website or application.

FIGURE 1-10

FIGURE 1-11

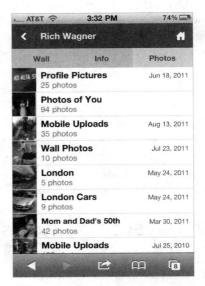

FIGURE 1-12

➤ **Level 4 — iOS web application:** The final approach is to provide a web application that is designed exclusively for iPhone and/or iPad and has a UI design that resembles a native app or one that takes full advantage of the capabilities of iOS devices (see Figure 1-13). One of the design goals is to minimize users' awareness that they are even inside of a browser environment. Moreover, a full-fledged iOS application will, as is relevant, integrate with iOS-specific services, including Phone, Mail, and Maps apps.

Therefore, as you consider your application specifications, be sure to identify which level of user experience you want to provide iOS users and design your application accordingly. In this book, I focus primarily on developing web applications optimized for iOS.

FIGURE 1-13

THE FINGER IS NOT A MOUSE

As you develop applications for iOS, one key design consideration that you need to drill into your consciousness is that *the finger is not a mouse*. On the desktop, a user can use a variety of input devices — such as an Apple Magic Mouse, a Logitech trackball, or a laptop touchpad. But, on screen, the mouse pointer for each of these pieces of hardware is always identical in shape, size, and behavior. However, on iOS, the pointing device is always going to be unique. Ballerinas, for example, probably input with tiny, thin fingers, while NFL players use big, fat input devices. Most of the rest of us will fall somewhere in between. Additionally, fingers are also not nearly as precise as mouse pointers are, making interface sizing and positioning issues very important, whether you are creating an iOS-friendly website or a full-fledged iPhone or iPad web application.

Additionally, finger input does not always correspond to a mouse input. A mouse has a left click, right click, scroll, and mouse move. In contrast, a finger has a tap, flick, drag, and pinch. However, as an application developer, you want to manage what types of gestures your application supports. Some of the gestures that are used for browsing websites (such as the double-tap zoom) are actually not something you normally want to support inside of an iOS web app. Table 1-2 displays the gestures that are supported on iOS as well as an indication as to whether this type of gesture should be supported on a website or full web application.

TABLE 1-2: Finger Gestures

GESTURE	RESULT	WEB SITE	APP
Tap	Equivalent to a mouse click	Yes	Yes
Drag	Moves around the viewport	Yes	Yes
Flick	Scrolls up and down a page or list	Yes	Yes

continues

TABLE 1-2 *(continued)*

GESTURE	RESULT	WEB SITE	APP
Double-tap	Zooms in and centers a block of content	Yes	No
Pinch open	Zooms in on content	Yes	No
Pinch close	Zooms out to display more of a page	Yes	No
Touch and hold	Displays an info bubble	Yes	No
Two-finger scroll	Scrolls up and down an `iframe` or element with CSS `overflow:auto` property	Yes	Yes

LIMITATIONS AND CONSTRAINTS

Because iPhone, iPad, and iPod touch are mobile devices, they are obviously going to have resource constraints that you need to be fully aware of as you develop applications. Table 1-3 lists the resource limitations and technical constraints. What's more, certain technologies (listed in Table 1-4) are unsupported, and you need to steer away from them when you develop for iOS devices.

TABLE 1-3: Resource Constraints

RESOURCE	LIMITATION
Downloaded text resource (HTML, CSS, JavaScript files)	10MB
JPEG images	128MB (all JPEG images over 2MB are subsampled — decoding the image to 16x fewer pixels)
PNG, GIF, and TIFF images	8MB (in other words, `width*height*4<8MB`)
Animated GIFs	Less than 2MB ensures that frame rate is maintained (over 2MB, only the first frame is displayed)
Non-streamed media files	10MB
PDF, Word, Excel documents	30MB and up (very slow)
JavaScript stack and object allocation	10MB
JavaScript execution limit	5 seconds for each top-level entry point (`catch` is called after 5 seconds in a `try`/`catch` block)
Open pages in Mobile Safari	8 pages

TABLE 1-4: Technologies Not Supported by iPhone and iPod touch

AREA	TECHNOLOGIES NOT SUPPORTED
Web technologies	Flash media (SWF and FLV), Java applets, SOAP, XSLT, and Plug-in installation
Mobile technologies	WML
File access	Local file system access
Security	Diffie-Hellman protocol, DSA keys, self-signed certificates, and custom x.509 certificates
JavaScript events	Several mouse-related events
JavaScript commands	`showModalDialog()`
Bookmark icons	`.ico` files
HTML	`Input type="file"`, tool tips
CSS	Hover styles, `position:fixed`

SETTING UP YOUR DEVELOPMENT ENVIRONMENT ON A LOCAL NETWORK

Because iOS does not allow you to access the local file system, you cannot place your application directly onto the device itself. As a result, you need to access your web application through another computer. On a live application, you obviously want to place your application on a publicly accessible Web server. However, testing is another matter. If you have a Wi-Fi network at your office or home, I recommend running a web server on your main desktop computer to use as your test server during deployment.

If you are running Mac OS X, you already have Apache web server installed on your system. To enable iOS access, go to System Preferences, Sharing Services and turn the Web Sharing option on (see Figure 1-14). When this feature is enabled, the URL for the website is shown at the bottom of the window. You use this base URL to access your web files from an iOS device.

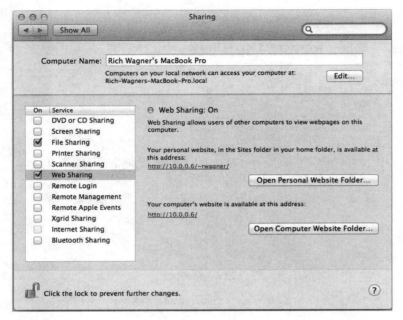

FIGURE 1-14

You can add files either in the computer's website directory (`/Library/WebServer/Documents`) or your personal website directory (`/Users/YourName/Sites`) and then access them from the URL bar on your iPhone or iPad (see Figure 1-15).

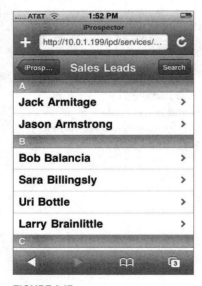

FIGURE 1-15

EXERCISES

1. What's the difference between a native iOS app and a web app?

2. Can a web app be placed on the Home screen alongside native apps?

3. Does finger input always correspond to mouse input?

Answers to the Exercises can be found in Appendix A.

▶ **WHAT YOU LEARNED IN THIS CHAPTER**

TOPIC	KEY CONCEPTS
Key Safari features for developers	Geolocation support, HTML5 media tags, CSS animation and effects, and SVG
Supporting mobile devices on your website	Level 1: Fully compatible website/application
	Level 2: Website/application optimized for Safari on iOS
	Level 3: Dedicated mobile website/application
	Level 4: iOS web application

Working with Core Technologies

WHAT YOU WILL LEARN IN THIS CHAPTER:

➤ Adding video to your app

➤ Discovering basic JavaScript coding techniques

➤ Working with functions and arrays

Although a native iPhone app is built entirely in Objective-C, an iPhone web app is composed of a variety of core technologies that serve as interlocking building blocks. HTML provides structure for the user interface and application data. CSS is used for styling and presentation. JavaScript and Ajax provide the programming logic used to power the app. And, depending on the app, it may have a back-end application server, such as Java or PHP.

Books on programming native iPhone apps often have a primer chapter on the basics of Objective-C to make sure everything is speaking the same language, so to speak. And, although it's outside the scope of this book to include a complete primer on the core web technologies you will work with to develop an iPhone web app, I do want to explore some of the key technologies you need to be sure you know about in order to be successful.

The information in this chapter is presented with the assumption that you at least know the basics of HTML and at least have a working knowledge of CSS. Most of the material covered here is about the scripting logic layer. However, first I want to highlight the HTML 5 tags that Safari on iOS supports for embedding media into your web app.

EXPLORING HTML 5 MEDIA ELEMENTS

In the early days of the iPhone, working with video inside of an iPhone web app usually consisted of a simple link to a YouTube clip, which would then launch the YouTube app. Because Safari on iOS doesn't support Flash video (.flv), there were few alternatives to an ordinary link when working with video. However, one of the key HTML 5 technologies that Safari on iOS now supports is the `video` element.

You use the `video` element to define a video clip or stream, much like an `img` tag defines an image on your page. The promise of the `video` tag is that it eliminates the complicated hoops that developers have to go through with embedded media content. Instead of mixing complicated `object` definitions and script, you can embed media with a simple tag definition.

Unfortunately for normal websites, the `video` element remains something of a tease because many desktop browsers don't yet support HTML 5. As a result, developers either have to add additional code for unsupported browsers or else avoid its use altogether.

However, if you are creating an iOS web app, you don't have this same dilemma. Safari on iOS provides full support for HTML 5. Therefore, if you need to utilize video in your app make sure to take advantage of the `video` tag.

Note that the video does not play inside of the web page as an embedded video; instead it launches the built-in iOS media player, which occupies the full screen of the device. The user then clicks the Done button to return to your app.

The basic syntax for the element is shown below:

```
<video src="../video/trailer.mov" controls="true" poster="picture.jpg"
   width="300" height="200"/>
```

TABLE 2-1: Attributes for the **video** Element

ATTRIBUTE	DESCRIPTION
autoplay	When set to `true`, the video plays as soon as it is ready to play.
controls	If `true`, the user is shown playback controls.
end	Specifies the end point to stop playing the video. If not defined, the video plays to the end.
height	Defines the height of the video player.
loopend	Defines the ending point of a loop.
loopstart	Defines the starting point of a loop.
playcount	Specifies the number of times a video clip is played. Defaults to `1`.
poster	Specifies the URL of a "poster image" to show before the video begins playing.
src	Defines the URL of the video.
start	Sets the point at which the video begins to play. If not defined, the video starts playing at the beginning.
width	Defines the width of the video player.

Supported video formats include QuickTime (`.mov`) and MPEG (`.mp4`). Note that Safari on iPhone does not support Flash media (`.flv`) and OggTheora (`.ogg`).

TRY IT OUT   Adding a Video

Adding a video into your app now becomes as easy as adding the video tag to your page.

1. Create the following HTML document in your text editor and then save the document as *BIDHJ-Ch02-Ex1.html.*

```
<!DOCTYPE html PUBLIC "-//W3C//DTD XHTML 1.0 Strict//EN"
        "http://www.w3.org/TR/xhtml1/DTD/xhtml1-strict.dtd">
<html xmlns="http://www.w3.org/1999/xhtml">
<head>
<title>Video</title>
<meta name="viewport" content="width=320; initial-scale=1.0;
  maximum-scale=1.0; user-scalable=0;"/>
<style type="text/css">

body
{
  background-color: #080808;
  margin: 10;
  color: #ffffff;
  font-family: Helvetica, sans-serif;
font-size:10px;
}

</style>

</head>
<body>
</body>
</html>
```

Code snippet BIDHJ-Ch02-Ex1.html

2. Add the following div element in the body and save your file:

```
<div style="text-align:center">
<p>Check out the new trailer for our upcoming video game release.</p>
<video src="../videos/tlr2_h.640.mov" controls="true" width="300"/>
</div>
```

Code snippet BIDHJ-Ch02-Ex1.html

How It Works

When this document loads, the poster image of the video is displayed in the rectangular area of the video element (see Figure 2-1). When the user touches the video player Safari displays the video in the built-in media player, as shown in Figure 2-2.

The audio element works in much the same way, though its attributes are a subset of the video tag's set. They include src, autobuffer, autoplay, loop, and controls. Figure 2-3 shows the audio file being played in the media player.

FIGURE 2-1

FIGURE 2-2

FIGURE 2-3

SCRIPTING JAVASCRIPT

The scripting layer of your iOS web app is often the "brains behind the operation" — the place on the client-side in which you add your programming logic. That's why as you begin to develop more and more sophisticated web apps for the iOS platform, you'll find that the technology you'll rely more and more on is JavaScript. Therefore, before you go any farther in this book, you need to have a solid grasp on how to script with JavaScript. Use this section as a primer for the core essentials of programming with JavaScript.

Syntax and Basic Rules

Like any other programming language, JavaScript has its own syntax rules and conventions. Consider the following script:

```
<script>

// Defining a variable
var message = "Hello";

// Creating a function, a module of code
function showGreeting(allow)
{
  // If allow is true, then show the message variable
  if (allow == true)
```

```
    {
      alert(message);
    }
    // Otherwise, show this message
    else
      alert("I withhold all greetings.");
}

// Call function
showGreeting(true)

</script>
```

Notice a few aspects of the JavaScript syntax:

➤ **Case sensitivity:** JavaScript is a case-sensitive language. The core language words (such as `var`, `function`, and `if` in the example) are all lowercase. JavaScript objects all use lowerCamelCase conventions, which is explained in the "JavaScript Naming Conventions" section later in this chapter. Variable names that you define can be in the case you choose, but note that the following terms are not equivalent:

```
var message = "Hello";
var MESSAGE = "Hello";
var Message = "Hello";
```

➤ **Whitespace:** Just like HTML, JavaScript ignores spaces, tabs, and new lines in code statements. Each of the following are equivalent:

```
var message="Hello";
var message = "Hello";
```

These are as well:

```
if (allow==true)
if ( allow == true )
```

➤ **Semicolons:** Each JavaScript statement ends with a semicolon (except for the descriptive comments lines).

➤ **Curly brackets:** Some JavaScript control structures, such as functions and `if` statements, use curly brackets (`{}`) to contain multiple statements between them. You can place these brackets on separate lines or on the same line as the other code. For example:

```
if (allow == true) {
  alert(message) }
```

is the same as:

```
if (allow == true)
{
  alert(message)
}
```

Variables

A *variable* is an alias that stores another piece of data — a text string, a number, a true or false value, or whatever. Variables are core to programming because they eliminate the need for having everything known while you are developing the script or application.

For example, suppose you want to capture the first name of the user and add it to a welcome message that appears when the user returns to your iOSWeb app. Without variables, you'd have to know the person's name beforehand — which is, of course, impossible — or you'd have to use a generic name for everyone.

By using a variable, you eliminate this problem. You can capture the name of the user and then store it in the code as a variable, such as `firstName`. Any time in my script in which I need to work with the user's name, I call `firstName`.

Declaring and Assigning Variables

When you want to use a variable, your first task is to declare it with the keyword `var` and then assign it a value. Here's how this two-step process can look:

```
var firstName;
firstName = "Jonah";
```

The `var` keyword instructs the JavaScript interpreter to treat the following word, `firstName` in this case, as a variable. The following line then assigns the literal string `Jonah` to the `firstName` variable.

While declaring and assigning a variable may be two separate actions, you usually want to combine these into one single step. For example, the following code is functionally equivalent to the preceding two lines of code:

```
var firstName = "Jonah";
```

Truth be told, you can actually assign a variable without even using the keyword `var`. For example, the following code still works:

```
firstName = "Jonah";
```

However, I strongly recommend regular use of `var` when you first define it to ensure your code is readable and manageable by both you and other developers.

Hanging Loose with Variable Types

You can assign a variety of data types to a variable. Here are a few examples:

```
// String value
var state = "CO";
// Boolean value
var showForm = true;
// Number value
var maxWidth = 300;
// HTML document "node"
```

```
var element = document.getElementById("container");
// Array item
var item = myArray[0];
```

If you are coming from a Java, ActionScript, or other stronger typed language, you are probably wondering where you declare the type of data that can be stored by the variable. Well, to put it simply, you don't have to. Because JavaScript is a loosely typed language, you do not need to declare the variable type.

Naming Variables

When you are naming variables, keep in mind the following general rules:

➤ A variable name must begin with a letter or underscore, not a number or other special character. For example:

```
// Valid
var helper;
var _helper;

// Invalid
var 2helper;
var ^helper;
```

➤ Although a number can't start off a variable name, you can include one elsewhere in the word, such as the following:

```
var doc1;
var doc2;
```

➤ As with other aspects of JavaScript, variable names are case sensitive. Therefore, each of the following are unique variable names:

```
var counter;
var Counter;
var COUNTER;
var counTer;
```

➤ A variable name can't contain spaces. For example:

```
// Valid
var streetAddress;
var street_address;

//Invalid
var street address;
```

➤ You can't use any reserved word (see the "Reserved Words" section later in the chapter) as a variable name. For example:

```
// Valid
var isDone;
var defaultValue;
```

```
var mainWindow;

// Invalid
var is;
var default;
var window;
```

Accessing a Variable

After you define a variable and assign it a value, each time you reference it in your code, the variable represents the value that was last assigned to it. In the following snippet of code, the company variable is assigned a string value and displayed in an alert box:

```
var company = "Cyberg Coffee";
alert( "Our company is proudly named " + company);
```

The alert box displays the following:

```
Our company is proudly named Cyberg Coffee.
```

You can also change the value of a variable inside your source code. After all, they are called variables, aren't they? A typical example is a counter variable that has a value that is incremented during a looping process. Consider the following example:

```
for (var i=1;i<=5;i++)
{
   document.write( "The value of the variable is: " + i + ".<br/>" );
}
```

I explain what the for loop does later in the chapter. For now, just focus on the variable named i. The variable starts out with a value of 1 during the execution of the first pass of the code inside of the for block. During the next pass, its value is incremented to 2. On the third pass, its value is incremented to 3. This same process continues until i is 5. In total, the document.write() method is called five times and outputs the following content:

```
The value of the variable is 1.
The value of the variable is 2.
The value of the variable is 3.
The value of the variable is 4.
The value of the variable is 5.
```

Scope

Variables can either have a limited or wide scope. If you define a variable inside of a function then that variable (called a *local variable*) is only available to the function itself and expires when the function is done processing. For example, check out the markup variable in the following code:

```
function boldText(textToDisplay)
{
   var markup = "<strong>" + textToDisplay + "</strong>";
   return markup;
}
```

The variable is created when the `boldText()` function runs, but it no longer exists after the function ends.

However, if you define the variable at the top level of the scripting block — in other words, outside of a function — then that variable (known as a *global variable*) is accessible from anywhere in the document. What's more, the lifetime of a global variable persists until the document itself is closed.

Table 2-2 summarizes the differences between local and global variables.

TABLE 2-2: Local Versus Global Variables

TYPE	SCOPE	LIFETIME
Local	Accessible only inside of a function	Exists until the function ends
Global	Accessible from anywhere in the document	Exists until the document itself closes

Scope deals with the context of the variable within the scripting hierarchy. However, the location at which a variable is defined also matters. Simply put, a variable is accessible after it is declared. Therefore, you typically want to define global variables at or near the top of the script and local variables at or near the top of the function.

I've put together a sample script that demonstrates the scope of variables. First, I define a global variable at the top of a script:

```
<script type="text/javascript">
var msg = "I am a global variable";
var msgEnd = ", and you cannot stop me."
```

Next, I add an alert box to display the variable:

```
alert(msg + msgEnd);
```

When this code runs, the alert message text that appears is:

```
I am a global variable, and you cannot stop me.
```

Now, check out what I do. I create a function that assigns a local variable with the same name (`msg`) and then simply references `msgEnd`, the global variable I already defined. Here's the code:

```
function displayAltMessage()
{
  var msg = "Don't hassle me, I'm a local variable';
  alert(msg + msgEnd);
}
```

I call this function in my script with the following line:

```
displayAltMessage();
```

When this function is executed the alert box displays the following text:

```
Don't hassle me, I'm a local variable, and you cannot stop me.
```

Notice that the local variable msg took precedence over the global variable msg. However, after that function finishes, the local variable msg is destroyed whereas the global variable msg remains.

Now suppose I reassign the value of the global variable msg later in my script and then display the alert box once again:

```
msg = "Reassigning now!";
alert(msg);
```

Yes, you've got it, the following text is displayed:

```
Reassigning now!
```

Notice that when I reassigned the variable, I did not need to add the var keyword again.

Here's the full script:

```
<script type="text/javascript">
  // Global variable
  var msg = "I am a global variable";
  var msgEnd = ", and you cannot stop me."

  // Displays "I am a global variable, and you cannot stop me."
  alert(msg + msgEnd);
function displayAltMessage()
  {
    // Local variable
    var msg = "Don't hassle me, I'm a local variable';
    // Displays "Don't hassle me, I'm a local variable, and you cannot stop me."
    alert(msg + msgEnd);
  }
  // Calls the function
  displayAltMessage();

  // Reassigning value to msg
  msg = "Reassigning now!";

  // Displays "Reassigning now!"
  alert(msg);
</script>
```

JavaScript Naming Conventions

Like other languages such as Java or ActionScript, JavaScript uses CamelCase conventions for naming parts of the language. Variables, properties, and methods use what is known as *lowerCamelCase*. When using lowerCamelCase convention, the name begins with a lowercase letter and the first letter of each subsequent new word in a compound word is uppercase with all other letters lowercase. You'll find that JavaScript and the DOM adhere to this convention. For example:

```
var divElements = document.getElementsByTagName("div");
```

In this example, `document` is the DOM object name for the HTML document and is all in lowercase. The method `getElementsByTagName()` is a compound word, so that the first letter of the additional words in the method are capitalized. My variable `divElements` uses lowerCamelCase style to make it clear that the term combines two words.

Another type of coding convention that some JavaScript developers follow is known as *Hungarian notation*. Following this coding style, variables are prefixed with a letter that indicates the data type of the variable. Table 2-3 shows several examples of this notation.

TABLE 2-3: Using Hungarian Notation with Your Variables

DATA/OBJECT TYPE	PREFIX	EXAMPLE
String	s	sFirstName
Number	n	nRating
Boolean	b	bFlag
Array	a	aMembers
Object (DOM elements, user objects, and so on)	o	oCustomer
Date	d	dTransactionDate

Working with Constants

As you work with variables, they often change values during the course of a script. However, there are other occasions in which you want to work with a variable that refers to a value that doesn't change. These are called *constants*.

ActionScript, Java, and many other programming languages actually have a constant built into the language that is different than a variable. JavaScript does not. However, from a practical standpoint, you can define a variable and treat it as a constant in your code.

If you do, I recommend following standard conventions for naming constants:

➤ Use uppercase letters

➤ Separate words with underscores

For example:

```
var APP_TITLE = "iOSWebApp";
var VERSION_NUM = "2.01";
var MAX_WIDTH = 320;
```

You can then use these constant-looking variables just as you would a variable throughout your script.

Operators

An operator is a no-frills symbol used to assign values, compare values, manipulate expressions, or connect pieces of code together.

The equal sign is perhaps the most common operator and you use it to assign a value to an expression. For example:

```
var i = 10;
```

Note that the operator you use to assign a value (=) is different than the operator you use to compare whether two values are equal. The == operator is charged with comparing two items and returning true if conditions are true. For example:

```
alert(n == 100);
```

As you may expect, you can use the + operator to add two number values together. However, you can also use it to combine two string literals or variables together. So, check out this code:

```
var s = "Welcome ";
var t = " to the world of operators.";
alert(s + t);
```

The text Welcome to the world of operators is displayed in a JavaScript alert box.

Tables 2-4 through 2-7 highlight the major operators. Some of the operators are pretty esoteric in most real-world situations, so the ones you typically use are shown in bold.

TABLE 2-4: Assignment Operators

OPERATOR	EXAMPLE	DESCRIPTION
=	x=y	The value of y is assigned to x
+=	x+=y	Same as x=x+y
-=	x-=y	Same as x=x-y
*=	x*=y	Same as x=x*y
/=	x/=y	Same as x=x/y
%=	x%=y	Same as x=x%y (modulus, division remainder)

TABLE 2-5: Comparison Operators

OPERATOR	EXAMPLE	DESCRIPTION
==	x==y	x is equal to y
!=	x!=y	x is not equal to y

OPERATOR	EXAMPLE	DESCRIPTION
===	x===y	Evaluates both for value and data type (for example, if x = "5" and y = 5, then x==y is true, but x===y is false)
<	x<y	x is less than y
<=	x<=y	x is less than or equal to y
>	x>y	x is greater than y
>=	x>=y	x is greater than or equal to y
?:	x=(y<5) ? -5 : y	If y is less than 5 then assign -5 to x; otherwise, assign y to x (known as the Conditional operator)

TABLE 2-6: Logical Operators

OPERATOR	EXAMPLE	DESCRIPTION
&&	if (x > 3 && y=0)	logical and
||	if (x>3 || y=0)	logical or
!	if !(x=y)	not

TABLE 2-7: Mathematical operators

OPERATOR	EXAMPLE	DESCRIPTION
+	x+2	Addition
-	x-3	Subtraction
*	x*2	Multiplication
/	x/2	Division
%	x%2	Modulus (division remainder)
++	x++	Increment (same as x=x+1)
--	x--	Decrement (same as x=x-1)

Reserved Words

JavaScript has a set of reserved words (see Table 2-8) that are set aside for use with the language. As a result, avoid using these words when you name variables, functions, or objects.

TABLE 2-8: JavaScript Reserved Words

abstract	boolean	break	byte	case
catch	char	class	const	continue
debugger	default	delete	do	double
else	enum	export	extends	false
final	finally	float	for	function
goto	if	implements	import	in
instanceof	int	interface	long	native
new	null	package	private	protected
public	return	short	static	super
switch	synchronized	this	throw	throws
transient	true	try	typeof	var
void	volatile	while	with	

Basic Conditional Expressions

JavaScript has three conditional statements that you can use to evaluate code:

➤ if

➤ if/else

➤ switch

These three statements are explained in the following sections.

if Statements

The if statement is used when you want to evaluate a variable and expression and then perform an action depending on the evaluation. The basic structure looks like the following:

```
if (condition)
{
// code to execute if condition is true
}
```

For example:

```
response = prompt("Enter the name of the customer.", "");
if (response == "Jerry Monroe")
{
alert("Yes!");
}
```

A prompt box is displayed to the user. The typed response of the user is assigned to the `response` variable. The `if` statement then evaluates whether `response` is equal to "Jerry Monroe." If so, then the alert box is displayed. Otherwise, `if` block is ignored.

I mentioned this in the operator section earlier in the chapter, but it bears repeating. The double equal signs are not a typo. A single equal sign (=) is used to assign a value to a variable whereas a double equals sign (==) compares one side of an expression with another.

If you are evaluating a Boolean variable, you write the `if` statements in two ways:

```
if (isValid == true)
{
  alert("Yes, it is valid!");
}
```

or, as a shortcut:

```
if (isValid)
{
  alert("Yes, it is valid!");
}
```

If you have a single line of code in the `if` block, you can actually forgo the curly brackets. So, the following syntax works, too:

```
if (isValid == true) alert("Yes, it is valid!");
```

You can also use `if` on a negative expression. Suppose, for example, that you want to perform an operation if a Boolean variable named `isValid` is `false`. The code would look something like this:

```
if (isValid == false)
{
  // do something to get validation
}
```

Notice that even though the `false` value is being used to evaluate the variable, the `if` block only executes if the expression (isValid == false) is true.

An alternative and usually preferred way to write this expression is to use the not operator (!):

```
if (!isValid)
{
  // do something to get validation
}
```

This expression says, in effect, *if isValid is not true, then do something . . .*

if/else Statements

The if/else statement extends the if statement so that you can also execute a specific block of code if the expression evaluates to true and a separate block if it is false. The basic structure is the following:

```
if (condition)
{
// code to execute if condition is true
}
else
{
// code to execute if condition is false
}
```

Here's an example of the if/else statement:

```
if (showName)
{
  document.write("My name is Sonny Madison.")
}
else
{
  document.write("I cannot disclose my name.");
}
```

Chaining if and if/else

You can also chain together if and if/else statements. Consider this scenario:

```
if (state = "MA")
{
  document.write("You live in Massachusetts.");
}
else if (state="CA")
{
  document.write("You live in California.");
}
else
{
  document.write("I have no idea where you live.");
}
```

switch Statements

Besides chaining the if and if/else statements, you can use the switch statement to evaluate multiple values. Its basic structure is like this:

```
switch (expression)
{
case label1:
  // code to be executed if expression equals label1
```

```
  break;
case label2:
  //code to be executed if expression equals label2
  break;
case label3 :
  //code to be executed if expression equals label3
  break;
default:
  // code to be executed if expression is different
  // from both label1, label2, and label3
}
```

The switch statement evaluates the expression to see if the result matches the first case value. If so, then the code inside of the first case statement is executed. Note break at the end of each of the case statements. It stops the switch statement from continuing to evaluate more of the case statements that follow. The default statement is executed if no matches are found.

Note that the case blocks do not use curly braces inside them.

Here's an example that uses the switch statement to evaluate the current time of day using the built-in Date() object:

```
var d = new Date()
var hrs = d.getHours()

switch (hrs)
{
case 7 :
  document.write( "Good morning." );
  break;
case 12 :
  document.write( "It must be time for lunch." );
  break;
case 15 :
  document.write( "Afternoon siesta. Zzzzz." );
  break;
case 23 :
  document.write( "Bed time. Boo!" );
  break;
default
  document.write( "Check back later." );
}
```

The hrs variable is assigned the current hour using the Date,getHours() method. The switch statement evaluates hrs, examining whether this value matches the case statements in sequence. If it finds a match then the code inside of the case is executed. Otherwise, the default statement is executed.

Loops

A common need that you will have in developing scripts in your iOS Web apps is the ability to perform a given task several times or on a series of objects. Or you might find you need to execute code until a condition changes. JavaScript provides two programming constructs for these purposes: for and while blocks. A for loop cycles through a block of code *x* number of times. A while loop executes a block of code as long as a specific condition is true.

for Loops

Along with the if statement, the for loop is likely the construct you'll use most often. The following snippet shows a for loop calling document.write() five times:

```
for (var i=1;i<=5;i++)
{
  document.write("Number:" i + "<br/>");
}
```

When run, the output is the following:

```
Number 1
Number 2
Number 3
Number 4
Number 5
```

Going back to the code, notice the three parts of the for statement inside of the parentheses:

> **Initialize variable:** The var i=1 initializes the variable used in the count. (The variable i is the typical name you see used for most loop counters.)

> **Looping condition:** The i<=10 indicates the condition that is evaluated each time the loop is cycled through. The condition returns true as long as the i value is less than or equal to 10.

> **Update:** The i++ statement is called after a pass of the loop completes. The ++ is the operator used to increment the value of i by 1.

while and do/while Loops

A while loop also cycles through a block of code one or more times. However, it continues as long as the expression evaluates to true. Here's the basic form:

```
while(expression)
{
  // statements
}
```

Here's an example:

```
var max = 100;
while(num>max)
{
document.write("Current count: " + num);
num++;
}
```

In this example, the code block loops as long as num is less than 100. However, suppose that num has the value of 101; the while code block is never executed.

The do/while loop is similar except that the condition evaluates at the end of the loop instead of at the start. Here's the basic structure:

```
do
{
    // statement
} while (expression)
```

In real-world practice, while loops are used more often than do/while loops.

Comments

As in HTML or other languages, you can add your own comments to your JavaScript code. Comments are useful for you personally when you go back into the code weeks or months later and need to understand your code and the thought process behind it. You also might use comments to note specific places in the code that you need to rework later.

You can add single-line or multiline comments.

Single-line Comments

To add a single-line comment, add two slashes (//) to a line. Any text on the same line to the right of the slashes is considered a comment and is ignored by the interpreter. For example:

```
// Define two string variables
var s = "Welcome ";
var t = " to the world of operators.";
// Display concatenated values in an alert box
alert(s + t);
```

Multiline Comments

You can also define a comment that spans multiple lines. To do so, enclose the comments inside /* and */ marks. Here's what a multiline comment looks like:

```
/*
 * Purpose: Converts Internet string date into Date object
 * RICH TO DO: Double-check that this works under all cases
 */
function getDateFromString(s)
{
  s = s.replace(/-/g, "/");
  s = s.replace("T", " ");
  s = s.replace("Z", " GMT-0000");
  return new Date(Date.parse(s));
}
```

Using JSDoc Comments

The Java world has a documentation generator called Javadoc, which is a tool that can generate HTML-based documentation from the comments a developer adds to the source code. JSDocToolkit is an open-source tool written in Perl that provides similar functionality.

You can download JSDoc at `http://code.google.com/p/jsdoc-toolkit/`.

To enable a script for JSDoc Toolkit, simply denote the comments you wanted to be included using a multiline comment, but use the following special syntax: Open the comment with a slash and two asterisks (`/**`) and close the comment the normal way (`*/`). Here's an example:

```
/**
 * Converts Internet string date into Date object
 */
function getDateFromString(s)
{
  s = s.replace(/-/g, "/");
  s = s.replace("T", " ");
  s = s.replace("Z", " GMT-0000");
  return new Date(Date.parse(s));
}
```

You can also add several attributes that can be used to better describe the code. These attributes are prefixed with an `@` sign. You can even add HTML tags for readability. Check this out:

```
/**
 * Converts Internet string date into Date object.
 * <p>
 * This function is called when the user selects the
 * Cyborg opton in the left-hand module of the doohing.
 *
 * @param   s string containing the
 * @returns  the date as a Date object
 */
function getDateFromString(s)
{
  s = s.replace(/-/g, "/");
  s = s.replace("T", " ");
  s = s.replace("Z", " GMT-0000");
  return new Date(Date.parse(s));
}
```

For full details on available attributes, formatting commands, and syntax rules, check out `http://code.google.com/p/jsdoc-toolkit/` as well the Javadoc conventions page at `http://java.sun.com/j2se/javadoc/writingdoccomments`.

Even if you don't plan on using JSDocToolkit to create source code documentation, the JSDocToolkit conventions are still very useful for creating well-documented code. Plus, you may find in the future that if you would like to use the JSDocToolkit, you're all set.

Functions

A *function* is the basic building block or organizing unit of JavaScript. A foundation of a house is composed of many building blocks. In the same way, a JavaScript script usually consists of a set of functions.

These building blocks may be easy to take for granted. But just as a beautifully decorated home means nothing apart from its foundation, a killer JavaScript animation routine is pretty meaningless without these building blocks to rest upon.

Creating a Function

A function is a module of JavaScript statements that together perform a specific action.

Follow the instructions below to create a JavaScript function.

1. Create the following HTML document in your text editor and then save the document as *BIDHJ-Ch02-Ex2.html.*

Available for download on Wrox.com

```
<!DOCTYPE html PUBLIC "-//W3C//DTD XHTML 1.0 Strict//EN"
        "http://www.w3.org/TR/xhtml1/DTD/xhtml1-strict.dtd">
<html xmlns="http://www.w3.org/1999/xhtml">
<head>
<title>Video</title>
<meta name="viewport" content="width=320; initial-scale=1.0;
  maximum-scale=1.0; user-scalable=0;"/>
<style type="text/css">

body
{
  background-color: #080808;
  margin: 10;
  color: #ffffff;
  font-family: Helvetica, sans-serif;
font-size:10px;
}

</style>
<script type="text/javascript">

</script>
</head>
<body>
</body>
</html>
```

Code snippet BIDHJ-Ch02-Ex2.html

2. Add the `addAndDisplay()` function inside the `script` element:

```
function addAndDisplay(a,b)
{
  var total = a + b;
  alert(total);
}
```

Code snippet BIDHJ-Ch02-Ex2.html

3. Inside the script element, add the following code just after the function you just defined:

```
addAndDisplay(3, 2);
```

Code snippet BIDHJ-Ch02-Ex2.html

4. Save the file.

How It Works

When the page loads the script, it executes `addAndDisplay(3, 2)` to display an Alert message box that displays the calculated total. As you can see, the function you created named `addAndDisplay()` takes two arguments: a and b. An **argument** (also called a **parameter**) is a variable or literal value that you want to pass on to the function to process. In this case, the calling function sends the 3 and 2 integer values to the function add them together. Inside the curly brackets the first line adds together the arguments and assigns the sum to the `total` variable. The second line displays the total in an alert box. When the alert box is closed the function ends and returns control to the code that called it.

As you can see from the preceding Try It Out, a function:

➤ Gets called by another section of code to perform a process, return a result, or both

➤ Hides the details of its programming logic from other parts of the code

A function can return a value to the calling code. For example, check out the following function:

```
function getTotal(subtotal)
{
  var t = subtotal * .05;
  return t;
}
```

The `getTotal()` function receives `subtotal` as an argument, multiplies it by the state tax percentage, and then returns the total value to the statement that called the function using the `return` command.

When `return` executes, the function stops executing at that line and returns to the calling function. For example:

```
function createProfile(el)
{
  if (el == null)
  {
    alert("Undefined DOM element. Cannot continue. :(");
    return;
  }
  else
  {
    // do something really important to el
  }
}
```

In this example, the function checks to see if the `el` parameter is null. If so, then the function ends processing after displaying an alert box. If not, then the function continues on.

Creating an Inline Function

JavaScript also supports inline functions, which enable you to define an unnamed function for use within a specific context. For example, suppose you want to display an alert message when the window loads. Using a normal function, you could structure your script as follows:

```
<script>
  function init()
  {
    alert("I am saying something important.");
  }

  window.onload = init;

</script>
```

The `onload` event is assigned the `init()` function as its event handler. However, you could also use an inline function and eliminate the specific function definition:

```
<script>
  window.onload = function(){alert("I am saying something important.")}
</script>
```

Another advantage is that you can reference variables within a specific scope without having to pass them to a function as arguments.

Overloading Functions

Function overloading is a concept of being able to pass varying numbers of arguments to a function. You can overload a function in JavaScript if you make use of the `arguments` property of a function. For example, suppose you want to create a function that adds two numbers together and then returns the result. You could code it like this:

```
function add(a, b)
{
  return a+b;
}
```

However, suppose your needs change over time. Instead of two numbers, you now need to add three or four or five numbers at a time. Instead of writing separate functions for each case, you could overload the `add()` function to do all of these summing tasks:

```
function add()
{
  var t = 0;
  for (var i=0, l=arguments.length; i<l; i++)
  {
    t += arguments[i];
  }
  return t;
}
```

The `add()` function creates a `for` loop to iterate through each of the supplied arguments. As it does so, it adds the current argument to the `t` variable. This total is then returned back to the statement that called the function. Each of the following calls now work:

```
var t = add(2,2);
var t1 = add(2,4,5);
var t2 = add(392,1230,3020202,1,2033);
```

You could also use the `typeof()` command to overload different data types inside of the same function. For example, if I want to expand the functionality of `add()` to "add" string values, I could modify the function as follows:

```
function add()
{
  var argType = typeof(arguments[0]);

  if (argType == "number")
  {
    var t = 0;
    for (var i=0, l=arguments.length; i<l; i++)
    {
      t += arguments[i];
    }
    return t;
  }
  else if (argType == "string")
  {
    for (var i=0, l=arguments.length; i<l; i++)
    {
      if (i == 0)
      {
        var s = arguments[i];
      }
      else
      {
        s += ", " + arguments[i];
      }
    return s;
```

```
    }
    else
      return "Unsupported data type";
  }
}
```

The `add()` function examines the type of the first parameter and assigns the result to `argType`. If the type is a number then the routine continues just like the earlier example. If the type is a string, however, then the function combines the arguments into a single comma-delimited string. If the type is neither a number nor a string then an error message is returned.

Data Types

JavaScript enables you to work with specific data types:

➤   String

➤   Number

➤   Boolean

➤   Null

➤   Undefined

➤   Array

➤   Object

Strings, numbers, and Booleans are often known as *primitive data types*, null and undefined as *special data types*, and objects and arrays as *composite data types*.

Strings

A *string* is a collection of characters enclosed in single or double quotation marks. A string is also called a *string literal*. The following lines are examples of strings:

```
var wd = 'Kitchen sink';
var el = "<p>This is HTML.</p>";
var n = "3.14";
var char = 'z';
var special = "@#(*&^%$#@!~<>S"}{+=";
var blank = "";
```

As you can see, you can include most anything in a string — normal text, HTML tags, numeric values, special characters, and even "the kitchen sink."

Notice that you can have an empty string (""), which is *not* the same as a `null` or `undefined` value.

Because you can enclose a string in either single or double quotation marks, you can easily embed a quotation mark and apostrophe by using the opposite type pair to enclose the string literal. For example:

```
var str =
'"I like living dangerously", said Jack. "I am enclosing a quote in this string."';
var str2 = "I'm happy, aren't I?";
```

Alternatively, you can use the backslash character (\) to "escape" an apostrophe or quotation mark if the string is enclosed by the same type of mark. Here are a couple cases:

```
var str2 = 'I\'m happy, aren\'t I';
var el = "<div id=\"container\"></div>";
```

The backslash character tells the interpreter to treat the following quote mark as part of the string rather than as the ending delimiter.

For many tasks, you can work with string values as string literals in the manner in which I described. However, if you are going to parse, manipulate, transform, or otherwise pick on a string, then you can also treat it as a `String` object.

Numbers

The number data type represents any sort of numeric value — integer, real floating-point number, octal, and even hexadecimal numbers.

Table 2-9 lists the variety of number values that are valid within JavaScript.

TABLE 2-9: Examples of Numbers

NUMBER	DESCRIPTION
32	Integer
.00223	Floating-point number
1.42e5	Floating-point number
0377	Octal value
0x32CF	A hexadecimal integer

In addition to these normal number types, JavaScript also contains a special value `NaN`, which stands for "not a number." As you might expect, if you perform an invalid math operation, you get `NaN` as the result.

Boolean Values

A Boolean type represents either a `true` or `false` value. You typically use it to determine whether a condition in your code is true or false. For example, suppose you assign `false` to the `flagUser` variable:

```
var flagUser = false;
```

You can then evaluate the `flagUser` variable to determine its Boolean state in an `if` control structure (see the "if/else Statement" section earlier in this chapter). For example:

```
if (flagUser == true)
{
  alert("Hey User! You are hereby flagged.");
}
```

The `if` statement displays the alert box if `flagUser` evaluates to `true`.

Note that a Boolean value is *not* wrapped in quotation marks. So notice the difference:

```
// Boolean
var isABoolean = true;
var isAString = "true";
```

Null Values

When a variable or object contains no value, then its value is expressed as `null`. (Not the literal string `"null"`, just `null`.) You can test whether or not a variable or object is null to determine if it has been defined earlier in the code. For example:

```
if (myArray != null)
{
  doSomethingReallyImportant();
}
```

This code block evaluates the variable `myArray`. If its value is not equal to `null` then the condition evaluates to true and something really important happens.

A `null` value is not the same as an empty string, the number `0` or `NaN`, or the undefined data type that I explain in the next section.

If you want to remove the contents of the variable, you can assign it a non-value by setting it to `null`:

```
if (loggedOut == true)
{
  userName = null;
}
```

So, in this example, if the `loggedOut` variable is true then the `userName` variable is reset.

Undefined Values

On first take, an undefined value sounds like just another name for `null`. But an `undefined` value is actually a different data type. An `undefined` value is returned by the interpreter when you access a variable that has been declared but never assigned a value. For example, the following snippet displays an alert box with `undefined` as the message.

```
var isSmiling;
alert (isSmiling);
```

You also get `undefined` if you try to call a property that does not exist. For example:

```
alert(document.theStreetThatHasNoName);
```

Arrays

So far, I've been talking about variables as individuals. An *array*, in contrast, is a collection of values. They are grouped together and indexed so that you can access a specific item stored in the group.

JavaScript stores arrays as `Array` objects, which means that it has a variety of properties and methods, which you can use to perform a variety of tasks.

Creating an Array

You can create a new array by assigning a variable to empty brackets:

```
var castMembers = [];
```

You can also create a new array by using `new Array()`. It goes like this:

```
var myArray = new Array();
```

However, using the `new` operator to create an array is considered old school and is not considered a good practice.

In some programming languages, you need to specify the number of items in an array at the time you define it. This is not so with JavaScript. The size of the array increases each time you add a new item to it.

Adding Items to an Array

To add items to the array, simply assign a value to a specific index in the array. The *index* is designated by a value within brackets, such as the following:

```
var castMembers = [];
castMembers[0] = "Jerry";
castMembers[1] = "George";
castMembers[2] = "Elaine";
castMembers[3] = "Kramer";
```

Notice that, because arrays are zero-based, you start counting at 0 rather than 1.

You can also define the array items by passing values in as parameters:

```
var primeNumbers = [1,3,5,7,11];
```

Storing Multiple Types in an Array

You can store most any kind of data in an array, including strings, numbers, Boolean values, undefined and null values, objects, and functions. You can even store an array within an array if you really want to. What's more, you can store various types of data within the same array. For example, consider the following array that contains a string, number, function, DOM object, and Boolean value:

```
var el = document.getDocumentById("easy_bake_oven");
var pieLove = ["pie", 3.14, function(){alert("Apple Pie")}, el, true];
```

Getting and Setting the Size of an Array

You can get the number of items in an array by accessing its `length` property. (Yes, an array is an object, so it has its own set of properties and methods.) For example:

```
var primeNumbers = [1,3,5,7,11];
alert(primeNumbers.length));
```

The alert box displays 5.

In most cases, you don't need to explicitly set the size of an array because it dynamically resizes on its own when you add or remove items from it. However, in cases in which you need to specify an array's size, you can assign a value to the `length` property. For example, the following line increases the size of the array to 10:

```
primeNumbers.length = 10;
```

Note that no new data items are created when you do this.

If you specify a `length` that is smaller than the current size of the array then the items that fall outside of that `length` value get the axe.

Keep in mind that the last item in the array has an index value one less than the total number of elements in an array.

Accessing Items in an Array

You can access any value in the array according to its index. For example, to write the third item in a `states` array to the document, you could use the following code:

```
function showHomeState(idx)
{
  document.write("<p>Your home state is " + states[idx] + "</p>");
}
```

You can also iterate through an array using a `for` loop if you want to work with each item in the group:

```
var castMembers = [];
castMembers[0] = "Jerry";
castMembers[1] = "Jan";
castMembers[2] = "Elias";
castMembers[3] = "Bob";
document.writeln("<ul>");
for(i=0, l=castMembers.length; i<l; i++)
{
  document.writeln("<li>" + castMembers[i] + "</p>");
}
document.writeln("</ul>");
```

In this example, the `castMembers` array defines four string items. The `length` property is used to determine the size of the array, so I know the number of times to loop through the `for` structure.

Notice that the length property is assigned to a variable rather than being included directly inside the `for` loop like this:

```
// Valid, but less efficient
for(i=0; i<castMembers.length; i++)
{
}
```

Although that loop is perfectly valid, it is not as efficient, particularly for large arrays. The reason is that the interpreter has to evaluate the length property on each pass rather than only one time. Therefore, it is a good habit to assign an array's length to a variable for loops.

The HTML output for this script is as follows:

```
<ul>
<li>Jerry</li>
<li>Jan</li>
<li>Elias</li>
<li>Bob</li>
</ul>
```

Passing by Reference or Value

When a primitive variable (string, number, or Boolean) is passed into an array, the array creates a *copy* of the variable's value rather than storing a reference to that variable. In programming lingo, this is known as *passing by value*. Here's an example that demonstrates the difference:

```
var n = 100;
var b = true;
var s = "string";
ar = [n, b, s];

document.write("<p>[First pass]</p>");
for (i=0; i<=2; i++)
  document.write("<p>"+ar[i]+"</p>");

n = 200;
b = false;
s = "new and improved string";

document.write("<p>[Second pass]</p>");
for (i=0; i<=2; i++)
  document.write("<p>"+ar[i]+"</p>");
```

Notice that the variables n, b, and s are passed as parameters in the ar array. The `for` loop then outputs the values of the array items as HTML content to the document. The variables are updated and given new assignments. However, when the same `for` loop is run again, the *original* values are output. Check out the HTML content that is output:

```
[First pass]
100
true
```

```
string
[Second pass]
100
true
string
```

However, when you pass an object or a function into an array, the array stores a reference to those advanced data types rather than a copy of it. As a result, any changes you make to the object or function outside of the array are reflected when you access its corresponding item in the array. This is called *passing by reference*.

EXERCISES

1. What keyword is used to declare a variable in JavaScript?

2. What is the difference between a local and global variable?

3. How are the = and == operators used differently?

4. What operator is used to compare whether two values are unequal to each other?

5. Write down the basic structure of a `for` loop that loops through 10 times.

6. Within a function, how would you check to the see the total number of parameters that were passed to the function?

7. Is an empty string `" "` the same as a `null` value?

Answers to the Exercises can be found in the Appendix.

▶ **WHAT YOU LEARNED IN THIS CHAPTER**

TOPIC	KEY CONCEPTS
Embedding video or audio into your app	Add a `video` or `audio` element to your HTML file.
Variables	A variable is an alias that stores another piece of data.
Scope of variables	Variable scope refers to the context of the variable, which can be local (specific to one piece of code) or global (accessible across the document).
Conditional expressions	Use `if`, `if/else`, or `switch` to add conditional logic to your JavaScript.
Loops	A `for` loop cycles through a block of code x number of times. A `while` loop executes a block of code as long as a specific condition is true.
Functions	A function is a basic organizing unit of JavaScript specified with the `function` keyword.

3

The Document Object Model

WHAT YOU WILL LEARN IN THIS CHAPTER:

➤ Looking at your document as a tree

➤ Accessing the DOM from your code

➤ Editing your document from the DOM

A web page is an HTML document containing markup tags and content. But, as you develop web apps, you'll find it more helpful to think of the document as a tree-like structure filled with branches, limbs, and leaf nodes. This "document as hierarchy" concept is exactly what is meant when you hear the term Document Object Model (DOM).

In this chapter, I introduce you to the DOM and walk you through the basics you need to access and manipulate the DOM from your application code.

WHAT IS THE DOM?

The Document Object Model provides a scripting interface into an HTML document so that you can work with all of its elements within a hierarchical structure. As a result, you can navigate through the document structure with JavaScript to access and manipulate anything inside it.

The DOM is a standard that was originated by the W3C, the Web standards body. There are three DOM levels:

➤ **Level 1:** Level 1 contains the core functionality to be able to script the DOM for an HTML or XML document. Any modern browser provides support for the Level 1 version of the DOM.

➤ **Level 2:** Level 2 support extends DOM support to include new core functionality, event listeners, and CSS DOM. Safari and other browsers provide generally strong support for most aspects of DOM2.

➤ **Level 3:** Level 3 adds support for newer properties and methods, keyboard events, and XPath. Safari provides strong support for Level 3.

DOM AS A TREE

As I mentioned at the start of the chapter, you'll find it helpful to think of the DOM as a hierarchical tree that contains all of the parts of the HTML document — elements, attributes, text, comments, and so on. In DOM lingo, these individual pieces are known as *nodes*.

When working with HTML markup, the primary building block of your document is the element. However, when working with the DOM, the basic piece you will work with is the node. Remember that all nodes are not identical. While the DOM tree is dominated by element nodes, there are several other types that you need to be aware of.

Just like a family tree in real life, each of the nodes are interconnected. A node can have a parent, a sibling, child, and the occasional half-crazy "grandparent" that no one talks about. The document object is the family patriarch and serves as the container for all of the nodes (the descendants) of the HTML file. The document object has no corresponding HTML element. The html, head, and body elements are all contained by document.

One point I should stress is that a DOM hierarchy is *not* identical to the natural element hierarchy you find in an HTML document. Take, for example, the following plain vanilla file:

```html
<html>
<head>
<title>Really Awesome Web Page</title>
</head>
<body>
<div id="container">
<h1>Pretty awesome heading</h1>
<p id="para1">Pretty lame paragraph</p>
</div>
</body>
</html>
```

The levels of indentation show the natural element hierarchy in the document. Or, I can express the same hierarchy in a visual tree, as shown in Figure 3-1.

Every HTML element in the DOM has properties that correspond to the element's attributes. For example, an img has src and alt properties. However, DOM elements also have a set of common properties and methods.

In the DOM, elements are just one type of node. As a result, you also have to express other nodes of the document, such as attributes and text content, in the

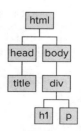

FIGURE 3-1

tree as well. The text content inside an element is a child node of the parent element. So, for example, `Pretty lame paragraph` is considered a child node of the p element that contains it.

Attributes are also considered nodes, but are a bit of a special case. They don't participate in the parent/child relationships that the other nodes do. Instead, they are accessed as properties of the element node that contains it. Figure 3-2 shows the same document in a DOM tree.

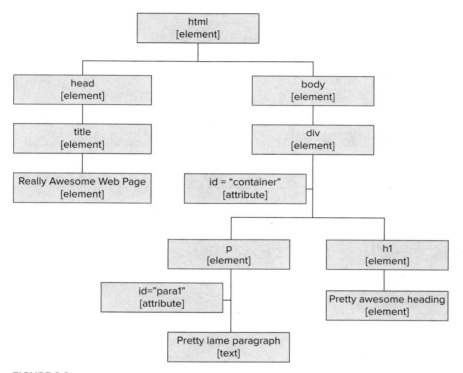

FIGURE 3-2

When working with the DOM in JavaScript, you typically work with the `document` object and DOM element objects. Each DOM element object has `childNodes` and `attributes` properties for accessing these nodes, as shown in Figure 3-3. As Figure 3-3 illustrates, each node has a `nodeType` property that you can use to determine the type of node you are working with.

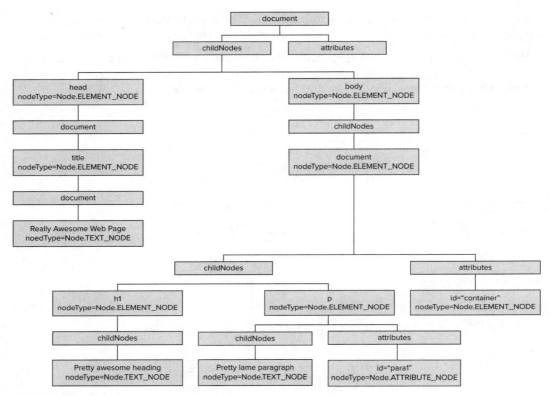

FIGURE 3-3

Before you begin to access the DOM, it is important to take a moment to identify the node types that the DOM contains that you'll work with. The nodeType property of each DOM node returns a constant from the Node object that represents the type of node. These include:

➤ Node.ELEMENT_NODE

➤ Node.ATTRIBUTE_NODE

➤ Node.TEXT_NODE

➤ Node.CDATA_SECTION_NODE

➤ Node.ENTITY_REFERENCE_NODE

➤ Node.ENTITY_NODE

➤ Node.PROCESSING_INSTRUCTION_NODE

➤ Node.COMMENT_NODE

➤ Node.DOCUMENT_NODE

➤ Node.DOCUMENT_TYPE_NODE

➤ Node.DOCUMENT_FRAGMENT_NODE

➤ Node.NOTATION_NODE

Each of the Node constants represent an unsigned short number. ELEMENT_NODE represents 1, ATTRIBUTE_NODE equals 2, and so on.

ACCESSING THE DOM FROM JAVASCRIPT

You access the document object through a named object called, appropriately enough, document. Therefore, if you want to access a document object's property or method, you can do so directly. For example:

```
document.open();
```

For other elements and nodes in the DOM, there are a variety of ways to access them, as described in the following sections.

Accessing a Specific Element

When you know the id of an element, the most common way in which you access the element node is by using getElementById(). This method searches through the DOM looking for the one node that has an id value that matches the string you specify. For example, consider the following:

```
<html>
<body>
<div id="header">
<p>Rawhide!</p>
</div>
</body>
</html>
```

If you want to access the div, you could use the following line:

```
var d = document.getElementById("header");
```

The variable d now references the div id="header" element. You can now use the d variable to access its properties and perform methods on it. For example, to set its text color, you could use the following:

```
d.style.color = #cccccc;
```

Accessing a Set of Elements

In addition to accessing a specific element, you'll also find occasions in which you'll want to access all element nodes of a given kind. You can also access a set of elements by using the document object's getElementsByTagName() method. This method takes an HTML element as its parameter:

```
var e  = document.getElementsByTagName(elementName);
```

This method returns all of the elements with the specified tag name as a *NodeList*, or a collection of nodes ordered by their appearance in the document.

For example, to get all of the p elements in a document and return as a NodeList, you could type the following:

```
var cPara = document.getElementsByTagName("p");
```

After you have the collection of elements through either of these techniques, you can access a particular node in the NodeList by using its index number. For example, to access the first p element in the document, you write this:

```
var p1 = cPara[0];
```

If you are accessing a specific p element, such as the first, you could combine both lines into a single call:

```
var p1 =  document.getElementByTagName("p")[0];
```

This returns the first p element and assigns it to the p1 variable.

More commonly, you could use it in a for loop to perform an action on each element:

```
for (var i=0; i<cPara.length; i++)
{
    var para = cPara[i];
    para.style.color = #000000;
}
```

This code block iterates through each p element in the document and changes its text color to black. Notice that because the cPara variable is a nodeList, you can access its length property to determine the number of elements returned.

In addition, you can use getElementsByTagName() to return *all* element nodes inside of the calling element by using * as the parameter:

```
var cElements = document.getElementsByTagName("*");
```

This call returns all of the descending elements inside the document, regardless of the level of hierarchy they sit on.

Accessing Family Members

You can access nodes related to other nodes through more "familial ways" through several node properties:

➤ parentNode returns the parent node of the current element.

➤ firstChild gets the first child of a node.

➤ lastChild gets the last child of a node.

➤ previousSibling gets the node just before the current one in the parent's NodeList.

➤ nextSibling gets the node just after the current one in the parent's NodeList.

➤ childNodes gets all of the children of a node.

For example, you can use parentNode property to get the parent node of a given element. For example, consider the following HTML snippet:

```
<div id="container">
<p id="p1"></p>
</div>
```

The following JavaScript returns a reference to the div element:

```
iParent = document.getElementById("p1").parentNode;
```

A parent node must be either the document, element node, or a document fragment.

In addition, suppose you want to return all of the nodes that are direct children under an element, you could use the childNodes property instead to retrieve its children as a NodeList and store it in a variable. Here's what you would code:

```
var c = document.getElementById("container");
var cChildren = c.childNodes;
```

In this code, the element with an id of container is assigned to the c variable. Its children are then assigned to the cChildren variable and are ready for action.

You can also use the hasChildNodes() method to check to see whether an element has child nodes. For example:

```
var c = document.getElementById("container");
if (c.hasChildNodes() == true)
{
    var cChildren = c.childNodes;
}
```

Retrieving Attributes

Attributes are technically nodes in a DOM, but don't think of them as being equal to element nodes. You cannot, for example, retrieve a list of id attribute nodes through some sort of GetAttributeByName() method. In fact, except in rare occasions, there is no practical reason for doing so because attributes are inextricably associated with an element. Not surprisingly, attributes are accessible through a DOM element by accessing its `attributes` property or by using one of three methods.

Accessing All Attributes

The object that returns from this property is called *NamedNodeMap* object, which is similar to a NodeList except that its items are listed in arbitrary order, rather than a specific defined order.

If I want to retrieve a list of attributes for a given element, I might write something like the following:

```
var atts = document.getElementById("container").attributes;
```

You can then work with the attributes by accessing their `name` and `value` properties. For example:

```
var atts = document.getElementById("container").attributes;
var str = "";

for(var i=0; i<atts.length; i++)
{
str += "Name:" + atts[i].name + " Value:" + atts[i].value + "<br/>";
}
```

This code block gets the attributes for an element and then outputs the name and value for each attribute into the `str` variable.

You can check to see whether an element has any attributes at all by using the `hasAttributes()` method:

```
var ctr = document.getElementById("container");
if (ctr.hasAttributes() == true)
{
    var atts = ctr.attributes;
}
```

Accessing a Specific Attribute

You can also access a specific attribute using the element's `getAttribute()` method. Simply enter the name of the attribute as the parameter. Suppose, for example, that I want to get the `href` attribute from a link:

```
var att = document.getElementById("book").getAttribute("href");
```

You can also check for the existence of an attribute with the `hasAttribute()` method. To check to see whether an element has a `style` attribute, use this code:

```
var cntMajor = document.getElementById("contentMajor");
if ( cntMajor.hasAttribute("style"))
{
    var att = c.getAttribute("style");
}
```

MANIPULATING THE DOM

You can do more than use the DOM to look at a document. In fact, you can also manipulate it — creating nodes, adding them to the DOM tree, editing nodes, and removing parts of a document for which you have no more use.

In the sections that follow, I show you how to add and remove various parts of a document to and from the DOM.

Creating an Element and Other Nodes

The document object has several methods used to create nodes. I'm covering the creation of element nodes now; read about other nodes in the "Creating Other Types Nodes" section later in this chapter.

To create an element, use the `document.createElement()` method. This method creates an instance of the element specified by the parameter. For example, to create a `p` element, use this:

```
var para = document.createElement("p");
```

The `createElement()` method creates the `p` element and returns the node, which is assigned to the `para` variable.

Note that the act of creating an element does not automatically add it to the DOM tree. The instance only exists in your script until you explicitly add it. It's in a sort of limbo land. A node without a country, if you will. Instead, you need to insert it into the document hierarchy to be a card-carrying node of the DOM.

Adding a Node to the DOM

DOM elements have two methods that you can use to add a node into the tree:

➤ `appendChild(node)` adds the node as a child at the end of the current element's `childNodes` list.

➤ `insertBefore(newNode, targetNode)` adds a new element as a child of the current node, but inserts it just before the node specified by the `targetNode` parameter.

TRY IT OUT Adding a DOM Node

To show you how to add a node, follow these steps.

1. Create the following HTML document in your text editor and then save the document as *BIDHJ-Ch03-Ex1.html*.

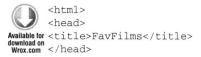

Available for
download on
Wrox.com

```
<html>
<head>
<title>FavFilms</title>
</head>
```

```
<body>
<div id="content">
<h1 id="header1">Welcome to the World of Cinema</p>
<p id="p1">Favorite films are shown below:</p>
<ol id="movieList">
<li id="film_30329">The Shawshank Redemption</li>
<li id="film_30202">Casablanca</li>
<li id="film_20216">Braveheart</li>
<li id="film_28337">Groundhog Day</li>
<ol>
</div>
</body>
</html>
```

Code snippet BIDHJ-Ch03-Ex1.html

2. Add the following script code in the document head and save your file:

```
<script type="application/x-javascript">
var fa = document.createElement("li");
document.getElementById("movieList").appendChild(fa);

var fb = document.createElement("li");
var casa = document.getElementById("film_30202");
document.getElementById("movieList.).insertBefore(fb, casa);

var fb = document.createElement("li");
var br = document.getElementById("film_20216");
document.getElementById("movieList.).insertBefore(fb, br.nextSibling);
</script>
```

Code snippet BIDHJ-Ch03-Ex1.html

How It Works

When this document loads, the script is executed. The first two lines of code append an empty `li` element to the end of the list. The next three add a blank `li` item in the spot just before Casablanca by using `insertBefore()`.

Although there is no `insertAfter()` method, you can perform the equivalent functionality by using `insertBefore()` in combination with the `nextSibling` property of the `targetNode`. That's exactly what I did in the final part of the script to add a node after Braveheart.

It's time to look at our results. The ordered list is now updated to include the new elements I added:

```
<ol id="movieList">
<li id="film_30329">The Shawshank Redemption</li>
<li/>
<li id="film_30202">Casablanca</li>
```

```
<li id="film_20216">Braveheart</li>
<li/>
<li id="film_28337">Groundhog Day</li>
<li/>
<ol>
```

Creating Other Elements

The `document` object contains methods for creating the rest of the common node types: attribute, text, comment, and document fragment. Each of these methods return a node that you can add into your document using `appendChild()` or `insertBefore()`.

An *attribute node* represent an element's attribute. To create an attribute, you use `createAttribute()`. For example:

```
var a = document.createAttribute("alt");
a.nodeValue = "Welcome to DOM and DOMMER."
document.getElementById("logo").appendChild(a);
```

A *text node* is as a container of text. When you are first introduced to the DOM, it is probably natural to think of text being a property of an element. But, text inside of an element is contained by a child text node. To create a text node, use `createTextNode()`. For example, the following code snippet creates a text node and adds it onto the end of a p element with an id of `para`:

```
var t = document.createTextNode("I scream for ice cream.");
document.getElementById("para").appendChild(t);
```

A *comment node* represents an HTML comment. To create a comment node, use `createComment()`:

```
var c = document.createComment("Insert new toolbar here.");
document.getElementById("toolbar_container").appendChild(c);
```

Finally, a *document fragment* is a temporary "off-line" document that you can use to create and modify part of a tree before you add the fragment to the actual DOM tree. When manipulating the DOM, working with a document fragment during the processing of a subtree is much more efficient (less overhead) than always working directly with the actual DOM itself. To create a document fragment, use `createDocumentFragment()`. For example, the following script creates a document fragment, adds nodes to it, and then finally adds it to the document:

```
var df = document.createDocumentFragment();

for(var i=0; i<30; i++)
{
var e = document.createElement("p");
var t = document.createTextNode("Line " + i);
e.appendChild(t);
```

```
df.appendChild(e);
    }

    document.getElementById("content").appendChild(df);
```

TRY IT OUT   **Adding a Complete Node**

Now that you know how to create the other node types, I want to revisit the movie list example.
Instead of adding empty `li` elements, add the attribute and text nodes needed to fill out the ordered list
appropriately. Use the following.

1.   Create the following HTML document in your text editor and then save the document as *BIDHJ-
Ch03-Ex2.html*.

```
<html>
<head>
<title>FavFilms</title>
</head>
<body>
<div id="content">
<h1 id="header1">Welcome to the World of Cinema</p>
<p id="p1">Favorite films are shown below:</p>
<ol id="movieList">
<li id="film_30329">The Shawshank Redemption</li>
<li id="film_30202">Casablanca</li>
<li id="film_20216">Braveheart</li>
<li id="film_28337">Groundhog Day</li>
<ol>
</div>
</body>
</html>
```

Code snippet BIDHJ-Ch03-Ex2.html

2.   Add the following script code in the document head and save your file:

```
<script type="application/x-javascript">
    var e; // Element
    var a; // Attribute
    var t; // Text
    var nd; // Target/Parent

    e = document.createElement("li");
    a = document.createAttribute("id", "film_29299");
    t = document.createTextNode("Babette's Feast");
    e.appendChild(a);
    e.appendChild(t);
    document.getElementById("movieList").appendChild(e);

    e = document.createElement("li");
```

```
    a = document.createAttribute("id", "film_29323");
    t = document.createTextNode("Amélie (Le Fabuleux destin d'Amélie Poulain)");
    e.appendChild(a);
    e.appendChild(t);
    nd = document.getElementById("film_30202");
    document.getElementById("movieList.).insertBefore(e, nd);
    e = document.createElement("li");
    a = document.createAttribute("id", "film_30276");
    t = document.createTextNode("Vertigo");
    e.appendChild(a);
    e.appendChild(t);
    nd = document.getElementById("film_20216");
    document.getElementById("movieList.).insertBefore(f, nd.nextSibling);
</script>
```

Code snippet BIDHJ-Ch03-Ex2.html

How It Works

In this example, the JavaScript is executed when the document is loaded. The script uses `createElement()`, `createAttribute()`, and `createTextNode()` methods of the `document` to create a full, complete `li` element to add to the list. It then uses `appendChild()` and `insertBefore()` to add the elements in the desired order in the list. The ordered list now looks like the following when the script is executed:

```
<ol id="movieList">
<li id="film_30329">The Shawshank Redemption</li>
<li id="film_29323">Amélie (Le Fabuleux destin d'Amélie Poulain)</li>
<li id="film_30202">Casablanca</li>
<li id="film_20216">Braveheart</li>
<li id="film_30276">Vertigo</li>
<li id="film_28337">Groundhog Day</li>
<li id="film_29299">Babette's Feast</li>
<ol>
```

Setting a Value to an Attribute

The `setAttribute()` method is a shortcut to creating an attribute and adding it to an element. This method sets the attribute value for an element, but if the attribute doesn't exist, the method goes ahead and creates it. It takes the attribute name and value as parameters:

```
setAttribute("name", "value")
```

For example, if you want to change the `href` of a link, you could use the following:

```
document.getElementById("myblog").setAttribute("href",
    "http://richwagnerwords.com");
```

Here's a little more detailed example of using setAtttribute() to clean up a document. Suppose you have an HTML document that has attributes with uppercase names. If you want to convert them to all lowercase, you could the following script:

```
var all = document.getElementsByTagName("*");
for(var i=0; i<all.length; i++)
{
    var e = all[i];

    for(var j=0; j<all.length; j++)
    {
        e.attributes[j].setAttribute(all.attributes[j].nodeName.toLowerCase());
    }
}
```

The script looks for all of the elements in a document and returns them as a NodeList. The first for loop iterates through all of the elements and assigns the e variable to be the current element in the loop. The second for loop cycles through all of the attributes of e and uses setAttribute() in combination with toLowerCase().

Moving a Node

Although there is no moveNode() method defined in JavaScript, appendChild() and insertBefore() do the same thing. In addition to adding new nodes you create, these two methods enable you to move a node from one location to another in the tree. For example, consider the following document:

```
<html>
<head>
</head>
<body>
<div id="header">
<img id="logoImg" src="logo.png"/>
</div>
<div id="footer">
</div>
</body>
</html>
```

If you want to move the image from the header to the footer, you write:

```
var i = document.getElementById("logoImg");
document.getElementById("footer").appendChild(i);
```

When this code is executed, the appendChild() method moves the logoImg from any location and adds it as a child to the footer div.

Cloning a Node

You can clone a node and add it elsewhere to the document tree by using a DOM element's cloneNode() method. This method copies the specified node and returns a new instance that is not part of the DOM. You can then add it wherever you want using the familiar `appendChild()` and `insertBefore()` methods.

This method takes a single Boolean parameter:

```
cloneNode(deepBoolean)
```

If the parameter is set to true then all subnodes of the current node are copied along with it.

When cloning nodes, there actually is a danger element. Using `cloneNode()`, every part of the node comes with it, including its `id`. As a result, you need to be sure to update the `id` before you add it to the document tree.

To demonstrate, I begin with the following document:

```
<html>
<head>
</head>
<body>
<div id="right_box">
<p id="main">All content should begin with this sentence.</p>
</div>
<div id="left_box">
</div>
</body>
</html>
```

Suppose I want to copy the paragraph to the `left_box` div. To do so, I could write this:

```
var cn = document.getElementById("right_box").cloneNode(true);
cn.setAtttribute("id", "main_left");
document.getElementById("left_box").appendChild(cn);
```

Removing a Node from the DOM

To remove a node, you call the `removeChild()` method of its parent, specifying it as the parameter. For example, to remove a paragraph with an `id="p1"`, you could use the following code snippet:

```
var cp = document.getElementById("p1");
cp.parentNode.removeChild(cp);
```

In this code, the `cp` variable is assigned the returning node of the specified paragraph element. Using `parentNode` to reference its parent, the `removeChild()` method is then called, specifying `cp` as the node to delete. The paragraph is removed from the DOM.

Or, suppose you want to remove all of the children in an element. To do so, you can loop through all of the child nodes and delete them one at a time. Here's the code you could use:

```
while ( bodyContent.childNodes[0] )
{
bodyContent.removeChild( bodyContent.childNodes[0];
}
```

In this routine, the `while` loop checks to see if there is a child node for the current node. If so, then the child node is removed using `removeChild()`. This process repeats until there no `childNodes[0]`.

Removing an Attribute

Suppose you have had it with an attribute and simply want to rid yourself of the pain and aggravation. Or maybe you just don't have a use for it anymore. If so, you can use the `removeAttribute()` method to delete an attribute from the DOM. The following, rather draconian script removes all the `alt` attributes from the document — simply out of spite! Here's the code:

```
var kitAndKaboodle = document.getElementsByTagName("*");
for(var i=0; i<kitAndKaboodle.length; i++)
{
    kitAndKaboodle[i].removeAttribute("alt");
}
```

EXERCISES

1. What is the primary "building block" of the DOM?

2. True or False? The DOM hierarchy must always be fully identical to the natural element hierarchy of an HTML document.

3. What is a *NodeList*?

4. What is a *document fragment*?

Answers to the Exercises can be found in Appendix A.

▶ **WHAT YOU LEARNED IN THIS CHAPTER**

TOPIC	KEY CONCEPTS
Accessing elements from the DOM	Use `document.getElementById()` or `document.getElementsByTagName()`.
Accessing attributes	Use the `attributes` property of a node to get a list of attributes; use `getAttribute()` to get a specific attribute value.
Adding to or editing the DOM	Use `document.createElement()` to create an element in your DOM. Add to the DOM using `appendChild()` or `insertBefore()`.

Writing Your First
Hello World Application

WHAT YOU WILL LEARN IN THIS CHAPTER:

➤ Creating your index page

➤ Adding styles

➤ Programming the UI with JavaScript

➤ Deploying your app

Okay, enough leg work. It's time to start developing your first app. In this chapter, I walk you through the full start-to-finish process of developing your first Hello World app that runs on all iOS platforms — iPhone, iPad, and iPod touch.

Whenever you create a web app, you can decide whether you want to create everything on your own from scratch or if you want to leverage a framework to get the basic app look and feel. The advantage of creating everything yourself is that you have complete control over all parts of the app. The downside is, of course, that you have to create everything yourself.

Throughout this book, I talk a lot about creating different parts of an app on your own. However, to start things off, I recommend you use a mobile framework to get rolling quickly. Therefore, in this chapter, I utilize one of the popular mobile frameworks available for Web apps — jQueryMobile — to create an iPhone web app. Using jQueryMobile, you can focus on just the content and meat of the app itself and let the framework do much of the styling and interactivity for you.

SETTING UP

Before you can begin developing an application, you need to set up a place for your app on a remote web server or on a server on your development machine. Make sure the server can be accessed via Wi-Fi from an iOS device.

TRY IT OUT   Creating a Location for Your Web App

Follow these steps to set up a location for your Hello World app.

1. Determine where you want to set up your developer server — either on a remote server or a server running on your development machine.

2. If the server is remote, connect to your server via FTP. If you are using your development machine, locate the main documents directory for your server. (If you are using Mac, this is the Sites folder in your user directory.)

3. Create a folder named `webapp`.

4. Inside of `webapp`, create another folder named `topfilmz`.

How It Works

Your first task is to prepare a home base where you will save your app files. It can be located on your development machine or on a remote server if you have one available. For this example, you are not going to be using an app server, so it really makes no difference.

If you are using a web server on your development machine, you need to know the address to access your web app. If you are running a Mac, an easy way to find this out is to do the following:

1. Go to System Preferences.

2. Click the Sharing icon.

3. Note the address to your personal website, which is your Sites folder. In my case, it is `http://10.0.0.6/~rwagner`.

CREATING YOUR INDEX PAGE

The app you're going to create demonstrates a popular style of mobile app — a navigation list-based app. The purpose of the app, which I am calling Top Filmz, is to display a list of top films. A user can click a film in the list to display a details page on the film. The details page displays a poster image of the film and two buttons — one that takes the user to the film's page on IMDB and a second that returns the user to the main films list.

Although the app will appear to have several different pages (one main list, individual pages for each of the dozen films), I am actually going to be able to place all of the code inside a single HTML file.

TRY IT OUT   Creating the Index Page

To create the basic shell of your app, follow these steps:

1. Create a new text file in your `topfilmz` folder and save it as index.html.

2. Enter the following HTML text:

```
<!DOCTYPE html>
<html>
<head>
<title>Top Filmz</title>
</head>
<body>
</body>
</html>
```

3. Add the viewport meta tag to the document head:

```
<meta name="viewport" content="width=device-width, initial-scale=1">
```

4. Add references to the core jQuery Mobile stylesheet and JavaScript files in the document head:

```
<link rel="stylesheet"
 href="http://code.jquery.com/mobile/1.0b3/jquery.mobile-1.0b3.min.css" />
<script
  type="text/javascript" src="http://code.jquery.com/jquery-1.6.3.min.js">
  </script>
<script type="text/javascript"
  src="http://code.jquery.com/mobile/1.0b3/jquery.mobile-1.0b3.min.js">
  </script>
```

5. Save your file.

How It Works

In these five steps, you created the basic shell for any jQuery Mobile app. The jQuery Mobile framework requires that the page start with an HTML5 `<!DOCTYPE html>` to ensure that all of the framework's features are available to you.

The viewport meta tag ensures that the browser sets the width of the page to be equal to the pixel width of the device screen, rather than zooming out to a page width of 900 pixels as Safari does by default.

For performance considerations, the links to the jQuery Mobile framework directly point to files hosted by jQuery rather than being placed on your own server.

CREATING THE MAIN SCREEN

Inside the `body` element of `index.html`, you are ready to add content for the home or main screen (or page) of your web app. In jQuery Mobile, you specify a page inside a `div` element and add a custom `data-role="page"` attribute.

Within an app, you can place anything that you want to on a page. However, a typical template that many apps use is a standard header-content-footer division. You can achieve this in jQuery Mobile by using the following code:

```
<div data-role="page">
<div data-role="header">
</div>

<div data-role="content">
</div>

<div data-role="footer">
</div>
</div>
```

Notice that the roles of the div elements are declared using the data-role attribute.

The content section of the page displays a scrolling navigation list of the names of movies. You can create a list quite simply by using an unordered list and adding a data-role="listview" attribute to it. The individual li items represent the rows of the scrolling list. The a link refers to the destination that you want to go to when the list item is tapped by the user.

```
<ul data-role="listview">
<li><a href=""></a></li>
<li><a href=""></a></li>
<li><a href=""></a></li>
<li><a href=""></a></li>
</ul>
```

Here's a case where there is an advantage of using a framework such as jQuery Mobile. When your page is processed by the jQuery Mobile framework, this list is transformed into a stylized scrolling list that spans the entire width of the device's screen.

TRY IT OUT Creating the Main Screen of Your App

Follow these instructions to set up the main screen of the Top Filmz app:

1. Inside of the body tag of your index.html file, add the following div structure:

Available for
download on
Wrox.com

```
<div data-role="page"id="home">
<div data-role="header">
</div>

<div data-role="content">
</div>

<div data-role="footer">
</div>
</div>
```

Code snippet index.html

2. Inside the header `div`, add the app title:

```
<div data-role="header">
<h1>Top Filmz</h1>
</div>
```

Code snippet index.html

3. Inside the footer `div`, add a credit line:

```
<div data-role="footer">
<h5>Hello World Apps</h5>
</div>
```

Code snippet index.html

4. Inside the content div, add the markup that will be transformed into the scrolling list:

```
<div data-role="content">
<ul data-role="listview" data-theme="b">
<li><a href="#theShawshankRemption">The Shawshank Redemption</a></li>
<li><a href="#casablanca">Casablanca</a></li>
<li><a href="#larsAndTheRealGirl">Lars and the Real Girl</a></li>
<li><a href="#babettesFeast">Babette's Feast</a></li>
<li><a href="#groundhogDay">Groundhog Day</a></li>
<li><a href="#lesMiserables">Les Miserables</a></li>
<li><a href="#thePrincessBride">The Princess Bride</a></li>
<li><a href="#chariotsOfFire">Chariots of Fire</a></li>
<li><a href="#signs">Signs</a></li>
<li><a href="#vertigo">Vertigo</a></li>
</ul>
</div>
```

Code snippet index.html

5. Save your file.

How It Works

You created the initial page of your app in this exercise by creating this `div` structure. The app title is added to the header using an `<h1>` tag whereas the footer displays a dummy credit line using an `<h5>` tag. The scrolling list of films is shown in the unordered list. Notice that the `href` attribute for each `a` link specifies an internal anchor-like link. I show you how those link to the other film detail pages in the next section.

Notice the `data-theme` attribute of the list element. jQuery Mobile has five color themes to choose from. For this example, I choose `b`, which displays the list items in a darkened color.

Although the app is not functional yet, go ahead and sneak a peek at the main screen by opening the page on your iPhone or other iOS device. You can do so by typing the URL of the app on your development server. In my case, I would enter `http://10.0.0.6/~rwagner/webapp/topfilmz`.

ADDING DETAIL PAGES

As I mentioned earlier, an HTML file can contain multiple "virtual pages" of your jQuery Mobile web app. Like the main screen shown in Figure 4-1 each additional page is represented as a `div` with a unique ID assigned to it. Then, to display that page from a link on another page, you simply specify the page ID as the `href` value prefixed with a # sign (`href="#mypage"`). When a user taps a `#link`, jQuery Mobile looks for a "virtual" page and displays it in the viewport.

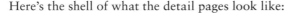

FIGURE 4-1

Here's the shell of what the detail pages look like:

```
<div data-role="page" id="uniqueID">
    <div data-role="header">
    <h1>Film Title</h1>
    </div>
    <div data-role="content" style="background-color:#ffffff">
    <img class="poster" src=""/>
    <a href=" " data-role="button">Go to IMDB Page</a>
    <a href="#home" data-role="button" data-icon="home">Return to List</a>
    </div>
    <div data-role="footer">
    <h5>Hello World Apps</h5>
    </div>
</div>
```

The header and footer look just as they appeared on the main screen, so there's not much new to say about them. However, in the content region of the page, there is an image and two links. Notice that the links have a `data-role="button"` attribute. When the page is displayed, jQuery Mobile transforms the link into a button.

Using that page template as a model, you can add detail pages for all the films in the list. The detail page code is shown under the Subpages section of the body in Listing 4-1.

LISTING 4-1: Full source of index.html

```
<!DOCTYPE html>
<html>
    <head>
    <title>Top Filmz</title>

    <meta name="viewport" content="width=device-width, initial-scale=1">

    <link rel="stylesheet"
```

```
        href="http://code.jquery.com/mobile/1.0b3/jquery.mobile-1.0b3.min.css" />
        <script
        type="text/javascript" src="http://code.jquery.com/jquery-1.6.3.min.js">
        </script>
        <script type="text/javascript"
         src="http://code.jquery.com/mobile/1.0b3/jquery.mobile-1.0b3.min.js">
        </script>

<style>
    img.poster
    {
        display: block;
        margin-left: auto;
        margin-right: auto;
    }
</style>

</head>

<body>

<!-- Page -->
<div data-role="page" id="home">
    <div data-role="header">
    <h1>Top Filmz</h1>
    </div>

    <div data-role="content">
    <ul data-role="listview" data-theme="b">
        <li><a href="#theShawshankRemption">The Shawshank Redemption</a></li>
        <li><a href="#casablanca">Casablanca</a></li>
        <li><a href="#larsAndTheRealGirl">Lars and the Real Girl</a></li>
        <li><a href="#babettesFeast">Babette's Feast</a></li>
        <li><a href="#groundhogDay">Groundhog Day</a></li>
        <li><a href="#lesMiserables">Les Miserables</a></li>
        <li><a href="#thePrincessBride">The Princess Bride</a></li>
        <li><a href="#chariotsOfFire">Chariots of Fire</a></li>
        <li><a href="#signs">Signs</a></li>
        <li><a href="#vertigo">Vertigo</a></li>
    </ul>
    </div>

    <div data-role="footer">
    <h5>Hello World Apps</h5>
    </div>
</div>


<!-- Subpages -->

<div data-role="page" id="theShawshankRemption">
    <div data-role="header">
    <h1>The Shawshank Redemption</h1>
    </div>
    <div data-role="content" style="background-color:#ffffff">
    <img class="poster"
```

continues

LISTING 4-1 *(continued)*

```
       src="http://ecx.images-amazon.com/images/I/519NBNHX5BL._SL500_AA300_.jpg"/>
       <a href="http://www.imdb.com/title/tt0111161/"
        data-role="button">Go to IMDB Page</a>
       <a href="#home" data-role="button" data-icon="home">Return to List</a>
       </div>
       <div data-role="footer">
       <h5>Hello World Apps</h5>
       </div>
</div>

<div data-role="page" id="casablanca">
       <div data-role="header">
       <h1>Casablanca</h1>
       </div>
       <div data-role="content" style="background-color:#ffffff">
       <img class="poster"
        src="http://ecx.images-amazon.com/images/I/51Mg3kdJ5KL._SL500_AA300_.jpg"/>
       <a href="http://www.imdb.com/title/tt0034583/"
        data-role="button">Go to IMDB Page</a>
       <a href="#home" data-role="button" data-icon="home">Return to List</a>
       </div>
       <div data-role="footer">
       <h5>Hello World Apps</h5>
       </div>
</div>

<div data-role="page" id="larsAndTheRealGirl">
       <div data-role="header">
       <h1>Lars and the Real Girl</h1>
       </div>
       <div data-role="content" style="background-color:#ffffff">
       <img class="poster"
        src="http://ecx.images-amazon.com/images/I/51Sn3wcuNGL._SL500_AA300_.jpg"/>
       <a href="http://www.imdb.com/title/tt0805564/"
        data-role="button">Go to IMDB Page</a>
       <a href="#home" data-role="button" data-icon="home">Return to List</a>
       </div>
       <div data-role="footer">
       <h5>Hello World Apps</h5>
       </div>
</div>

<div data-role="page" id="babettesFeast">
       <div data-role="header">
       <h1>Babette's Feast</h1>
       </div>
       <div data-role="content" style="background-color:#ffffff">
       <img class="poster"
        src="http://ecx.images-amazon.com/images/I/51A2BJ1WTML._SL500_AA300_.jpg"/>
       <a href="http://www.imdb.com/title/tt0092603/"
        data-role="button">Go to IMDB Page</a>
       <a href="#home" data-role="button" data-icon="home">Return to List</a>
       </div>
```

```
        <div data-role="footer">
        <h5>Hello World Apps</h5>
        </div>
</div>


<div data-role="page" id="groundhogDay">
        <div data-role="header">
        <h1>Groundhog Day</h1>
        </div>
        <div data-role="content" style="background-color:#ffffff">
        <img class="poster"
         src="http://ecx.images-amazon.com/images/I/51EVxBEKg6L._SL500_AA300_.jpg"/>
        <a href="http://www.imdb.com/title/tt0107048/"
          data-role="button">Go to IMDB Page</a>
        <a href="#home" data-role="button" data-icon="home">Return to List</a>
        </div>
        <div data-role="footer">
        <h5>Hello World Apps</h5>
        </div>
</div>

<div data-role="page" id="lesMiserables">
        <div data-role="header">
        <h1>Les Miserables</h1>
        </div>
        <div data-role="content" style="background-color:#ffffff">
        <img class="poster"
         src="http://ecx.images-amazon.com/images/I/51MeImdd92L._SL500_AA300_.jpg"/>
        <a href="http://www.imdb.com/title/tt0119683/"
          data-role="button">Go to IMDB Page</a>
        <a href="#home" data-role="button" data-icon="home">Return to List</a>
        </div>
        <div data-role="footer">
        <h5>Hello World Apps</h5>
        </div>
</div>

<div data-role="page" id="thePrincessBride">
        <div data-role="header">
        <h1>The Princess Bride</h1>
        </div>
        <div data-role="content" style="background-color:#ffffff">
        <img class="poster"
         src="http://ecx.images-amazon.com/images/I/51%2BOCP1DUSL._SL500_AA300_.jpg"/>
        <a href="http://www.imdb.com/title/tt0093779/"
          data-role="button">Go to IMDB Page</a>
        <a href="#home" data-role="button" data-icon="home">Return to List</a>
        </div>
        <div data-role="footer">
        <h5>Hello World Apps</h5>
        </div>
</div>


<div data-role="page" id="chariotsOfFire">
```

```
        <div data-role="header">
        <h1>Chariots of Fire</h1>
        </div>
        <div data-role="content" style="background-color:#ffffff">
        <img class="poster"
         src="http://ecx.images-amazon.com/images/I/51PyP5bti7L._SL500_AA300_.jpg"/>
        <a href="http://www.imdb.com/title/tt0082158/"
         data-role="button">Go to IMDB Page</a>
        <a href="#home" data-role="button" data-icon="home">Return to List</a>
        </div>
        <div data-role="footer">
        <h5>Hello World Apps</h5>
        </div>
    </div>

    <div data-role="page" id="signs">
        <div data-role="header">
        <h1>Signs</h1>
        </div>
        <div data-role="content" style="background-color:#ffffff">
        <img class="poster"
         src="http://ecx.images-amazon.com/images/I/51c02AOAyCL._SL500_AA300_.jpg"/>
        <a href="http://www.imdb.com/title/tt0286106/"
         data-role="button">Go to IMDB Page</a>
        <a href="#home" data-role="button" data-icon="home">Return to List</a>
        </div>
        <div data-role="footer">
        <h5>Hello World Apps</h5>
        </div>
    </div>

    <div data-role="page" id="vertigo">
        <div data-role="header">
        <h1>Vertigo</h1>
        </div>
        <div data-role="content" style="background-color:#ffffff">
        <img class="poster"
          src="http://ecx.images-amazon.com/images/I/51JF1C6DF5L._SL500_AA300_.jpg"/>
        <a href="http://www.imdb.com/title/tt0052357/"
         data-role="button">Go to IMDB Page</a>
        <a href="#home" data-role="button" data-icon="home">Return to List</a>
        </div>
        <div data-role="footer">
        <h5>Hello World Apps</h5>
        </div>
    </div>

    </body>
    </html>
```

When you save your file and then refresh it inside your iOS device you can tap any of the films from the main screen and jump to its detail page. Notice that when you tap a list item, jQuery Mobile automatically adds a sliding transition effect as it displays the corresponding detail page.

Figures 4-2 and 4-3 show the contents of the Casablanca page.

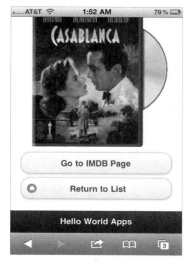

FIGURE 4-2

FIGURE 4-3

That's it! You have created your first iPhone app. However, here's an Easter egg bonus for what you already created. If you have an iPad, open the web app from the iPad version of Safari. Surprise! jQuery Mobile automatically displays the app in a customized manner suited perfectly for the iPad, as shown in Figures 4-4 and 4-5. As you conclude this Hello World chapter, you can see one of the practical benefits of using a mobile framework such as jQuery Mobile — you created an iPad app without even knowing it.

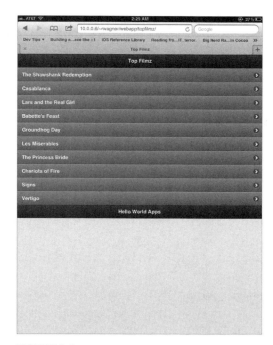

FIGURE 4-4

FIGURE 4-5

EXERCISES

1. What are the benefits to using a mobile framework such as jQuery Mobile?

2. For a jQuery Mobile-based app, do all app pages need to be stored in separate files?

3. How do you link to another page that is stored in the same HTML file?

Answers to the Exercises can be found in the Appendix.

► WHAT YOU LEARNED IN THIS CHAPTER

TOPIC	KEY CONCEPTS
Find a location for your web app	Determine where you want to set up your developer server — either on a remote server or on a server running on your development machine.
Use jQuery Mobile as a mobile app framework	Use `<!DOCTYPE html>` and add links to jQuery stylesheet and JavaScript files
Add a page in a jQuery Mobile app	Use a `div` element with a `data-role="page"` attribute

5

Enabling and Optimizing Web Sites for the iPhone and iPad

WHAT YOU WILL LEARN IN THIS CHAPTER:

➤ Making your website compatible with iOS devices

➤ Making your site easy to navigate from iPhone and iPad

➤ Adding custom style sheets for iOS devices

Although this book is focused on developing web apps for iOS devices, the reality is that you'll probably also need to deal with designing a website that is compatible with iPhone and iPad.

I remember having trouble browsing the Web on the iPhone when it was first released in 2007. I recall one evening in which my boys and I were watching the third quarter of a Monday Night Football game. The electricity suddenly went out because of a town-wide outage. Because my son's favorite team was playing, he was frantic. *What's happening in the game? Are the Titans still winning?* I immediately pulled out my iPhone and confidently launched Safari in search of answers. But upon going to NFL.com, I discovered that its live updating scoreboard was Adobe Flash media. All I could see was a gray box with a Lego-like block in its place. I then pointed the browser to the official Tennessee Titans site, only to discover more useless empty blocks scattered across its front page as well. We spent the rest of the outage using the iPhone to scour the Web, looking for a sports site to help us.

Fast forward to today. The expectations of the iPhone and iPad user are far different than what I had in 2007. At that time, I would just accept the lack of mobile support as something to be expected for being on the cutting edge of technology. However, today, if you design or run a website, your visitors won't be nearly as forgiving.

In the past, you could design a minimalist, text-only style sheet for mobile users with the expectation that your normal website would be viewed only by desktop browsers. However, expectations of iOS users are not so modest. They are expecting to view the *full web* in the palm of their hands. Therefore, as you design and develop your website, you need to consider the level of support you want to provide for these Apple devices. Do you offer mere compatibility and device friendliness, or do you even create a design specifically targeting iOS users? This chapter goes over the four tiers of enabling your website for Safari on iOS:

- ➤ Tier 1: iOS compatibility
- ➤ Tier 2: Navigation friendliness
- ➤ Tier 3: Device-specific style sheets
- ➤ Tier 4: Dedicated alternative site

TIER 1: IOS COMPATIBILITY

The first tier of support for iOS is simply making your website work inside Safari on iOS. Fortunately, because Safari is a sophisticated browser, far closer in capability to a desktop than a typical mobile browser, this is usually not problematic. However, there are some "gotchas," including the following:

- ➤ Adobe Flash media, Java applets, and plug-ins are not supported.
- ➤ You cannot use the CSS property `position:fixed`.
- ➤ The JavaScript functions `showModalDialog()` and `print()` do not function under Safari on iOS.
- ➤ Downloads and uploads (including HTML element `input type="file"`) are not supported.

Given its widespread popularity and desktop install base, Flash is the thorniest incompatibility for many web designers and developers. Until the original iPhone's release, Flash support was typically considered a given except in the case of a relatively small percentage of users. In fact, many designers could take it for granted that if a user was coming to a website without Flash support, then that user was probably not a target visitor anyway and so the designer could either ignore that user or simply refer him to the Adobe download page. However, with the ubiquitous nature of iOS devices, those assumptions are now invalid. Web designers over the past three years have been forced to rethink their site's reliance on a technology that they had become dependent upon. Figures 5-1 and 5-2 demonstrate the harsh reality in which a state-of-the-art website that looks amazing in Safari for Mac OS X never accounts for iPhone users.

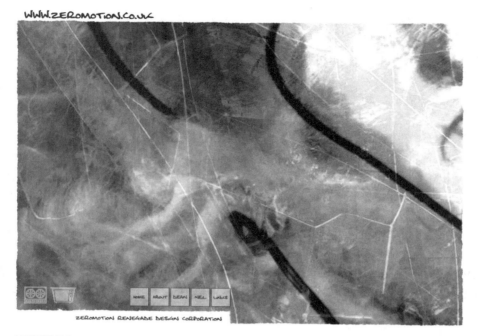

FIGURE 5-1

Therefore, if you plan on using Flash for an interactive portion of a page then you should also plan to degrade gracefully to a static graphic or alternative content. At a minimum, you should place a disclaimer over Flash content. It's not ideal, but it is better than the empty block. Or if you have a Flash-driven site (such as the one shown in Figure 5-1) then you should consider an alternative HTML site or, if warranted, even an iOS or mobile-specific site.

In order to detect Flash support, one solution is to use SWFObject, an open source JavaScript library that is used for detecting and embedding Flash content (available at http://code.google.com/p/swfobject/). SWFObject is not iOS specific, but it encapsulates the Flash Player detection logic, making it easy for you to degrade gracefully for Safari on iOS. For example, the following code displays a Flash file for Flash-enabled desktop browsers but displays a splash .png graphic for non-Flash visitors, including iOS users:

FIGURE 5-2

```
<!DOCTYPE html PUBLIC "-//W3C//DTD XHTML 1.0 Strict//EN"
          "http://www.w3.org/TR/xhtml1/DTD/xhtml1-strict.dtd">
<html xmlns="http://www.w3.org/1999/xhtml">
```

```
<head>
<title>Company XY Home Page</title>
<meta name="viewport" content="width=780">
<script type="text/javascript" src="swfobject.js"></script>
</head>
<body>
<div id="splashintro">
<a href="more.html"><img src="splash_noflash.png"/></a>
</div>
<script type="text/javascript">
    var so = new SWFObject("csplash.swf", "company_intro", "300", "240", "8",
      "#338899");
    so.write("splashintro");
</script>
</body>
</html>
```

As you can see, the swfobject.js library file is added to the homepage. When Flash is available, the script replaces the content of the splashintro div with Flash media. When Flash is not supported then appropriate content is substituted inside the splashintro div.

Therefore, at a minimum, you should seek to make your website fully aware and compatible for Safari on iPhone users.

TIER 2: NAVIGATION-FRIENDLY WEBSITES

When your website degrades gracefully for iOS users, you have achieved a base level of support for Apple mobile devices. However, while a user may be able to see all of the website's content, it still might not be easy for Safari on iOS users to navigate and read. A wide section of text, for example, may be perfectly fine for iPad, but it can become a stumbling block for iPhone and iPod touch users to read because horizontal scrolling is required when the user zooms in to read it. With this in mind, the second tier of support is to structure the site in a manner that is easy for Safari to zoom and navigate.

Working with the Viewport

A *viewport* is a rectangular area of screen space within which a web page is displayed. It determines how content is displayed and scaled to fit onto the iPhone or iPad. Using the viewport is analogous to looking at a panoramic scenic view of a mountain range through a camera zoom lens. If you want to see the entire mountainside you zoom out using the wide-angle zoom. As you do, you see everything, but the particulars of each individual mountain become smaller and harder to discern. Conversely, if you want to see a close-up picture of one of the peaks then you zoom in with the telephoto lens. Inside the camera's viewfinder you can no longer see the range as a whole, but the individual mountain is shown in terrific detail. The viewport meta tag in Safari works much the same way, enabling you to determine how much of the page to display, its zoom factor, and whether you want the user to zoom in and out or whether she needs to browse using one scale factor.

The way in which Safari renders the page is largely based on the width (and/or initial-scale) property of the viewport meta tag. With no viewport tag present, Safari considers the web page it is loading as being 980 pixels in width, and then shrinks the page scaling so that the entire page width can fit inside of the 320-pixel viewport (see Figure 5-3). Here is the default declaration:

```
<meta name="viewport" content="width=980;user-scalable=1;"/>
```

Suppose your website is only 880 pixels wide. If you let Safari stick with its default 980-pixel setting then the page scales more than it needs to. Therefore, to adjust the viewport magnification, you can specify a width optimized for your site:

```
<meta name="viewport" content="width=880"/>
```

Figures 5-4 and 5-5 show the noticeable difference between a 980- and an 880-width viewport for an 880-pixel width site.

With this declaration, instead of trying to fit 980 pixels into the 320 pixels of width, it only needs to shrink 880 pixels. Less scaling of content is needed (.363 scale instead of .326), making the site easier to use for iPhone and iPod touch users. Note that the `viewport` meta tag does not affect the rendering of the page in a normal desktop browser.

FIGURE 5-3

FIGURE 5-4

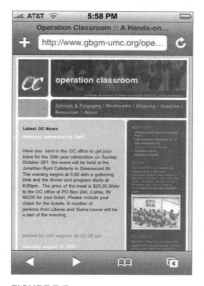

FIGURE 5-5

In addition to the `width` property, you can also programmatically control the scale of the viewport when the page initially loads through the `initial-scale` parameter. For example, if you want to set the initial scale to be .90, the declaration is the following:

```
<meta name="viewport" content="initial-scale=.9;user-scalable=1;"/>
```

After the page loads, however, the user is able to change the scale factor as he wants using pinch and double-tap gestures as long as the `user-scalable` property is set to true (the default). If you want to limit the scale range, you can use the `minimum-scale` and `maximum-scale` properties:

```
<meta name="viewport"
    content="initial-scale=.9;maximum-scale=1.0;minimum-scale=.8;user-scalable=1;"/>
```

In this way, the user has the ability to pinch and zoom but only to the extent that you want to allow.

If you develop a site or app specifically for iPhone or iPad, you need to size the page to the viewport by setting the `width=device-width` (`device-width` is a constant) and `initial-scale=1.0`. Because the scale is 1.0, you don't want the user to be able to rescale the application interface, so the `user-scalable` property should be disabled. Here's the declaration:

```
<meta name="viewport" content="width=device-width;
    initial-scale=1.0; maximum-scale=1.0; user-scalable=0;">
```

The `device-width` constant is treated as 320px on an iPhone and 1024px on iPad. In general, you need to avoid hardcoding a specific width and height for the viewport by making use of `device-width` and `device-height`. This is especially important for iPad because viewing with a viewport that has a width less than 1024 can affect the rendering quality of the content.

Table 5-1 lists the `viewport` properties. You don't need to set every property. Safari infers values based on the properties you have set.

Keep in mind that the `width` attribute does not refer to the size of the Safari browser window. It refers to the perceived size of the page in which Safari shrinks down to be displayed properly on the mobile device.

TABLE 5-1: viewport Meta Tag Properties

PROPERTY	DEFAULT VALUE	MINIMUM VALUE	MAXIMUM VALUE	DESCRIPTION
`width`	980	200	10000	Width of viewport
`height`	Based on aspect ratio	223	10000	Height of viewport
`initial-scale`	Fit to screen	Minimum-scale	Maximum-scale	Scale to render when page loads
`user-scalable`	1 (yes)	0 (no)	1 (yes)	If yes, user can change scale through pinch and double-tap

PROPERTY	DEFAULT VALUE	MINIMUM VALUE	MAXIMUM VALUE	DESCRIPTION
minimum-scale	0.25	>0	10	Use to set the lower end for scaling
maximum-scale	1.6	>0	10	Use to set the higher end for scaling

Although it's not generally recommended, you can specify the width of the content to be greater than the viewport width, but that requires the user to scroll horizontally.

Turning Your Page into Blocks

One of the most important ways to make your website friendly for iOS users is turn your web page into a series of columns and blocks. Columns make your page readable like a newspaper and help you avoid wide blocks of text that cause users to horizontally scroll left and right to read.

When a user double-taps an element, the iPhone or iPad looks at the element that is double-tapped and finds its closest block (`div`, `ol`, `ul`, `table`, and so on) or image ancestor. If a block is found then Safari zooms the content to fit the block's content based on the `viewport` tag's `width` property value and then centers it. If the user taps an image then Safari zooms to fit the image and centers it. If the image is already zoomed then zoom out occurs.

Figure 5-6 shows a sample page with a relatively simple structure, but it's one that makes it difficult for the iPhone to zoom in. The table is defined at a fixed width of 1000px, and the first column takes up 875px of that space. The text above the table spans the full document width, but, because it is outside of any block, Safari can do no zooming when the user double-taps. The user is forced to go to landscape mode and pinch to get readable text, but it still scrolls off the right of the screen (see Figure 5-7).

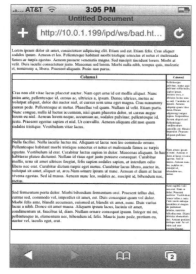

FIGURE 5-6

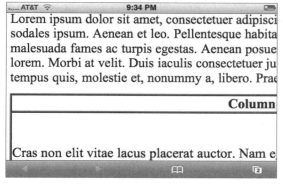

FIGURE 5-7

TRY IT OUT Making a Web Page Easy to Navigate for iOS Users

With a few simple tweaks, you can transform the page into something far easier for smaller devices (iPhone and iPod touch) to work with. Follow the instructions below on a page you want to work with.

1. Open the desired page of your website in a text editor.

2. Add a `viewport` meta tag to gain greater control over the width:

```
<meta name="viewport" content="width=780"/>
```

3. If your body content is not enclosed in any sort of block container, add a `div` block element and, if it makes sense for the design of your page, transform it into a column (say 50% of the page):

```
<div style="width:50%">
</div>
```

4. Locate any fixed-width tables and change to sized by percentage (90% of width). For example:

```
<table width="90%" border="1" cellspacing="1" cellpadding="1">
<tr>
<th width="75%" valign="top" scope="col"><div align="center">Column1</div></th>
<th width="25%" valign="top" scope="col">Column2</th>
</tr>
<tr>
</table>
```

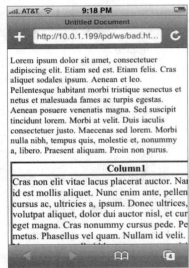

5. Save your page.

How It Works

In this exercise, we just performed some simple general purpose tasks that can make your website easier for iOS visitors to navigate. You added a viewport meta tag, added block containers for your content, and converted fixed-width tables into percentage-based. Even with these rudimentary changes, your page becomes easier to browse when you double-tap the page, as shown in Figure 5-8.

Figure 5-9 shows the model block-based web page that is easily navigated with double-tap and pinch gestures of iPhone.

FIGURE 5-8

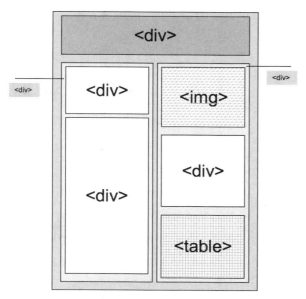

FIGURE 5-9

Defining Multiple Columns (Future Use)

The latest versions of WebKit (Safari) and Mozilla-based browsers provide support for new CSS3 properties that enable you to create newspaper-like, multicolumn layouts. For a content block, you can specify the number of columns, width of the columns, and the gap between them. Because not all browsers currently support multiple columns, these style properties are prefixed with -webkit and -moz:

```
-webkit-column-count: 2;
-moz-column-count: 2;
-webkit-column-width: 200px;
-moz-column-width: 200px;
-webkit-column-gap: 13px;
-moz-column-gap: 13px;
```

Unfortunately, the current version of Safari does not support these properties. However, be watching for their future support. When Safari does support multicolumns, it can offer an easy way to transform existing content into the columnar structure that iPhone users love.

TIER 3: CUSTOM STYLING

An iPhone user can navigate a Tier 2 website with double-tap, pinch, and flick gestures, but that does not necessarily mean that it is easy or enjoyable to do so. Panning and scrolling across the screen can become quickly tiresome. Users will quickly find themselves returning to sites that provide a richer, more tailored experience for Safari on iOS. The easiest way to do this is to create custom styles specifically for iPhone and iPad.

Media Queries

If you want to specify a style sheet for iOS usage, you can use a CSS3 `screen` media query. You can then use the `link` element to set specific styles for iPhone and iPad by looking for devices that only support screen display and have appropriate widths:

```
<!-[if !IE]>->
<link media="only screen and (max-device-width: 480px)" type="text/css"
   rel="stylesheet" href="iPhone.css" />
<link
   media="only screen and (min-device-width: 768px) and (max-device-width: 1024px)"
   type="text/css" rel="stylesheet" href="iPad.css" />
<!-<![endif]->
<link
   media="screen and (min-device-width: 1025px)" href="default.css"
   type="text/css" rel="stylesheet"/>
```

The first media query targets the iPhone and the second targets iPad. The `only` keyword prevents non-compliant browsers from selecting one of the mobile style sheets. However, the problem is that, under certain situations, earlier versions of Internet Explorer (versions 6 and 7) fail to ignore this rule and render the page anyway using the iPhone-specific style sheet. As a result, you need to guard against this possibility by using IE's conditional comments. When you do, Internet Explorer ignores this link element because the `[if !IE]` indicates that the enclosed code should only be executed outside of IE.

You can also set iOS-specific styles inside a single CSS style sheet, by using a `@media` query:

```
@media only screen and (max-device-width: 480px)
{
   /* Add iPhone styles here */
}

@media only screen and (min-device-width: 768px) and (max-device-width: 1024px)
{
   /* Add iPad styles here */
}
```

Text Size Adjustment

Normally, the font size of a web page adjusts automatically when the viewport is adjusted. For instance, after a double-tap gesture, Safari looks at the zoomed width of the content block and adjusts the text to zoom in proportion. This behavior makes the text easier to read for typical uses, though it can affect absolute positioning and fixed layouts. If you would like to prevent the text from resizing then use the following CSS rule:

```
-webkit-text-size-adjust: none;
```

In general, for most website viewing, you will want to keep this property enabled. For iPhone-specific contexts in which you want more control over scaling and sizing, you need to disable this option.

Case Study: Enabling an Existing Web Site

Consider a case study example, the website of Operation Classroom, a nonprofit organization doing educational work in Africa. Keep in mind that the style sheet of each website needs to be optimized in a unique manner, but this case study demonstrates some of the common issues that crop up.

The website renders nicely on iPad as is, but less optimally on a smaller iOS device. Figure 5-10 displays a page from the site with a basic `viewport` meta tag set at `width=780`, which gives it the best scale factor for the existing page structure. However, even when the viewport setting is optimized, a user still needs to double-tap in order to read any of the text on the page. What's more, the top-level links are difficult to tap unless you pinch and zoom first.

However, by creating an iPhone and iPod touch-specific style sheet, you can transform the usability site for Safari on iOS users without affecting any of the HTML code.

Each website is going to have individual needs and customizations to work well with iPhone users, so the specific transformations that I performed with this website may or may not apply to you. However, in general, these provide a good example of the types of modifications you should think about for your site.

Looking at the page (see Figure 5-10), notice that several transformations need to occur:

➤ Shrink the page width.

➤ Shrink the Operation Classroom logo at the top of the page.

➤ Increase the font size for the menu links, page header, rabbit trail links, and body text.

➤ Move the sidebar to appear below body text.

FIGURE 5-10

Updating the HTML files

As a first step, I add a media query to the document head of each page in the site:

```
<!-[if !IE]>->
<link media="only screen and (max-device-width: 480px)" type="text/css"
```

```
   rel="stylesheet" href="iPhone.css" />
<!-<![endif]->
<link media="screen and (min-device-width: 1025px)" href="default.css"
   type="text/css" rel="stylesheet"/>
```

Next, inside the HTML files I change the `viewport` meta tag to a smaller width:

```
<meta name="viewport" content="width=490"/>
```

The 490px width is wide enough to be compatible with the existing site structure but small enough to minimize the scaling.

That's all of the work that I need to do to the HTML files.

Creating iPhone.css

To create the new custom style sheet, I begin by opening the default style sheet already being used and then save as a new name — iphone.css. My first task is to change the width of the document from 744px to 490px. Here's the updated style:

```
@media all {
  #wrap {
    position:relative;
    top:4px;
    left:4px;
    background:#ab8;
    width:490px;
    margin:0 auto;
    text-align:left;
  }
```

Next, I change the original `font-size:small` property defined in `body` to a more specific pixel size:

```
body {
  background:#cdb;
  margin:0;
  padding:10px 0 14px;
  font-family: Verdana,Sans-serif;
  text-align:center;
  color:#333;
  font-size: 15px;
  }
```

Although this size is not as large as what an iPhone web app would use, it is the largest font size that works with the current structure of the Operation Classroom website. Fortunately, the *rabbit trail* (pathway) and page header fonts are relative to the body font, as shown in the style below:

```
#pathway {
  margin-top:3px;
  margin-bottom: 25px;
  letter-spacing: .18em;
  color: #666666;
  font-size: .8em;
```

```
   }
#pageheader {
   font-family:Helvetica,Arial,Verdana,Sans-serif;
   font-weight: bold;
   font-size: 2.2em;
   margin-bottom: 1px;
   margin-top: 3px;
}
```

The next issue is to shrink the size of the banner at the top of the page. Here's the pre-iPhone style for the banner text:

```
#banner-text{
   background:url("./images/bg_header.jpg") no-repeat left top;
   margin:0;
   padding:40px 0 0;
   font:bold 275%/97px Helvetica,Arial,Verdana,Sans-serif;
   text-transform:lowercase;
   }
```

The two properties you need to try to shrink are the `padding` and the `font` size. Here's a workable solution:

```
#banner-title {
   background:url("./images/bg_header.jpg") no-repeat left top;
   margin:0;
   padding:10px 0 10px;
   font: Bold 35px Helvetica,Arial,Verdana,Sans-serif;
   text-transform:lowercase;
   }
```

The final and perhaps most important change is to enable the sidebar to follow the main text rather than float alongside it. Here's the original pre-iPhone definition:

```
#sidebar {
   background:#565 url(".images/corner_sidebar.gif") no-repeat left top;
   width: 254px;
   float: right;
   padding:0;
   color:#cdb;
   }
```

To move the sidebar content below the main body text, I remove the `float` property and add a `clear: both` declaration to prevent the sidebar from any side wrapping. I also change the small width of 254px to 100 percent, which enables it to take up the entire contents of the `content` `div`. Here's the code:

```
#sidebar {
   background:#565 url("./images/corner_sidebar.gif") no-repeat left top;
   width:100%;
   clear: both;
   padding:0;
   color:#cdb;
   }
```

Figures 5-11, 5-12, and 5-13 show the results of the transformation.

FIGURE 5-11

FIGURE 5-12

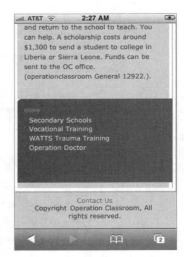

FIGURE 5-13

As you can see, you can often transform your existing website into an iPhone-friendly site with a handful of well-thought-out style changes.

TIER 4: PARALLEL SITES

Unless you are creating an iPhone or iPod touch application, developing for Tier 2 or 3 support provides sufficient support for most sites. However, you might find a compelling need to actually develop a site specifically written for iPhone or iPad. The content may be the same, but it needs to be structured in a manner discussed throughout this book.

If you are going to offer an mobile version of your site, you need to offer your users the freedom to choose between the mobile site and your normal full site. Don't auto-redirect based on user agent. Because Safari on iOS can navigate a normal website, you should always allow users to make the decision themselves. Therefore it is standard practice to add a link at the bottom of the page to your full site for users who access the home page with their iPhones.

A second alternative is to do the reverse: When an iOS device loads the page, the site asks whether or not the user would prefer to go to the dedicated mobile site instead.

TRY IT OUT   Prompting iOS Users to a Dedicated Site

Follow the instructions below to add this capability to your site.

1. Open up the home page of your website in a text editor.

2. Add an empty `div` element at the top of your content, just below a top navigation menu if it exists on your page:

```
<div id="ios-notify"></div>
```

3. Add the following script to the document head:

```
<script type="application/x-javascript">
function isiPhone()
{
  result ((navigator.platform.indexOf("iPhone") != -1) ||
          (navigator.userAgent.indexOf('iPod') != -1))
}
function isiPad()
{
  result ((navigator.platform.indexOf("iPad") != -1)
}

function init()
{
  if (isiPhone())
  {
    var o = document.getElementById( 'ios-notify' );
    o.innerHTML = "<h1 style='text-align:center;border: 1px solid #a23e14;" +
    " -webkit-border-radius: 10px;'><a href='iphone-index.html'>" +
    "Tap here to go to our<br/>iPhone web site.</a></h1>";
  }
  else if (isiPad())
  {
  if (isiPad)
  {
    var o = document.getElementById( 'ios-notify' );
    o.innerHTML = "<h1 style='text-align:center;border: 1px solid #a23e14;" +
    " -webkit-border-radius: 10px;'><a href='ipad-index.html'>" +
    "Tap here to go to our<br/>iPad web site.</a></h1>";
  }

  }
}
</script>
```

4. Save the file.

How It Works

This example shows you a simple way in which you can offer iPhone and iPad visitors the option of viewing a site designed for each device. The empty `div` element serves as the placeholder for the message that you display to iOS visitors.

The `init()` function calls the `isiPhone()` function to determine whether the user agent is an iPhone or iPod touch. If the device is an iPhone or iPod touch then HTML content is added to the placeholder `div` element. If not, then the `isiPad()` function is called to see if the user is coming to the site using an iPad. The `init()` function is then called from the `onload` handler of the `body`. Figure 5-14 shows the results when viewed from an iPhone.

FIGURE 5-14

EXERCISES

1. Is Flash supported on iOS devices?

2. What is the purpose of a `viewport` meta tag?

3. What constant should you use to size the page to the width of the device's viewport?

4. Why is it a good idea to make frequent use of columns in your web page structure?

5. What is the link syntax for defining an iPad media query?

Answers to the Exercises can be found in the Appendix.

▶ **WHAT YOU LEARNED IN THIS CHAPTER**

TOPIC	KEY CONCEPTS
Making your website compatible with iOS devices	Avoid using Adobe Flash media, Java applets, and Plug-ins. Also, avoid using the CSS property `position:fixed`.
Making your site easy to navigate with iOS devices	Add a `viewport` meta tag, which determines how content is displayed and scaled to fit onto the iPhone or iPad. Turn your Web page into a series of columns and blocks, which are much easier for an iPhone to zoom and navigate.
Add custom iOS styling to your website	Use a CSS3 `screen` media query to set specific styles for iPhone and iPad.
Maintaining a parallel website for mobile devices	Allow mobile users the choice of using the mobile site or the full site.

PART II
Application Design

Designing the iPhone UI

WHAT YOU WILL LEARN IN THIS CHAPTER:

➤ Understanding the iPhone viewport

➤ Exploring iOS design patterns

➤ Designing for touch

More than anything else, the iPhone and iPad are known for their usability, intuitiveness, and overall positive user experience. The native iOS user interface (UI) is known by novices and geeks alike as being easy to use; no instruction manual needed.

An iOS web app doesn't need to copy or perfectly emulate native iOS UI design and controls. In fact, some developers even argue that developers shouldn't try to create iOS-focused web apps. Regardless of your position on that issue, there's one thing you will want to do when you create an iOS web app — create a usable and navigable UI.

That's why, in this chapter, you explore many of the common design patterns that Apple uses in its UI as well as the key design patterns used to present data in a mobile device. In this chapter, I focus primarily on iPhone; in Chapter 7, I focus on iPad.

EVOLVING UI DESIGN

User interface design has been evolutionary rather than revolutionary over the past decade. Most would argue that Mac OS X Lion and Windows 7 both have much more refined UIs than their predecessors. As true as that may be, their changes improve upon existing ideas rather than offer groundbreaking new ways of interacting with the computer. Web design is no different. All of the innovations that have transpired — such as HTML5 and Ajax — have revolutionized the structure and composition of a website but not how users interact with it. Moreover, mobile and handheld devices offered a variety of new platforms to design for, but these were either lightweight versions of a desktop OS or a simplistic character-based menu.

Enter iOS.

An iOS interface is not a traditional desktop interface, though it has a codebase closely based on Mac OS X. It is also not a traditional mobile interface, though the iPhone and the iPad are obviously mobile devices. Despite the fact that you build web apps using web technologies, an iOS interface is not a normal web application interface.

Because the underlying guts of iOS web applications are based on tried and true web technologies, many are tempted to come to the iOS platform and naturally want to do the same things they've always done — except customizing it for the new device. That's why the biggest mindset change for developers is to grasp that they are creating iOS web apps, not web applications that happen to run on iOS. The difference is significant. In many ways, iOS web applications are far more like Mac or Windows desktop applications — users have a certain look and feel and core functionality that they expect to see in it.

On the Web, users expect every interface design to be one-offs. Navigation, controls, and other functionality are usually unique to each site. However, when working on a platform — be it Windows, Mac OS X, or iOS — the expectation is much different. Users anticipate a consistent way to do tasks — from application to application. Operating systems provide application program interfaces (APIs) for applications to call to display a common graphical user interface (GUI). Because iOS web apps do not have such a concept, it is up to you as an application developer to implement consistency.

THE IPHONE VIEWPORT

A *viewport* is a rectangular area of screen space within which an application is displayed. Traditional Windows and Mac desktop applications are contained inside their own windows. Web apps are displayed inside a browser window. A user can manipulate what is seen inside of the viewport by resizing the window, scrolling its contents, and, in many cases, changing the zoom level. The actual size of the viewport depends entirely on the user, though an average size for a desktop browser is roughly 1000×700 pixels.

The entire iPhone display is 320×480 pixels in portrait mode and 480×320 in landscape. However, application developers don't have access to all of that real estate. Instead, the viewport in which an iPhone developer is free to work with is a smaller rectangle: 320×416 in portrait mode without the URL bar displayed (320×356 with the URL bar shown), and 480×268 in landscape mode (480×208 with the URL bar). Figures 6-1 and 6-2 show the dimensions of the iPhone viewport in both orientations.

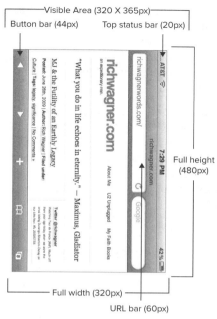

FIGURE 6-1

FIGURE 6-2

Users can scroll around the viewport with their fingers. However, they cannot resize it. To use desktop lingo, an iOS application is always "full screen" and takes up all available space.

If the on-screen keyboard is displayed, the visibility of the viewport is further restricted with the keyboard overlay, as shown in Figures 6-3 and 6-4.

FIGURE 6-3

FIGURE 6-4

Because users have a much smaller viewport than they are used to working with on their desktop, the iPhone viewport has a scale property that you can manipulate. When Safari on iOS loads a web page, it automatically defines the page width as 980 pixels, a common size for most fixed width pages. It then scales the page to fit inside of the 320 or 480 pixel width viewport. Although 980 pixels may be acceptable for browsing a scaled-down version of a website, an iPhone application avoids scaling by customizing the `viewport` meta tag.

As I talked about in Chapter 5, you use the `viewport` meta tag to set the width and scale of the viewport. If you are creating a web app targeting iPhone, then you need to set the viewport to be the exact width of the device — `320px` in portrait mode and `480px` in landscape mode. (For iPad, you'd use `640px` in portrait mode and `1024px` in landscape.) To make things easier, Safari on iOS supports constants so you can avoid the specific numeric values. Therefore, to set the viewport for a normal iPhone web app, you should add the following meta tag to the head of your HTML document:

```
<meta name="viewport" content="width=device-width; initial-scale=1.0;
    maximum-scale=1.0; user-scalable=no;"/>
```

The `width=device-width` attribute sets the width to a fixed size and ensures that the viewport is not resized when the user rotates to landscape mode. The `initial-scale=1.0` sets the scale at 1.0, whereas the `maximum-scale` and `user-scalable` settings disable user zooming of the web page.

EXPLORING IOS DESIGN PATTERNS

Before you begin designing your iOS web application, a valuable exercise is exploring the native iOS applications on the device or from the App Store. As you do so, you can consider how other designers handled a small viewport as well as how to design an intuitive interface for touch screen input.

TRY IT OUT   Exploring User Interface Patterns

To get an idea how the user interfaces of other apps are designed, follow these steps.

1. Open three different types of apps: Mail, Camera, and Calculator.

2. Note the purpose of the app and examine the design decisions that went into each of the different apps.

3. Pick some third-party apps that you have downloaded from the App Store and note what you liked and did not like about them.

4. Based on your review of native apps, make a list of UI design ideas that could work and are appropriate in a Web context.

How It Works

The purpose of this activity is simply to get you to think differently about apps that you work with on a daily basis. Why did the developers make the design decisions that they did? Why did they employ the UI design elements and schemes that they did? What would you have done differently? These are exactly the sorts of questions that you should ask as you begin to design your own app UI.

Categorizing Apps

To fully appreciate the design decisions that went into these applications, you need to understand the differences in the way in which users use iOS applications compared to their desktop counterparts. After all, consider the types of applications that you find installed on your desktop computer. An overly simplistic categorization is as follows:

> ➤ **Task-based applications:** The typical desktop application, whether it is on Mac, Windows, or Linux, is designed to solve a particular problem or perform a specific task. These applications, (such as Word, Excel, PowerPoint, Photoshop, or iCal) tend to act upon one file or a few files at a time. The UI for these applications is often quite similar, including a top-level menu, toolbar, common dialogs for open/save, main destination window, and side panels.

> ➤ **Aggregators:** The second category of desktop application is aggregators — those applications that manage considerable amounts of data in which you tend to work with many pieces of data at a time rather than just one or two. iTunes manages your songs and videos, iPhoto and Picasa manage your photos, and Outlook and Apple Mail store your emails. The UI for aggregator applications is typically navigation-based, consisting of top-level navigable categories in a left-side panel (playlists in iTunes, folders in Mail, albums in iPhoto) and scrolling listings in the main window.

> ➤ **Widgets:** A third category is widget-style applications, which are mini applications that display system or other information (battery status meter, weather, world clock), or perform a very specific task (lyrics grabber, radio tuner). A widget UI typically consists of a single screen and a settings pane.

On the desktop, task-based applications have traditionally been the dominant category, though aggregators have become more and more important over the past decade with the increasing need to manage digital media. Although widgets are quite popular now that Apple and Microsoft have added this functionality directly into their OS, they remain far less important.

When you look at built-in iOS applications, you can see that they generally fall into these three categories as well. However, because of the device's viewport and file-storage constraints, task-based applications take a back seat role to the aggregators (see Table 6-1).

TABLE 6-1: Categorizing Apple's Built-in iOS Applications

AGGREGATORS	TASK-BASED	WIDGETS
Mail	Safari	Stocks
Messages	Phone	Weather
Photos	Camera	Clock
YouTube	Calendar	Calculator

continues

TABLE 6-1 *(continued)*

AGGREGATORS	TASK-BASED	WIDGETS
Notes	Maps	
Contacts (Address Book)	Compass	
iPod	Voice Memos	
iTunes		
App Store		

The document is the primary point of focus in a traditional desktop application, but it is not surprising for a document on an iOS device to be consumable and temporary. You have the Pages, Numbers, and Keynote applications for iOS, but many of the documents that users work with are consumable: web pages, SMS messages, YouTube videos, quick notes, and Google maps.

Navigation List-based UI Design

Because the focus of many iOS apps is to consume various amounts of information, navigation list–based design becomes an essential way to present large amounts of information to users on the iPhone. As I mentioned earlier, desktop applications typically relegate navigation lists to a side panel on the left of the main window, but many iPhone applications use "edge-to-edge" navigation as the primary driver of the UI.

Not all navigation list designs are equal. In fact, the iPhone features at least eight distinct varieties of navigation lists. For example, the Contacts list uses a single line to display the name of a contact in bold letters (see Figure 6-5), whereas Mail uses a four-line list style to display both message header information and optional text preview (see Figure 6-6). Finally, YouTube sports a wealth of information in its four-line item (see Figure 6-7). Table 6-2 lists each of the various navigation style lists.

FIGURE 6-5

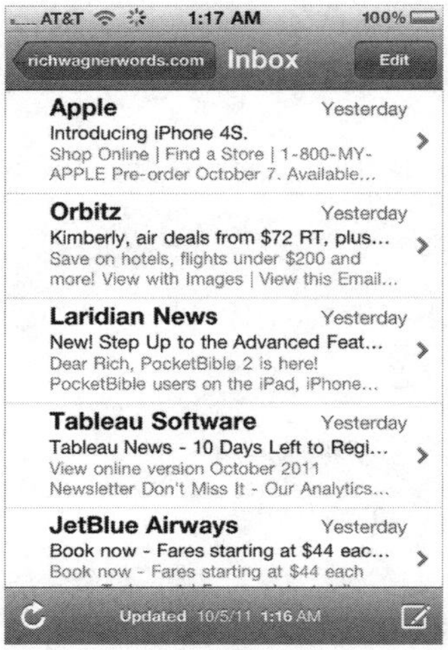

FIGURE 6-6

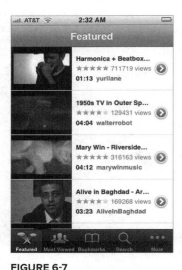

FIGURE 6-7

TABLE 6-2: Different Types of Navigation Lists

APPLICATION	STYLE	DISPLAYS
Contacts	1 line	Name of contact (last name bolded)
Mail	2.7 lines (default 4)	Message title and optional text preview
Maps List	2 lines	Location name, address
SMS	3 lines	Message title and text preview
Photos	1 line	Album title and thumbnail image
YouTube	3 lines	Thumbnail, title, rating, length, views, and submitter
Notes	1 line	First line of note text
iPod Playlists	1 line	Playlist name
Settings	1 line	Grouped items with icons

However, no matter the style of the navigation lists, they are each designed to quickly take you to a destination page in as few interactions as possible.

What's more, the top title bar of the app usually provides contextual information to help users understand where they are in the hierarchy of the application. The left side often has a back button that enables users to return to the previous screen. Read more on this in the "Title Bar" section later in the chapter.

Application Modes

Native iPhone applications also often have modes or views to the information or functionality with which you can work. These modes are displayed as icons or buttons on the bottom toolbar (see Figure 6-8). Interestingly, in the initial release of iCal, the buttons were on the top. However, in subsequent releases, Apple moved the bottoms to the bottom to adhere to the convention of *navigation on top, modes on bottom* (see Figure 6-9).

Table 6-3 details these modes.

TABLE 6-3: Application Modes and UI Access

APPLICATION	MODES	UI CONTROLS
iCal	List, Day, Month	Bottom button bar
Phone	Favorites, Recents, Contacts, Keypad, Voicemail	Bottom toolbar
iPod	Playlists, Podcasts, Albums, Videos, and so on	Bottom toolbar
YouTube	Featured, Most Viewed, Bookmarks, Search	Bottom toolbar
Clock	World Clock, Alarm, Stopwatch, Timer	Bottom toolbar

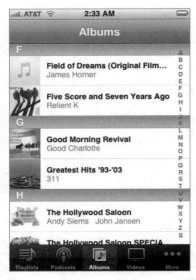

FIGURE 6-8   **FIGURE 6-9**

Therefore, as you begin to examine how you should design the UI of your application, look to see what parallels there are with the built-in iPhone application design. Even if you don't emulate its look and feel, you might want to have a consistent approach.

EXPLORING SCREEN LAYOUT

By the time you have studied and evaluated the UI design of the built-in applications, you can then begin to determine what parallels may exist with the type of application in which you are building.

For applications that need to use a navigation list design, you need to download one of the frameworks that I discuss in Chapter 15. Each of these enables you to easily implement edge-to-edge navigation list–based applications.

The four common components of a typical mobile app are a title bar, a navigation list, a destination page, and a button bar.

Title Bar

Most iOSWeb applications should include a title bar to emulate the look of the standard title bar available in nearly all native iOS applications. When the URL bar is hidden (as I explain later in this chapter) the custom title bar displays just below the status bar at the top of the viewport (see Figure 6-10). The title bar includes the following elements:

> **Back button:** A back button should be placed on the left-hand side of the toolbar to allow the user to return to the previous page. The name of the button should be the same name as the title of the previous screen. This "bread crumb" technique lets the user know how he got

to the page and how to get back. If the page is at the top level of the application then there is no back button.

➤ **Screen title:** Each screen should have a title displayed in the center of the toolbar. The title of the page should be one word and appropriately describe the content of the current screen. You do not want to include the application name in each screen title of the application, as you would for a standard web application.

➤ **Command button:** For some screens, you want to employ a common command, such as Cancel, Edit, Search, or Done. If you need this functionality, place a command button at the top right of the title bar.

Edge-to-Edge Navigation Lists

If you are designing an app specifically for the iPhone that aggregates or organizes lists of information, you typically want to follow iPhone's edge-to-edge navigation list design pattern, as shown in Figure 6-11. Each of the cells, or subsections, is extra large to allow for easy touch input. In addition, to ensure that a user never loses context and gets lost, the title shows the current page, and a back button indicates the screen to which the user can return. When a list item expands to a destination page or another list, an arrow is placed on the right side indicating a next page is available.

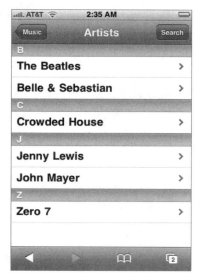

FIGURE 6-10

FIGURE 6-11

When a list item is selected, the navigation list should emulate Apple's slide-in animation, appearing as if the new page is coming in from the right side of the screen to replace the old.

Table 6-4 lists each of the specific metrics to emulate the same look and feel of the Apple design in edge-to-edge navigation lists.

TABLE 6-4: Metrics for Apple's Edge-to-Edge Design

ITEM	VALUE
Cell height (including bottom line)	44px
Cell width	320px (portrait), 480px (landscape)
Font	Helvetica, 20pt bold (normal text acceptable for less important text)
Font color	Black
Horizontal lines (between cells)	#d9d9d9 (RGB=217, 217, 217)
Left padding	10px
Bottom padding	14px
Control height	29px
Control alignment	Right, 10px
Control shape	Rounded rectangle of 7-degree radius
Control text	Helvetica, 12pt
Background color	White

Rounded Rectangle Design Destination Pages

In a navigation-list UI design, a user ultimately winds up at a destination page that provides a full listing of the specific piece of information for which she was looking. Apple implements a rounded rectangle design, as shown in Figure 6-12. Labels are displayed on a blue background, and items are grouped together logically and surrounded by a rounded rectangle box. Table 6-5 describes the specifications you should follow to implement this Apple design.

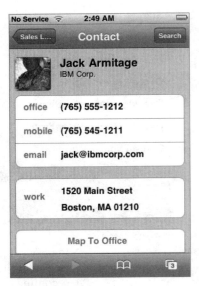

FIGURE 6-12

TABLE 6-5: Metrics for Apple's Rounded Rectangle Design

ITEM	VALUE
Cell height	44px
Rounded rectangle corner radius	10px × 10px radius (-webkit-border-radius:10px)
Rounded rectangle left and right margins	10px
Rounded rectangle top and bottom margins	17px
Horizontal lines (between cells)	#d9d9d9 (RGB=217, 217, 217)
Label font	Helvetica 17pt, bold
Label font color	#4c566c (RGB=76, 86, 108)
Cell font	Helvetica 17pt, bold
Cell font color	Black
Cell text position	10px from left edge, 14px bottom edge
Background color	#c5ccd3 (RGB= 197, 204, 211)

DESIGNING FOR TOUCH

One of the most critical design considerations you need to take into account for iPhone interfaces in particular is that that you are designing an interface that interacts with a finger, not a mouse or other mechanical pointing device. A mouse pointer has a small point that's just a couple pixels in height, but a finger can touch 40 pixels or more of the screen during a typical click action. Therefore, when laying out controls in an application, make sure the height of controls and spacing between controls are easy to use even for someone with large fingers.

NOTE Because iPhone is a mobile device, keep in mind that users may be on the go when they are interacting with your application. Maybe they are walking down the street, waiting in line at a coffee shop, or perhaps even jogging. Therefore, you should allow enough space in your UI to account for shaky fingers.

Standard navigation list cells should be 44px in height. Buttons should be sized about the size of a finger, typically 40px in height or more and have sufficient space around them to prevent accidental clicks. You can get by with a button of 29 to 30 pixels in height if no other buttons are around it, but be careful. Table 6-6 lists the recommended sizes of the common elements.

In addition to sizing and spacing issues, another important design decision is to minimize the need for text entry. Use select lists rather than input fields where possible. What's more, use cookies to remember last values entered to prevent constant data reentry.

TABLE 6-6: Metrics for Touch Input Screen

ELEMENT METRIC	RECOMMENDED SIZE
Element height	40px (minimum 29px)
Element width	Minimum 30px
Select, Input height	30px
Navigation list cell height	44px
Spacing between elements	20px

WORKING WITH FONTS

With its Retina Display and anti-aliasing support, iPhone is an ideal platform to work with typefaces. Quality fonts render beautifully on the iPhone display, enhancing the overall attractiveness of your application's UI.

Helvetica, Apple's font of choice for iOS, should generally be the default font of your application. However, iOS does offer several font choices for the developer. Unlike a typical web environment in which you must work with font families, iOS enables you to make some assumptions on the exact fonts that users have when they run your application. Table 6-7 lists the fonts that are supported on iOS.

TABLE 6-7: iOS Fonts

NAME
American Typewriter (no italics)
Arial
Arial Rounded MT Bold (no italics)
Courier New
Georgia
Helvetica
Marker Felt
Times New Roman
Trebuchet MS
Verdana
Zapfino

Safari on iOS automatically substitutes three unsupported fonts with their built-in counterparts. Courier New is substituted when Courier is specified. Helvetica is substituted for Helvetica Neue, and Times New Roman is used in place of Times.

BEST PRACTICES IN IOS UI DESIGN

When you are designing for iOS, there are several best practices to keep in mind:

➤ **Remember the touch!** Perhaps no tip is more critical in iPhone UI design than always double-checking every design decision you make with the reality of touch input.

➤ **Make sure you design your application UI to work equally well in portrait and landscape modes.** Some native applications, such as Mail, optimize their UI for portrait mode and ignore any changes the user makes to orientation. Third-party iOS web app developers do not have that same level of control. Therefore, any UI design you create needs to work in both orientation modes.

➤ **Avoid UI designs that require horizontal scrolling.** If your interface design requires the user to scroll from side to side within a single display screen, change it. Horizontal scrolling is confusing to users and leaves them feeling disoriented within your application.

➤ **Keep your design simple.** As attractive as the iOS interface is, perhaps its most endearing quality is its ease of use and simplicity. Your UI design should follow suit. Avoid adding complexity where you do not need to — either in functionality or design (see Figure 6-13).

➤ **Use familiar lingo.** You know the saying, "When in Rome." Well, when designing for iOS, be sure you do not bring along the UI baggage you are used to elsewhere (Windows, Mac, or even the Web).

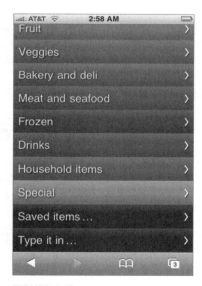

FIGURE 6-13

➤ **Use UI frameworks, but use them wisely.** Mobile web app frameworks (see Chapter 16) are major assets to the iOS web app developer community and provide a major head start in developing applications. However, don't automatically assume that their prebuilt designs are the best way to go for your application. You may find another approach is better for your specific needs.

➤ **Restrict use of a black button bar.** A translucent black button bar (such as the one used by the iPod app in Figure 6-8) should only be used in your application for displaying modes or views, not for commands. Use the other button types for commands.

➤ **Minimize the rabbit trail.** Because iOS users are primarily concerned with consuming data, you should get them to the destination page as soon as possible. Therefore, make sure you are optimally organizing the information in a way that enables a user to get to the data he needs in just a couple of flicks and clicks.

➤ **Place text entry fields at the top of the page.** When your application requires data-entry fields, work to place these input fields as near to the top of the page as possible. Top positioning of text entry fields helps minimize the chances of the user losing context when the on-screen keyboard suddenly appears at the bottom of the screen.

➤ **Communicate status.** Because your application may be running from a 3G connection, its response may be relatively slow. As a result, be sure to provide status to the user when performing a function that requires server processing. This visual cue helps users feel confident that your application is working as expected and is not in a hung state.

➤ **Label the title bar appropriately.** Make sure each screen or page has its own title. The Back button should always be named with the title of the previous screen.

➤ **Unselect previously selected items.** When a user clicks the Back button in a navigation-list UI, be sure that the previously selected item is unchecked.

➤ **Break the rules — competently.** Although it is often wisest to design your app to be consistent with the design patterns that I've been discussing in this chapter, not every iOS application UI needs to rigidly conform to a design implemented already by Apple. You may have an application in which a different look-and-feel works best for its target users. However, if you decide to employ a unique design, be sure it complements overall iOS design, not clashes with it.

ADDING FINISHING TOUCHES

In order to transform your web app into something that looks and feels like a native iOS app, you need to put some finishing touches on it. In this final section, I show you how to launch the app in full screen, customize the status bar, and create a WebClip icon.

TRY IT OUT Adding Finishing Touches to Your App

To make your web app appear much more like a native iOS app, follow these steps.

1. Create or obtain PNG images that you want to use as the icon for your app on the home screen of the iOS device. For iPhone 4 and above, you need 114 x 114. For iPad, you need 72 x 72. For iPod touch and older iPhone models, you need the default size of 57 x 57. Name the images as follows: `touch-icon-iphone.png` (57 x 57), `touch-icon-ipad.png` (72 x 72), and `touch-icon-iphone4.png` (114 x 114).

2. Save the image in the root directory of your web app.

3. Open the main page of your web app in a text editor.

4. Add an `apple-mobile-web-app-capable` meta tag to the document head and assign it a `yes` value:

```
<meta name="apple-mobile-web-app-capable" content="yes" />
```

5. Add a `status-bar-style` meta tag to the document head and set it to a value of `black`:

```
<meta name="apple-mobile-web-app-status-bar-style" content="black" />
```

6. Add the following link tags to the document head:

```
<link rel="apple-touch-icon" href="icon.png"/>
<link rel="apple-touch-icon" sizes="72x72" href="icon-ipad.png" />
<link rel="apple-touch-icon" sizes="114x114" href=" icon-iphone4.png" />
```

7. Save your file.

How It Works

By default, when you run your web app in Safari on iOS, Safari still takes up a sizable majority of the viewport with its URL bar and bottom bar. However, to take back that wasted space and to make your app look more like a native app, you should launch your application in full-screen mode, which your app does when the an `apple-mobile-web-app-capable` meta tag is provided in the document. However, full-screen mode only takes effect when you launch your app from the Home screen via a WebClip icon. When you access the page from the URL bar, Safari retains its URL bar and button bar.

When you use the `apple-mobile-web-app-capable` meta tag to go into full-screen mode, Safari still displays the top status bar. This behavior is not that unexpected because most native apps show it in the same way. However, if you prefer to mark the status bar, you can customize its appearance to be transparent black by using the `status-bar-style` meta tag and setting it to a value of `black`. However, this meta tag only takes effect if you also use the `apple-mobile-web-app-capable` meta tag to turn on full-screen mode.

Finally, the `<link rel="apple-touch-icon/>` tag enables you to add your app to the Home screen just like a native application. The graphic file you point to needs to adhere to the following conventions:

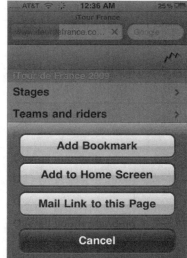

FIGURE 6-14

➤ Must be in .png format.

➤ Located in the root directory.

➤ As stated earlier, use 114 x 114 for iPhone 4 and above. For iPad, use 72 x 72. And for iPod touch and older iPhone models, use the default size of 57 x 57.

➤ Must be a rectangle — iOS automatically adds the rounded corners.

➤ It must be named `apple-touch-icon.png` or `apple-touch-icon-precomposed.png`. If you use `apple-touch-icon.png`, the iPhone OS adds round corners, drop shadow, and a "shiny coating" to the graphic. If you use `apple-touch-icon-precomposed.png` then the OS won't add these effects.

Users can add the WebClip icon of your app by clicking the + button on the button bar when they navigate to the URL. In the pop-up dialog, users click the Add to Home Screen button (see Figure 6-14).

Unfortunately, because there is no formal install process of a web app, there is no programmatic way to automatically add a WebClip icon to the Home screen. The process must be carried out by the user.

EXERCISES

1. When would you use the edge-to-edge navigation list design pattern?

2. What is the minimum pixel size a button or other UI element should generally be for touch?

3. True or False? Comic Sans is a font available on iOS.

4. True or False? Safari on iOS enables you to control screen orientation via JavaScript.

Answers to the Exercises can be found in the Appendix.

▶ **WHAT YOU LEARNED IN THIS CHAPTER**

TOPIC	KEY CONCEPTS
Viewport	A *viewport* is a rectangular area of screen space within which an application is displayed. A user can manipulate what is seen inside of the viewport by resizing the window, scrolling its contents, and, in many cases, changing the zoom level.
iOS UI design patterns	Navigation list–based design becomes an essential way to present large amounts of hierarchical or list-based info.
	Navigation on top, modes on bottom.
Best practices	Remember the touch.
	Avoid horizontal scrolling.
	Keep your design simple.
	Use familiar terminology.
	Communicate status to user.

Designing for iPad

The iPad is mobile, but it is not a phone device. That statement is a "no-brainer" obviously, but when designing for the iPad it is easy to fall into the trap of thinking of it as a "giant iPhone." On the contrary, the iPad is almost a perfect blend between the mobile and touch qualities of an iPhone and the larger visual experience and interaction capabilities of a desktop computer. Therefore, as you design web apps for the iPad, you need to give it the individual attention it deserves rather than just treating it as a bigger iPhone viewport.

In this chapter, I highlight some of the special considerations you should think about when designing an app for iPad. I then focus on creating a split view UI (user interface) design that emulates the look of a native iPad app.

SPECIAL IPAD CONSIDERATIONS

When you create a web app for iPad, you need to perform many of the same things you do when creating an iPhone app. Chapters 5 and 6 discuss the process of creating apps in full detail, but the following are a few of the key ways you can transform a normal web page into a web app that targets iPad:

➤ Adding the `viewport` meta tag to the document head:

```
<meta name="viewport" content="width=device-width; initial-scale=1.0;
    maximum-scale=1.0; user-scalable=no;"/>
```

➤ Adding an iPad-specific media query:

```
<link media="only screen and (min-device-width: 768px)
    and (max-device-width: 1024px)" type="text/css"
    rel="stylesheet" href="iPad.css" />
```

➤ Adding iPad-specific styles:

```
@media only screen and (min-device-width: 768px) and (max-device-width: 1024px)
{
    /* Add iPad styles here */
}
```

➤ Enabling the iPad app to run in full screen mode when launched from the iPad home screen:

```
<meta name="apple-mobile-web-app-capable" content="yes">
```

Design Essentials

The following are some additional essentials to keep in mind as you design for iPad:

➤ Design for both portrait and landscape modes. You need to design your app at 1024 × 768 in landscape and 768 × 1024 in portrait.

➤ Be sure your design is flexible enough for both portrait and landscape modes. If needed, add a listener for the `orientationchange` event and adjust your design dynamically. The exercise later in this chapter demonstrates one way to do this.

➤ Minimize your use of modal windows. This enables users to work with your app in more flexible, non-linear behavior. When you do want to use a modal view for users to perform a given task, I recommend a popover-like window, which I demonstrate later in the chapter.

➤ For edit elements, don't use the `contenteditable` attribute, as Safari on iOS doesn't support it. Instead, use a `textarea` for multi-line editing.

➤ Unless you use one of the popular mobile frameworks or iScroll (discussed in the next section), avoid using the `position:fixed` CSS property. It will not display as you intend. Specifically, fixed elements can scroll off screen if users zoom or pan on a page.

Dealing with Scrolling

Scrolling inside of Safari on iPad doesn't behave as you expect from the desktop browser world. A single or double finger swipe triggers `window.scroll()`. As a result, there is no way to scroll overflowing content inside a fixed-sized block, as Safari interprets a swipe inside the element as a window scrolling action. What's more, Safari on iOS doesn't support single finger scrolling for `div` elements.

In order to overcome these limitations, a handful of open source solutions have been developed. Arguably the most popular of these is iScroll 4, a project originally developed by Matteo Spinelli. You can add this JavaScript library to your project to have the kind of scrolling experience that users will be looking for in an app that targets the iPad device. You can download it at `http://cubiq.org/iscroll-4`.

In addition to more native-like scrolling capabilities, iScroll 4 also provides several additional touch event capabilities including pinch/zoom of content, pull down to refresh, snap to element, and custom scrollbars.

Split View Design Pattern

One of the key iPad design patterns for native apps that you should look to emulate when it makes sense is a master-detail view known as *split view*. The split view design pattern consists of two side-by-side panes in which a list of items is displayed on the left and detailed information about the currently selected item from the list is shown on the right.

On the desktop, you see this pattern utilized all of the time. It's used in most email applications, such as Outlook or Apple Mail, in which the list of messages is displayed next to a message viewer.

The iPhone makes use of the master-detail concept, but can't show both master and detail views in a split manner due to space limitations. However, the iPad — the man in the middle of the phone and desktop worlds — behaves like either the desktop or the phone depending on the context. In landscape mode, both master and detail views are displayed (see Figure 7-1). However, in portrait mode the master view is shown in a popover box (Figure 7-2).

FIGURE 7-1

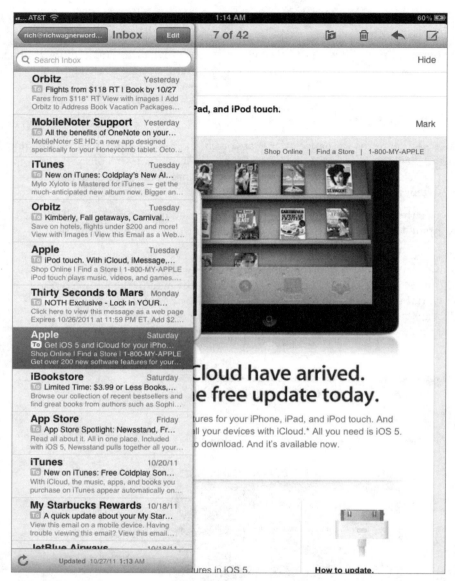

FIGURE 7-2

DESIGNING A UI FOR IPAD

When you read Chapter 16 you find out that you can create a web app for iPad using popular mobile frameworks, such as jQuery Mobile, and have it behave nicely within the Safari on iOS environment. However, because most of these frameworks are cross-platform, they don't attempt to emulate iOS design standards. Instead they provide a more neutral, agnostic-looking UI. The Hello

World app I created in Chapter 5 is a perfect example of this technique. However, suppose you would like your web app to follow closely the native iOS UI guidelines, so that it has a basic "look and feel" that is similar to the native apps that users are familiar with. You can create this "look and feel" from scratch using CSS and JavaScript or you can explore open-source options available on the Web. One such option is Slablet, an open source framework that you can add to your web app to re-create a native-looking iPad UI. You can download it from `https://github .com/fellowshiptech/slablet`.

Although Slablet and other templates of its ilk are not the full, comprehensive solutions that jQuery Mobile, Sensa Touch, or iWebKit are, Slablet is a great example of a lean, easy-to-use add-on that you can quickly use to transform your app into a rather impressive-looking app for iPad users. The following exercise walks you through the steps needed to create a Slablet-based app.

TRY IT OUT   Creating a Split View App Shell

Get an idea of how to create an iPad app by following these steps.

1.   Download the Slablet library from `https://github.com/fellowshiptech/slablet`.

2.   Unzip the contents of the zip file into your app folder. Make sure that Slablet's assets folder is directly inside your root app folder.

3.   Create the following HTML document in your text editor and then save the document as *BIDHJ-Ch07-Ex1.html*.

```
<!DOCTYPE html>
<html lang="en">
<head>
<!--
        Credit: This example utilizes the Slablet template
        URL: https://github.com/fellowshiptech/slablet
-->
<meta http-equiv="content-type" content="text/html; charset=utf-8" />
<meta http-equiv="x-ua-compatible" content="ie=edge" />
<title>iOS WebAppster Conference</title>
<meta name="apple-mobile-web-app-capable" content="yes" />
<meta name="viewport" content="width=device-width, initial-scale=1,
    maximum-scale=1, user-scalable=no" />
<link rel="stylesheet" href="assets/stylesheets/master.css" />
<!--[if IE 8]>
<link rel="stylesheet" href="assets/stylesheets/ie8.css" />
<![endif]-->
<!--[if !IE]><!-->
<script src="assets/javascripts/iscroll.js"></script>
<!--<![endif]-->
<script src="assets/javascripts/jquery.js"></script>
<script src="assets/javascripts/master.js"></script>
</head>
<body>


</body>
</html>
```

Code snippet BIDHJ-Ch07-Ex1.html

4.   Add the main page content inside of the document body:

```
<!-- Begin Page (shown in both landscape and portrait -->
<div id="main" class="abs">

    <!-- Begin Page Header -->
    <div class="abs header_upper chrome_light">
        <!-- Main menu button -
                shown only in Portait mode
                displays popover menu when pressed
        -->
        <span class="float_left button" id="button_navigation">
            Menu
        </span>
        <!-- Left toolbar button -->
        <!--a href="#" class="float_left button">
            Back
        </a-->
        <!-- Right toolbar button -->
        <!--a href="#" class="float_right button">
            Command
        </a-->
        My Title
    </div>
    <!-- Toolbar -->
    <!--div class="abs header_lower chrome_light">

    </div-->
    <!-- End Page Header -->
    <!-- Begin Page content -->
    <div id="main_content" class="abs">
        <div id="main_content_inner">
            <!-- Add content here -->
        </div>
    </div>
    <!-- End Page content -->

    <!-- Begin Page Footer -->
    <div class="abs footer_lower chrome_light">
        <!--a href="#" class="float_left button">
        </a-->
        <a href="#">View full site</a>
    </div>
    <!-- End Page Footer -->

</div>
<!-- End Page -->
```

Code snippet BIDHJ-Ch07-Ex1.html

5. Add the following sidebar-related code after the previous content block inside the document body:

```
<!-- Begin Sidebar (shown as sidebar in landscape, shown as popover in portrait -->
<div id="sidebar" class="abs">
    <span id="nav_arrow"></span>
    <!-- App Name -->
    <div class="abs header_upper chrome_light">
    My App Name
    </div>
    <!-- Begin Sidebar Menu -->
    <div id="sidebar_content" class="abs">
        <div id="sidebar_content_inner">
            <ul id="sidebar_menu">
            </ul>
        </div>
    </div>
    <!-- End Sidebar Menu -->
    <!-- Begin Sidebar Footer -->
    <div class="abs footer_lower chrome_light">
        <a href="#" class="icon icon_gear2 float_left"></a>
        <span class="float_right gutter_right">Slogan</span>
    </div>
    <!-- End Sidebar Footer-->
</div>
<!-- End Sidebar -->
```

Code snippet BIDHJ-Ch07-Ex1.html

How It Works

In this exercise, you created a basic split view UI shell that, although devoid of content, enables you to build a complete app on top of the basic shell. You begin by adding the essential meta tags and links required to create the app structure. The `app-mobile-web-app-capable` and `viewport` meta tags are discussed in Chapter 6. The remaining code in the head adds all the essential CSS style sheets and JavaScript libraries (including `jquery.js`) that are utilized by the Slablet template.

The Slablet style sheets and JavaScript libraries make heavy use of the `id` and `class` attributes of an element to define its look and behavior, so each of the core parts of the UI are given a specific `id` and/or `class` attribute value.

Figures 7-3 and 7-4 show the empty app shell in both landscape and portrait modes. As happens in a native iPad app, the sidebar appears when in landscape mode and is hidden in portrait mode. Notice also that the Menu button appears in portrait but is not visible in landscape.

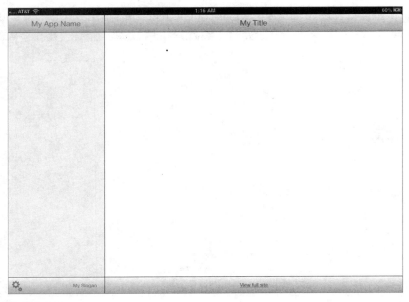

FIGURE 7-3

FIGURE 7-4

As you can see from this simple example, Slablet offers you considerable functionality when you have correctly defined the right elements in your HTML file. Looking under the Slablet hood, there are a few key parts of the template that are worth looking at. First, the `master.js` file is used to define all of the behavior of the template. Particularly noteworthy is how Slablet adjusts to orientation and toggles the visibility of the sidebar. Here's the relevant code:

```
function adjust_angle() {
        var angle = window.orientation;
        var body = $('body');
        var body_width = body.outerWidth();
        var sidebar = $('#sidebar');

        if (angle === 0 || angle === 180 || body_width < 1024) {
            body.addClass('is_portrait');
            $('#button_navigation').removeClass('button_active');
            sidebar.hide();
        }
        else {
            body.removeClass('is_portrait');
            sidebar.show();
        }
    }

    adjust_angle();

    $(window).bind('resize orientationchange', function() {
        adjust_angle();
    });
```

As you can see from this code, the `adjust_angle()` function is assigned as the event handler for the browser's `orientationchange` event. Therefore, when the iPad orientation changes the `window.orientation` property is evaluated. When it is determined that the iPad is in portrait mode, the sidebar is hidden using `sidebar.hide()`, but if the iPad is in landscape mode, then the sidebar is shown.

Although the app so far is purely a shell with no content or working parts, it doesn't take much to transform this UI shell into a usable application. The following exercise walks you through the steps needed to do just that.

TRY IT OUT   Creating a Split View Conference App

Use the following steps to turn the empty UI shell into a conference app.

1. Open the `BIDHJ-Ch07-Ex1.html` file you created in the previous exercise and save it as *index.html*.

2. Replace the empty page content so that it looks like the following:

```
<!-- Begin Page (shown in both landscape and portrait -->
<div id="main" class="abs">

    <!-- Begin Page Header -->
    <div class="abs header_upper chrome_light">
```

```
        <!-- Main menu button -
                shown only in Portait mode
                displays popover menu when pressed
        -->
        <span class="float_left button" id="button_navigation">
            Menu
        </span>
        <!-- Left toolbar button -->
        <!--a href="#" class="float_left button">
            Back
        </a-->
        <!-- Right toolbar button -->
        <!--a href="#" class="float_right button">
            Command
        </a-->
        iOS WebAppster Conference
    </div>
    <!-- Toolbar -->
    <!--div class="abs header_lower chrome_light">

    </div-->
    <!-- End Page Header -->
    <!-- Begin Page content -->
    <div id="main_content" class="abs">
        <div id="main_content_inner">
            <h1>Welcome to iOS WebAppster Conference 2013</h1>
            <p>You are now at the most amazing conference in the
               history of the Web. Ok, maybe
            that's hyperbole. But we think you are going to like it.</p>
        </div>
    </div>
    <!-- End Page content -->

    <!-- Begin Page Footer -->
    <div class="abs footer_lower chrome_light">
        <a href="#" class="float_left button">
            About the Salsa Conference Center
        </a>
        <!--a href="#" class="float_left button">
            Bar
        </a-->
        <!--a href="#" class="icon icon_bird float_right"></a-->
        <a href="#">View full site</a>
    </div>
    <!-- End Page Footer -->

</div>
<!-- End Page -->
```

Code snippet index.html

3. Replace the empty sidebar content so that it includes the following code:

```
<!-- Begin Sidebar (shown as sidebar in landscape, shown as popover in portrait -->
<div id="sidebar" class="abs">
    <span id="nav_arrow"></span>
    <!-- App Name -->
    <div class="abs header_upper chrome_light">
    ConfApp
    </div>
    <!-- Begin Sidebar Menu -->
    <div id="sidebar_content" class="abs">
        <div id="sidebar_content_inner">
            <ul id="sidebar_menu">
                <li id="sidebar_menu_home" class="active">
                    <a href="#"><span class="abs"></span>Home</a>
                </li>
                <li>
                    <a href="#">Welcome to iOS WebAppster</a>
                </li>
                <li>
                    <a href="#">Sessions</a>
                    <ul>
                        <li>
                            <a href="#">Session 100: Hello World</a>
                        </li>
                        <li>
                            <a href="#">Session 110: Designing for Mobile</a>
                        </li>
                        <li>
                            <a href="#">Session 210: Styling with CSS</a>
                        </li>
                        <li>
                            <a href="#">Session 220: Advanced JavaScript</a>
                        </li>
                        <li>
                            <a href="#">Session 225: Designing for iPad</a>
                        </li>
                        <li>
                            <a href="#">Session 300: Touch Events</a>
                        </li>
                        <li>
                            <a href="431.html">Session 431: Distributing Your
                                App</a>
                        </li>
                    </ul>
                </li>
                <li>
                    <a href="#">Speakers</a>
                    <ul>
                        <li>
                            <a href="#">Doug Majoring</a>
                        </li>
                        <li>
```

```
                                <a href="#">Kyle Exwhi</a>
                    </li>
                    <li>
                                <a href="#">Jason Masters</a>
                    </li>
                    <li>
                                <a href="#">Samantha Goodface</a>
                    </li>
                    <li>
                                <a href="#">Jess Gentleman</a>
                    </li>
                    <li>
                                <a href="#">Lex Landry</a>
                    </li>
                    <li>
                                <a href="#">Rachel Furgeson</a>
                    </li>
                </ul>
            </li>

        </ul>
    </div>
</div>
<!-- End Sidebar Menu -->
<!-- Begin Sidebar Footer -->
<div class="abs footer_lower chrome_light">
    <a href="#" class="icon icon_gear2 float_left"></a>
    <span class="float_right gutter_right">Bringing Conferences to Life</span>
</div>
<!-- End Sidebar Footer-->
</div>
```

Code snippet index.html

4. Save the file.

5. Using this file as starting point, save the file twice under the names `welcome.html` and `431.html`.

6. Open `welcome.html` in your editor.

7. Replace the code in the `main_content_inner` div with the following code:

```
<div id="main_content_inner">
    <h1>Welcome to the Conference</h1>
    <p>We're going to have a great time!</p>
</div>
```

Code snippet welcome.html

8. Save the file.

9. Open `431.html` in your editor.

10. Replace the code in the `main_content_inner` div with the following code:

```
<div id="main_content_inner">
    <h1>Session 431: Distributing Your App</h1>
    <p>In this compellings session, Doug Majoring leads you through how
        to distribute your
        web app in the App Store.</p>

    <p><button onclick="alert('View Slides')">View Slides</button></p>

    <h1>Session Details</h1>
    <p>Lorem ipsum dolor sit amet, consectetur adipiscing elit. Fusce suscipit
      diam id ipsum sagittis ac rhoncus enim dignissim. Phasellus venenatis
      risus in eros sollicitudin vel posuere magna convallis. Aenean malesuada
      luctus arcu ac tincidunt. Ut ultricies mattis metus, vel tempus elit
      cursus ut. Pellentesque dui orci, rutrum id facilisis vitae, porta sed
      tellus. Morbi venenatis ornare eros a varius. Integer convallis euismod
      urna, sed imperdiet purus tempor elementum. Pellentesque metus tortor,
      fringilla a ullamcorper eu, semper ut nulla. Phasellus ullamcorper leo
      in lectus vestibulum lobortis. Lorem ipsum dolor sit amet, consectetur
      adipiscing elit. Sed at est ut turpis venenatis lacinia consectetur et
      ante. Maecenas feugiat pulvinar sagittis.</p>

    <p>In eu velit magna. Phasellus felis lectus, rhoncus ut ultricies nec,
      porttitor sed nunc. Nulla sit amet purus metus, sed molestie diam. Nam
      pellentesque dui vitae mauris tincidunt venenatis. Cras a adipiscing risus.
      Morbi lorem turpis, suscipit iaculis hendrerit non, auctor ut augue.
      Phasellus at urna a nisl tempor sodales. In hac habitasse platea dictumst.
      Cras at augue massa, non suscipit nulla. Morbi bibendum ultricies luctus.
      Phasellus rutrum blandit dui ac facilisis. Mauris vitae augue eros.
      Suspendisse fermentum ultricies risus quis viverra. Donec ut ante id nisi
      fringilla mollis sed nec velit. Phasellus ornare, nulla ut rutrum
      hendrerit, felis diam cursus purus, quis fermentum erat lacus posuere
      odio. Fusce ac odio tortor.</p>

    <p>Nullam tempor, est in ultrices luctus, diam lectus tincidunt sem, nec
      ornare dolor lectus a magna. Vestibulum accumsan suscipit aliquet.
      Mauris at lorem quam. Aenean ac augue quis sem commodo accumsan a vitae
      nunc. Maecenas luctus velit et erat dignissim ut commodo arcu malesuada.
      Vestibulum ante ipsum primis in faucibus orci luctus et ultrices posuere
      cubilia Curae; Nulla viverra, enim sit amet placerat venenatis, tortor
      odio feugiat mauris, sit amet vehicula purus tellus pulvinar libero.
      Phasellus id feugiat turpis. Donec aliquam luctus iaculis. In faucibus
      neque in lorem tincidunt pellentesque. Vestibulum condimentum augue vel
      ante euismod euismod sed ac urna. Phasellus scelerisque, quam id dapibus
      sagittis, nulla nibh hendrerit est, vel aliquam tellus augue vitae sem.
      Aenean commodo, urna a sagittis varius, nulla metus tempor nunc, ac
```

```
suscipit elit odio sed leo. Vivamus ut lobortis velit. Nam pretium
vestibulum tellus non vehicula.</p>

<p>Proin dolor diam, laoreet vel faucibus nec, malesuada sit amet purus.
Proin turpis orci, ultrices at laoreet quis, vulputate ac mi. Sed nec
tristique justo. Maecenas cursus sem et tellus gravida nec semper neque
suscipit. Curabitur vitae convallis metus. Fusce porta elementum molestie.
Quisque neque eros, vehicula nec cursus ac, tincidunt accumsan lacus.
Nulla facilisi. Donec id nisl ligula, eget cursus quam. Donec euismod
iaculis rhoncus. Aliquam malesuada dignissim libero nec scelerisque.
Donec mauris sapien, dignissim ac blandit a, consequat bibendum felis.</p>

<p>In dignissim varius eros, eu mattis metus fringilla ut. In ultrices
orci nec libero sollicitudin a dapibus mi tempor. Donec neque justo,
condimentum ac vehicula quis, iaculis eget lacus. In at elit nisl.
Donec vel aliquam dolor. Phasellus hendrerit justo in elit ultrices
ac pulvinar turpis viverra. Nullam ornare nisi vitae risus vulputate
malesuada. Nam vulputate lobortis velit, sed iaculis arcu fermentum
pharetra. Aliquam dolor massa, pretium sit amet ultrices sed, pellentesque
ut lectus. Sed aliquet pharetra dolor eget pharetra. Mauris sit amet purus
odio. Vestibulum ante ipsum primis in faucibus orci luctus et ultrices
posuere cubilia Curae; Quisque lobortis, dui pulvinar dapibus facilisis,
lectus enim pretium odio, ut imperdiet sem sem nec augue. Nulla facilisi.
Integer et risus eget purus posuere varius. Donec ac nibh quis mi lobortis
sagittis quis ut est.</p>

</div>
```

Code snippet 431.html

11. Replace the code in the `float_left` link in the page footer with the following code:

```
<a href="#" class="float_left button">
View Doug's Bio
</a>
```

Code snippet 431.html

12. Save the file.

How It Works

In this exercise, you transformed the UI shell into a sample app that could be filled out to serve as an app that a conference presenter could utilize. To demonstrate it, you created the main index page, the welcome page, and an example session page. The main app page is shown in Figure 7-5. The pages are accessible via the list of links defined in the sidebar, as shown in Figure 7-6. As discussed earlier, when the app runs in portrait mode, the sidebar is hidden and displayed as a popup when the user clicks the Menu button (see Figure 7-7).

FIGURE 7-5

FIGURE 7-6

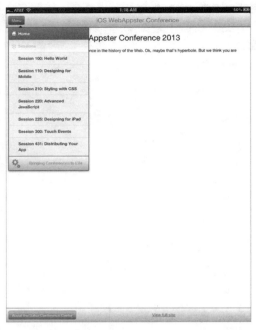

FIGURE 7-7

Figure 7-8 shows the example session page. However, what's important to note about this page is that the content scrolls inside the page `div` using the popular `iScroll.js` library.

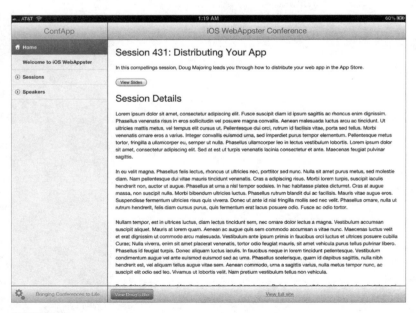

FIGURE 7-8

EXERCISES

1. True or False? Although the iPhone should use the `viewport` meta tag for web apps, the `viewport` tag is not needed for iPad web apps.

2. Is it better to design for landscape or portrait modes?

3. How can you overcome the limitation of being unable to scroll overflowing content inside of a fixed size `div`?

Answers to the Exercises can be found in the Appendix.

▶ **WHAT YOU LEARNED IN THIS CHAPTER**

TOPIC	KEY CONCEPTS
Key meta tags to add for most every iPad web app	`Viewport` meta tag, `apple-mobile-web-app-capable` meta tag
Design for portrait and landscape	Design your app to work at 1024 × 768 in landscape and 768 × 1024 in portrait
Split view design pattern	A core iPad design pattern, used frequently in native iPad apps

Styling with CSS

WHAT YOU WILL LEARN IN THIS CHAPTER:

➤ Working with text styles and shadows

➤ Styling block elements

➤ Creating CSS buttons

Like its Mac and Windows cousins, the mobile version of Safari on iOS provides some of the best CSS support of all web browsers. As you develop iOS web applications, you can utilize CSS to make powerful user interfaces.

Safari provides support for much of CSS 2.1 as well as parts of CSS3. However, Safari also supports some properties technically called "experimental CSS3" that are not currently part of the W3C CSS standard; these properties will be supported by Apple going forward. (Hint: A -webkit- prefix is added to the names of these properties.) For a normal web app, most developers typically stay away from these experimental properties, or at least they don't rely upon them for their application's design. However, because you know that your app will be accessed exclusively by an iOS device, you can safely use these more advanced styles as you create your UI.

In this book, you've already been introduced to using CSS to create iOS interfaces. In this chapter I'm continuing that discussion and diving deeper into various CSS techniques.

CSS SELECTORS SUPPORTED IN SAFARI

Many would contend that the real power of CSS is not so much in the properties that you can apply, but in CSS's ability select the exact elements within a DOM that you want to work with. If you have worked with CSS before, you are probably familiar with the standard type, class, and ID selectors. However, Safari provides selector support that includes many new selectors that are part of the CSS3 specification. Table 8-1 lists a set of CSS selectors that

Safari provides support for, and Table 8-2 lists the set of pseudo-classes and pseudo-elements that Safari works with.

Note that the following CSS3 selectors are not supported with Safari:

➤   :last-child

➤   :only-child

➤   nth-child()

➤   nth-last-child()

➤   last-of-type

➤   only-of-type

➤   :nth-of-type()

➤   :nth-last-of-type()

➤   Empty

TABLE 8-1: Safari CSS Selectors

SELECTOR	DEFINITION
E	Type selector
.class	Class selector
#id	ID selector
*	Universal selector (all elements)
E F	Descendant selector
E > F	Child selector
E + F	Adjacent sibling selector
E ~ F	Indirect adjacent selector[a]
E[attr]	attr is defined
E[attr=val]	attr value matches val
E[attr~=val]	One of many attribute value selectors[b]
E[attr|=val]	attr value is a hyphen-separated list and begins with val[b]
E[attr^=val]	attr value begins with val[a,b]
E[attr$=val]	attr value ends with val[a,b]
E[attr*=val]	attr value contains at least one instance of val[a,b]

[a]New to CSS3

[b]Case-sensitive, even when unnecessary

TABLE 8-2: Safari Pseudo-Classes and Pseudo-Elements

PSEUDO-CLASS/PSEUDO-ELEMENT	DEFINITION
E:link	Unvisited link
E:visited	Visited link
E:lang([Code])	Selector content uses the language code specified
E:before	Content before an element
E::before	Content before an element (new double-colon notation in CSS3)[a]
E:after	Content after an element
E::after	Content after an element (new double-colon notation in CSS3)[a]
E:first-letter	First letter of element
E::first-letter	First letter of element (new double-colon notation in CSS3)[a]
E:first-line	First line of element
E::first-line	First line of element (new double-colon notation in CSS3)[a]
E:first-child	First child[b]
E:first-of-type	First child of type[a,b]
E:root	Root[a]
E:not()	Negation[a]
E:target	Target[a]
E:enabled	Enabled state[a]
E:disabled	Disabled state[a]
E:checked	Checked state[a]

[a]New to CSS3
[b]When new first child/child of type is created programmatically using JavaScript, the previous maintains the :first-child or :first-of-type attributes.

TEXT STYLES

When you are styling text inside your iOS web apps, keep in mind three text-related styles that are important to effective UI design: -webkit-text-size-adjust, text-overflow, and text-shadow. These properties are explained in this section.

Controlling Text Sizing with -webkit-text-size-adjust

When a page is rendered, Safari on iOS automatically sizes the page's text based on the width of the text block. However, by using the `-webkit-text-size-adjust` property, you can override this setting. The `none` option turns off auto-sizing of text:

```
body { -webkit-text-size-adjust: none; }
```

Or, you can specify a multiplier:

```
body { -webkit-text-size-adjust: 140%; }
```

Figures 8-1 and 8-2 show the results of these two options on the same page.

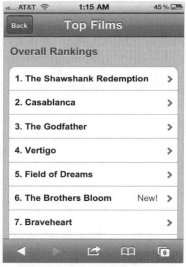

FIGURE 8-1

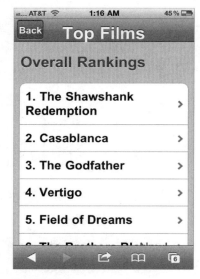

FIGURE 8-2

Finally, you can set it to the default value of `auto`:

```
body { -webkit-text-size-adjust: auto; }
```

For a normal website, `-webkit-text-size-adjust: auto` is recommended for improving the readability of text. However, if you are developing an application, you almost always want to use `-webkit-text-size-adjust: none` to maintain precise control over the text sizing, particularly when you switch between portrait and landscape modes.

Handling Overflowed Text with text-overflow

Because the width of the viewport in Safari on iPhone is either 320 (portrait) or 480 (landscape) pixels (and Safari on iPad is 768 (portrait) or 1024 (landscape), effectively managing the physical length of dynamic text on UI elements can be tricky. This is particularly important for headings or button text in which a fixed amount of real estate is available. The best example of the need to handle text overflow is in the top toolbar that is a standard part of the iPhone application interface. By default, any content that does not fit inside of the container box of the element is clipped, which can potentially lead to confusion, such as the back button example shown in Figure 8-3. Because there is not enough space to display the text iProspector, only iProspect is shown.

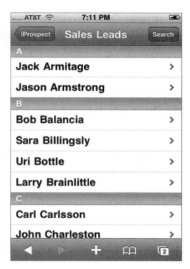

FIGURE 8-3

Therefore, to prevent this situation from happening, you should provide a visual hint that the text has been clipped. Fortunately, the text-overflow property enables developers to specify what they want to have done when the text runs on. The two values are ellipsis and clip. The ellipsis value trims the content and adds an ellipsis character (. . .) to the end. Suppose you assign the following property to the toolbar's button and heading element:

```
text-overflow: ellipsis;
```

Now, when text overflows, an ellipsis is added, as shown in Figure 8-4.

The text-overflow property is particularly useful for web apps that target the iPhone because a heading that displays fully in landscape mode may need to be clipped in the much thinner portrait mode. iPad apps will probably not experience this problem, unless you have a really, really long title.

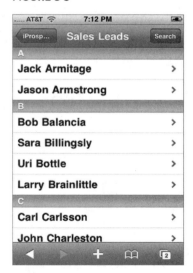

FIGURE 8-4

TRY IT OUT | **Creating Ellipsis Text**

To demonstrate how to work with an ellipsis in text, follow these steps.

1. Create the following HTML document in your text editor and then save the document as *BIDHJ-Ch8-Ex1.html*.

```
<html>
<meta name="viewport" content="width=320; initial-scale=1.0; maximum-scale=1.0;">
<body>
<div> this is a test this is a test this is a test
this is a test this is a test this is a testthis is a test </div>
<br><br>
<div> this is a test this is a test this is a test
this is a test this is a test this is a testthis is a test </div>
<br><br>
<div> this is a test this is a test this is a test
this is a test this is a test this is a testthis is a test </div>
</body>
</html>
```

Code snippet BIDHJ-Ch8-Ex1.html

2. Add the following `style` section to the document head:

```
<style>
.ellipsis
{
    text-overflow: ellipsis;
    width: 200px;
    white-space: nowrap;
    overflow: hidden;
}

.ellipsisBroken1
{
    text-overflow: ellipsis;
    width: 200px;
    /* white-space: nowrap; */
    overflow: hidden;
}

.ellipsisBroken2
{
    text-overflow: ellipsis;
    width: 200px;
    white-space: nowrap;
    /* overflow: hidden; */
}
</style>
```

Code snippet BIDHJ-Ch8-Ex1.html

3. Add a class attribute to each of the three div elements, associating each with a corresponding style.

```
<div class="ellipsis"> this is a test this is a test this is a test
this is a test this is a test this is a testthis is a test </div>
<br><br>
<div class="ellipsisBroken1"> this is a test this is a test this is a test
this is a test this is a test this is a testthis is a test </div>
<br><br>
<div class="ellipsisBroken2"> this is a test this is a test this is a test
this is a test this is a test this is a testthis is a test </div>
```

Code snippet BIDHJ-Ch8-Ex1.html

4. Save your document.

5. View it on your iPhone or iPod touch, as shown in Figure 8-5.

FIGURE 8-5

How It Works

This example demonstrates the fact that `text-overflow` may require specifying additional CSS properties to display as intended. In this case, it needs to have `overflow` or `white-space` properties set to ensure that the `text-overflow` property works.

Creating Subtle Shadows with text-shadow

In the iOS UI, Apple makes subtle use of text shadows, particularly on buttons and larger heading text. In addition to aesthetics, text shadows are also useful in making text more readable by increasing its contrast with the background.

You can add drop shadows to your text through the `text-shadow` property. The basic declaration is as follows:

```
text-shadow: color offsetX offsetY blurRadius;
```

The first value is the color of the shadow. The next two give the shadow's offset position — the second value is the x-coordinate and the third is the y-coordinate. (Negative values move the shadow left and up.) The fourth parameter indicates the shadow's Gaussian blur radius. So, in the following example, a gray shadow is added 1 pixel above the element's text with no blur:

```
text-shadow: #666666 0px -1px 0;
```

However, text shadows can be a distraction and look tacky if they are too noticeable. Therefore, you can use an rgba (red, green, blue, alpha) color value in place of a solid color value in order to define the transparency value of the shadow. (See the "Setting Transparencies" section later in this chapter.) Therefore, the following declaration defines a white shadow with a .7 alpha value (0.0 is fully transparent, and 1.0 is fully opaque) that is positioned 1 pixel under the element's text:

```
text-shadow: rgba(255, 255, 255, 0.7) 0 1px 0;
```

STYLING BLOCK ELEMENTS

There are several styles that you can apply to block elements to transform their appearance that go beyond ordinary CSS styles that you may have used on traditional websites. These include three so-called experimental properties (`-webkit-border-image`, `-webkit-border-radius`, and `-webkit-appearance`) and a CSS3 enhancement of the `background` property. These are described in this section.

Image-Based Borders with -webkit-border-image

The `-webkit-border-image` property enables you to use an image to specify the border rather than the `border-style` properties. The image appears behind the content of the element, but on top of the background. For example:

```
-webkit-border-image: url(image.png) 7 7 7 7;
```

The four numbers that follow the image URL represent the number of pixels in the image that should be used as the border. The first number indicates the height of the top (both the corners and edge) of the image used. Per CSS conventions, the remaining three numbers indicate the right, bottom, and left sides. Pixel is the default unit, though you can specify percentages.

If the image URL you provide cannot be located or the style is set to none then border-style properties are used instead.

You can optionally specify one or two keywords at the end of the declaration. These determine how the images for the sides and the middle are scaled and tiled. The valid keywords are stretch or round. If you use stretch as the first keyword, the top, middle, and bottom parts of the image are scaled to the same width as the element's padding box. You can also use round , which is far less common for iOS use, as the first keyword. When this setting is present, the top, middle, and bottom images are reduced in width so that a whole number of the images fit in the width of the padding box. The second keyword acts on the height of the left, middle, and right images. If both keywords are omitted then stretch is implied.

When rendered, Safari looks at the -webkit-border-image property and divides the image based on the four numbers specified.

The -webkit-border-image property plays an important role in creating CSS-based iOS buttons, which is explained later in this chapter.

Rounded Corners with -webkit-border-radius

The -webkit-border-radius is used to specify the radius of the corners of an element. Using this property, you can easily create rounded corners on your elements rather than resorting to image-based corners. For example:

```
-webkit-border-radius: 10px;
```

This declaration specifies a 10 pixel radius for the element, which is the standard radius value for the Rounded Rectangle design for destination pages. You can also specify the radius of each individual corner using the following properties:

```
-webkit-border-top-left-radius
-webkit-border-top-right-radius
-webkit-border-bottom-left-radius
-webkit-border-bottom-right-radius
```

If, for example, you want to create a div with rounded top corners and square bottom corners, the style code looks like the following:

```
div.roundedTopBox
{
-webkit-border-top-left-radius: 10px;
-webkit-border-top-right-radius: 10px;
-webkit-border-bottom-left-radius: 0px;
-webkit-border-bottom-right-radius: 0px;
}
```

Results are shown in the text box in Figure 8-6.

FIGURE 8-6

Gradient Push Buttons with -webkit-appearance

The -webkit-appearance property is designed to transform the appearance of an element into a variety of different controls. Safari on iOS supports just two of the possible values: push-button and button. But it is the push-button that holds the most promise for iOS web app developers. Suppose, for example, you would like to turn a link element into a gradient push button. You could do it with an image, but -webkit-appearance: push-button enables you to do it entirely within CSS. To demonstrate, begin with a link assigned to a class named special:

```
<a href="tel:202-558-1212" class="special">Call Headquarters</a>
```

Then, define the a.special style:

```
a.special
{
    display: block;
    width: 246px;
    font-family: Helvetica;
    font-size: 20px;
    font-weight: bold;
    color: #000000;
    text-decoration: none;
    text-shadow: rgba(255, 255, 255, 0.7) 0 1px 0;
    text-align: center;
    line-height: 36px;
    margin: 15px auto;
    -webkit-border-radius:10px;
    -webkit-appearance: push-button;
}
```

The display:block and width:246px properties give the link a wide rectangular block shape. The -webkit-appearance: push-button property transforms the appearance to have a gradient gray push button look. The -webkit-border-radius rounds the edges using the standard

Call Headquarters

FIGURE 8-7

10px value. Although the shape of the push button is now set, the text needs to be tweaked using not just standard text formatting properties, but also a line-height property of 36px, which vertically centers the 20px text in the middle of the push button. If you add a simple background-color: #999999 style to the body tag, then you get the result shown in Figure 8-7.

Multiple Background Images

In earlier versions of CSS, there was always a 1:1 correspondence between an element and a background image. Although that capability worked for most purposes, some page designs could not work effectively with a single background image defined. So, in order to get around the 1:1 limitation, designers would resort to adding extra div tags here or there just to achieve the intended visual design.

CSS3 addresses this issue by giving you the ability to define multiple background images for a given element. Most browsers don't support this feature yet, but fortunately for iOS web app developers, Safari on iOS does.

You define a set of background images by listing them in order after the background property name declaration. Images are rendered with the first one declared on top, the second image behind the first, and so on. You can also specify the background-repeat and background-position values for each of the images. If background-color is defined then this color is painted below all of the images. For example:

```
div.banner
{
background: url(header_top.png) top left no-repeat,
    url(banner_main.png) top 6px no-repeat,
    url(header_bottom.png) bottom left no-repeat,
    url(middle.png) left repeat-y;
}
```

In this code, the header_top.png serves as the background image aligned to the top left portion of the div element. The banner_main.png is positioned 6px from the top, and the header_bottom.png image is positioned at the bottom of the div. Finally, the middle.png is treated as a repeating background.

SETTING TRANSPARENCIES

Developers have long used rgb to specify an RGB color value for text and backgrounds. CSS3 adds the ability to set an alpha value when specifying an RGB color with the new rgba declaration. Using the rgba declaration, you can add translucent color overlays without transparent PNGs or GIFs. The syntax is the following:

```
rgba(r, g, b, alpha)
```

The r, g, and b values are integers between 0 and 255 that represent the red, green, and blue values; alpha is a value between 0 and 1 (0.0 is fully transparent, and 1.0 is fully opaque). For example, to set a red background with a 50% transparency, you would use:

```
background: rgba(255, 0, 0, 0.5);
```

Keep in mind that the alpha value in the rgba declaration is not the same as the opacity property. rgba sets the opacity value only for the current element, whereas opacity sets the value for the element and its descendants.

The following example shows five div elements, each with a different alpha value for the black background:

```
<!DOCTYPE html PUBLIC "-//W3C//DTD XHTML 1.0 Strict//EN"
        "http://www.w3.org/TR/xhtml1/DTD/xhtml1-strict.dtd">
<html xmlns="http://www.w3.org/1999/xhtml">
<head>
<title>RGBA Declaration</title>
<meta name="viewport" content="width=320; initial-scale=1.0;
    maximum-scale=1.0; user-scalable=0;">
<style type="text/css" media="screen">
div.colorBlock {
    width: 50px;
    height: 50px;
```

```
        float: left;
        margin-bottom: 10px;
        font-family: Helvetica;
        font-size: 20px;
        text-align:center;
        color:white;
        text-shadow: rgba(0,0, 0, 0.7) 0 1px 0;
        line-height: 46px;
    }
    </style>
    </head>
    <body>
    <div style="margin: 10px 0 0 30px;">
    <div class="colorBlock" style="background: rgba(0, 0, 0, 0.2);"><span
    >20%</span></div>
    <div class="colorBlock" style="background: rgba(0, 0, 0,
    0.4);"><span>40%</span></div>
    <div class="colorBlock" style="background: rgba(0, 0, 0,
    0.6);"><span>60%</span></div>
    <div class="colorBlock" style="background: rgba(0, 0, 0,
    0.8);"><span>80%</span></div>
    <div class="colorBlock" style="background: rgba(0, 0, 0,  1.0)
    ;"><span>100%</span></div>
    </div>
    </body>
    </html>
```

Code snippet BIDHJ-Ch8-Ex2.html

Figure 8-8 shows the page.

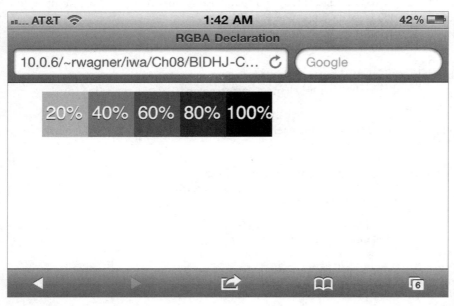

FIGURE 8-8

CREATING CSS-BASED IOS BUTTONS

Using `-webkit-border-image`, you can create buttons that closely emulate Apple's standard button design. This technique, inspired by developer Matthew Krivanek, involves using a pill-shaped button image (available for download at www.wrox.com) and stretching the middle of the button image, but ensuring that the left and right sides of the button are not distorted in the process.

TRY IT OUT   Using CSS to Create an iOS Button

1. Create the following empty HTML document in your text editor and then save the document as *BIDHJ-Ch8-Ex3.html*.

Available for download on Wrox.com

```
<!DOCTYPE html PUBLIC "-//W3C//DTD XHTML 1.0 Strict//EN"
        "http://www.w3.org/TR/xhtml1/DTD/xhtml1-strict.dtd">
<html xmlns="http://www.w3.org/1999/xhtml">
<head>
<title>Basic Button/title>
<meta name="viewport" content="width=320; initial-scale=1.0;
    maximum-scale=1.0; user-scalable=0;">
</head>
<body>
<a href="mailto:me@company.net" class="fullSizedButton">Send to Client</a>
</body>
</html>
```

Code snippet BIDHJ-Ch8-Ex3.html

2. Add the following `<style>` element to your document head:

Available for download on Wrox.com

```
<style type="text/css" media="screen">
a.fullSizedButton
{
    font-family: Helvetica;
    font-size: 20px;
    display: block;
    width: 246px;
    margin: 15px auto;
    text-align:center;
    text-decoration: none;
    line-height: 46px;
    font-weight: bold;
    color: #000000;
    text-shadow: rgba(255, 255, 255, 0.7) 0 1px 0;
    border-width: 0 14px 0 14px;
    -webkit-border-image: url(images/whiteButton.png) 0 14 0 14;
}
body
{
    background-color: black;
}
</style>
```

Code snippet BIDHJ-Ch8-Ex3.html

3. Add an <a>link with a `fullSizedButton` class:

```
<a href="mailto:rich@company.com" class="fullSizedButton">Send to Client</a>
```

4. Save your document.

5. View it on your iPhone or iPod touch.

How It Works

In this example, the `display` property is set to `block` and the width is set to 246px, the width of the buttons used by Apple. The `line-height` is set to 46px, which gives the block element the standard height and vertically centers the button text. A `border-width` property sets the left and right borders to 14px and eliminates the borders for the top and bottom by defining their values as 0.

Now that everything else is set up, look at the `-webkit-border-image` property definition. In this example, 0 pixels are used from whiteButton.png on the top and bottom. However, the first 14 pixels of the image are used for the left border of the element, whereas the 14 rightmost pixels are used for the right border. Because the `whiteButton.png` image is 29 pixels in width, a 1-pixel section is used as the middle section. This middle section is then repeated over and over to fill the width of the element. Figure 8-9 shows how `-webkit-border-image` divides the image.

Figure 8-10 shows the button when rendered by Safari on iOS.

FIGURE 8-9

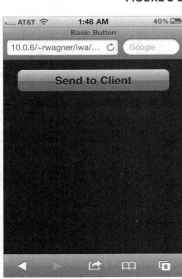

FIGURE 8-10

IDENTIFYING INCOMPATIBILITIES

Although Safari on iOS is closely related to its Mac and Windows counterparts, it is not identical in terms of CSS support. The latest versions of Safari on Mac and Windows support most of the newer CSS3 and experimental properties (prefixed with `-webkit-`). Safari for iPhone, however, provides limited support of several properties.

The following CSS properties are not supported (or have limited support) in Safari on iOS:

➤ `box-shadow`

➤ `-webkit-box-shadow`

➤ `text-stroke`

➤ `-webkit-text-stroke`

➤   `text-fill-color`

➤   `-webkit-text-fill-color`

➤   `-website-appearance` (`push-button` supported, but no other values are)

EXERCISES

1.   What experimental CSS extensions are supported by Safari on iOS?

2.   For a website (not an app) would you typically use `-webkit-text-size-adjust: auto` or `-webkit-text-size-adjust: none`?

3.   What CSS property would you use to specify an image border?

Answers to the Exercises can be found in Appendix A.

▶ **WHAT YOU LEARNED IN THIS CHAPTER**

TOPIC	KEY CONCEPTS
Transforming an element into a button using CSS	The `-webkit-appearance` property is designed to transform the appearance of an element into a button.
Specify transparency in CSS	Use the `rgba()` function, in which the last parameter specifies the alpha setting.
Create CSS-based iOS buttons	Use `-webkit-border-image` to create iOS-looking buttons.

PART III
Application Development

Programming the Interface

WHAT YOU WILL LEARN IN THIS CHAPTER:

➤ Using iUI to program and style your iOS web app

➤ Developing a web app that closely resembles native iOS apps

➤ Discovering how CSS and JavaScript can work together

The previous two chapters surveyed the UI standards and guidelines that you need to keep in mind as you design a web app that works well on iPhone and iPad. With these design principles in hand, you are ready to apply them as you develop and program your web app.

In order to demonstrate how to implement an iOS interface, I walk you through a case study application I am calling iRealtor. The concept of iRealtor is to provide a mobile *house-hunter* application for potential buyers. The current pattern for Internet-based house hunting is to search MLS listings online, print out individual listing addresses, get directions, and then travel to these houses. However, with iRealtor, all of those tasks can be done on the road with an iOS-based application. The design goals of iRealtor are to provide a way for users to do the following:

➤ Browse and search the MLS listings of a local realtor

➤ Get a map of an individual listing directly from its listing page

➤ Access information about the realtor and easily contact the realtor using iOS phone or mail services

➤ Browse other helpful tools and tips

Because the target user for this app uses an iPhone, most design decisions need to target the smaller iPhone UI. However, because some users may use an iPad, I want to make sure that the app is fully functional and usable when used on the larger iPad device.

As you look at these overall objectives, an edge-to-edge navigation design looks like an obvious choice given the task-based nature of the application. The realtor information is relatively static, but the MLS listings need to be database-driven. Therefore, the app takes advantage of Ajax to seamlessly integrate listing data into the application.

Here's an overview of the technologies that are for iRealtor:

➤ XHTML/HTML and CSS for presentation layer

➤ JavaScript for client-side logic

➤ PHP or other server-side technology to serve MLS listing data (not included in case study example)

As I walk you through the application, I examine both the custom code I am writing for iRealtor as well as the underlying styles and code that power it. I am using the iUI framework (available at `http://code.google.com/p/iui`) to achieve a native-looking iOS UI. However, no matter the framework you decide to choose after working through this case study you will have a solid grasp on the key design issues you need to consider.

TOP LEVEL OF APPLICATION

The top level of iRealtor is best presented as an edge-to-edge navigation-style list that contains links to the different parts of the application. When assembled, the iPhone design looks like Figure 9-1. The iPad design is shown in Figure 9-2.

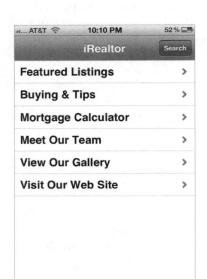

FIGURE 9-1

FIGURE 9-2

TRY IT OUT   Creating the index.html of Your Web App

Follow the steps below to create the iUI-based shell for your web app.

1.   Create a new blank document in your text editor.

2.   Add the following HTML to your document:

Available for download on Wrox.com

```
<!DOCTYPE html>
<html>
<head>
<title>iRealtor</title>
<meta content="yes" name="apple-mobile-web-app-capable" />
<meta name="viewport"
   content="width=device-width; initial-scale=1.0;
   maximum-scale=1.0; user-scalable=0;"/>
<link rel="stylesheet" href="iui/iui.css" type="text/css" />
<link rel="stylesheet" href="iui/t/default/default-theme.css" type="text/css"/>
<script type="application/x-javascript" src="iui/iui.js"></script>
<body>
</body>
</html>
```

Code snippet index.html

3.   Save your file.

How It Works

In this short exercise, you built the initial shell of your web app. You start off with a basic HTML document, linking the iUI style sheet and scripting library files that you're using for this web app. The `apple-mobile-web-app-capable` instruction opens the app full screen when a user launches it from the iOS device home screen. The `viewport` `meta` tag tells Safari exactly how to scale the page and sets 1.0 scale and does not change layout on reorientation. It also specifies that the width of the viewport is the size of the device (`device-width` is a constant). These properties ensure that iRealtor behaves like a web application, not a web page.

Examining Top-Level Styles

The iUI framework uses a core set of base styles in `iui.css` and allows more platform-specific and theme-based styles to be defined in a secondary style sheet. The default style sheet for iOS is `default-theme.css`.

The default style sheet used by iUI sets up several top-level styles. The `body` style in `default-theme.css` sets up the default `margin`, `font-family`, and colors.

```
body {
    font-family:     Helvetica, Arial, Sans-serif;
    margin:          0;
    color:           #000000;
    background:      #FFFFFF;
}
```

The iui.css adds additional styles, uses -webkit-user-select and -webkit-text-size-adjust to ensure that iRealtor behaves as an application rather than a web page. Here's the definition in iui.css:

```
body {
    overflow-x: hidden;
    -webkit-text-size-adjust: none;
}
```

For iOS web apps, it is important to assign -webkit-text-size-adjust: none to override the default behavior.

All elements, except for the .toolbar class, are assigned the following properties in iui.css:

```
body > *:not(.toolbar) {
    box-sizing: border-box;
    -webkit-box-sizing: border-box;
    -moz-box-sizing: border-box;
    -o-box-sizing: border-box;
    display: none;
    position: absolute;
    width: 100%;
    height: auto;
    -webkit-transition-duration: 300ms;
    -webkit-transition-property: -webkit-transform;
    -webkit-transform: translate3D(0%,0,0);
}
```

In landscape mode, the padding-top changes for these elements in default-theme.css:

```
body[orient="landscape"] > *:not(.toolbar) {
    padding-top:      32px;
}
```

The orient attribute changes when the orientation of the viewport changes between portrait and landscape. You can see how this works later in the chapter.

The iUI framework uses a selected attribute to denote the current page of the application. From a code standpoint, the page is typically either a div or a ul list. Here's the reference in iui.css:

```
body > *[selected="true"] {
    display: block;
}
```

Links also are assigned the selected attribute:

```
ul > li > a[selected],
ul > li > a:active,
.panel > ul > li > a[selected],
.panel > ul > li > a:active {
    color: #fff;
    background-color:#194fdb;
    background-repeat: no-repeat, repeat-x;
```

```
        background-position: right center, left top;
        background-image: url(listArrowSel.png), url(selection.png);
    }

    ul > li > a[selected="progress"] {
        background-image: url(loading.gif), url(selection.png);
    }
```

The `ul > li > a[selected="progress"]` style in `default-theme.css` is used to display an animated GIF showing the standard iOS loading animation.

Adding the Top Toolbar

The first UI element to add is the top toolbar, which serves a common UI element throughout the application. To create the toolbar, use a `div` element assigning it the `toolbar` class:

```
<!—Top iUI toolbar—>
<div class="toolbar">
    <h1 id="pageTitle"></h1>
    <a id="backButton" class="button" href="#"></a>
    <a class="button" href="#searchForm">Search</a>
</div>
```

The `h1` element serves as a placeholder for displaying the active page's title. The `a backbutton` is not shown at the top level of the application, but is used on subsequent pages to go back to the previous page. The Search button allows access to the search form anywhere within the application. Here are the corresponding style definitions for each of these elements.

In `iui.css`:

```
.toolbar {
    box-sizing:          border-box;
    -webkit-box-sizing:  border-box;
    -moz-box-sizing:     border-box;
    -o-box-sizing:       border-box;
    -webkit-transform:   translateX(0);
}

.toolbar > h1,
.button {
    overflow:          hidden;
    white-space:       nowrap;
    text-overflow:     ellipsis;
    -o-text-overflow:  ellipsis;
    -ms-text-overflow: ellipsis;
}

.button {
    text-decoration:              none;
    white-space:                  nowrap;
    -webkit-tap-highlight-color:  rgba(0,0,0,0);
}

.leftButton {
```

```
    left:             6px;
    right:            none;
}


#backButton {
    display:          none;
}
```

The `default-theme.css` adds some iOS-specific styling:

```
.toolbar {
    padding:          0 10px 10px 10px;
    height:           45px;
    background:       url(toolbar.png) #6d84a2 repeat-x;
    background-size:auto 100%;
}
.toolbar > h1 {
    position:         absolute;
    left:             50%;
    width:            150px;
    margin:           1px 0 0 -75px;
    padding:          10px 0;
    height:           auto;
    font-size:        20px;
    color:            #FFFFFF;
    font-weight:      bold;
    text-shadow:      rgba(0,0,0,.6) 0 -1px 0;
    text-align:       center;
}
body[orient="landscape"] .toolbar > h1 {
    width:            300px;
    margin:           1px 0 0 -150px;
    padding:          6px 0;
    font-size:        16px;
}


.button {
    position:         absolute;
    top:              8px;
    right:            6px;
    width:            auto;
    margin:           0;
    padding:          0 3px;
    color:            #FFFFFF;
    line-height:      30px;
    font-family:      inherit;
    font-size:        12px;
    font-weight:      bold;
    text-shadow:      rgba(0,0,0,.6) 0px -1px 0;
    border-width:     0 5px;
    background:       none;
    -webkit-border-image:    url(toolButton.png) 0 5 0 5;
    -moz-border-image:       url(toolButton.png) 0 5 0 5;
    border-image:            url(toolButton.png) 0 5 0 5;
}
```

```
body[orient="landscape"] .button {
    top:            3px;
    right:          3px;
    line-height:    26px;
}

#backButton {
    left:           6px;
    right:          auto;
    padding:        0;
    max-width:      55px;
    border-width:   0 8px 0 14px;
    -webkit-border-image:   url(backButton.png) 0 8 0 14;
    -moz-border-image:      url(backButton.png) 0 8 0 14;
    background:             url(backButton.png) repeat-x;
}
#backButton[selected],#backButton:active {
    -webkit-border-image:   url(backButtonSel.png) 0 8 0 14;
    -moz-border-image:      url(backButtonSel.png) 0 8 0 14;
    background:             url(backButtonSel.png) repeat-x;
}
```

The `body > .toolbar` class style is set to 45px in height. The `.toolbar > h1` header emulates the standard look of an application caption when in portrait mode and `body[orient="landscape"] > .toolbar > h1` updates the position for landscape mode. Notice that the limited width of the iPhone viewport dictates use of `overflow:hidden` and `text-overflow:ellipsis`.

Adding a Top-Level Navigation Menu

After the toolbar is created then the top-level navigation menu needs to be created. Under the iUI framework, use a `ul` list, such as the following:

Available for download on Wrox.com

```html
<ul id="home" title="iRealtor" selected="true">
    <li><a href="#featuredListings">Featured Listings</a></li>
    <li><a href="#">Buying & Tips</a></li>
    <li><a href="#calculator">Mortgage Calculator</a></li>
    <li><a href="#meetOurTeam">Meet Our Team</a></li>
    <li><a href="#">View Our Gallery</a></li>
    <li><a href="http://www.myirealtor.com" target="_self">Visit Our Web Site</a>
    </li>
</ul>
```

Code snippet index.html

The `title` attribute is used by iUI to display in the toolbar's `h1` header. The `selected` attribute indicates that this `ul` element is the active block when the application loads. Each of the menu items is defined as an `a` link inside of `li` items. The `href` attribute can point to either another `div` or `ul` block inside the same file (called a *panel*) using an anchor reference (such as `#meetOurTeam`). Alternatively, you can also use Ajax to load a block element from an external URL. Table 9-1 displays the four types of links you can work with inside iUI.

TABLE 9-1: iUI Link Types

LINK TYPE	DESCRIPTION	SYNTAX
Internal URL	Loads a panel that is defined inside the same HTML page	`<a href="#meet_our_team">`
Ajax URL	Loads document fragment via Ajax	`<a href="listings.html">`
Ajax	Loads document fragment via Ajax replacing contents of the calling link	`<a href="listings1.html" target="_replace">`
External URL	Loads external web link	`<a href="index.html" target="_self">`

The styles for the list items and links are as follows in `default-theme.css`:

```
body > ul > li {
    margin:           0;
    border-bottom:    1px solid #E0E0E0;
    padding:          8px 0 8px 10px;
    font-size:        20px;
    font-weight:      bold;
    list-style-type:none;
}
body[orient="landscape"] > ul > li {
    font-size:        18px;
}

body > ul > li > a {
    margin:     -8px 0 -8px -10px;
    padding:    8px 32px 8px 10px;
    color:      inherit;
    background: url(listArrow.png) no-repeat right center;
    text-decoration:    none;
}
```

Notice that `listArrow.png` is displayed at the right side of the list item's `a` link.

DISPLAYING A PANEL WITH AN INTERNAL URL

If you are linking to another block section inside the same page then you simply need to add the code. For example, the Meet Our Team item links to the following `div`:

```
<div id="meetOurTeam" class="panel" title="Meet Our Team">
    <h2>J-Team Reality</h2>
    <fieldset>
        <div class="row">
```

```
            <p class="normalText">Lorem ipsum dolor sit amet, consect etuer adipis
cing elit. Suspend isse nisl. Vivamus a ligula vel quam tinci dunt posuere.
Integer venen atis blandit est. Phasel lus ac neque. Quisque at augue.
Phasellus purus. Sed et risus. Suspe ndisse laoreet consequat metus. Nam
nec justo vitae tortor fermentum interdum. Aenean vitae quam eu urna
pharetra ornare.</p>
            <p class="normalText">Pellent esque habitant morbi tristique
senectus et netus et malesuada fames ac turpis egestas. Aliquam congue.
Pel lentesque pretium fringilla quam. Integer libero libero, varius ut,
faucibus et, facilisis vel, odio. Donec quis eros eu erat ullamc orper
euismod. Nam aliquam turpis. Nunc convallis massa non sem. Donec non
odio. Sed non lacus eget lacus hend rerit sodales.</p>
        </div>
    </fieldset>
</div>
```

Code snippet index.html

The `id` attribute value of the block element is identical to the `href` value of the source link (except for the # sign). The `div` element is assigned the `panel` class, and the `title` attribute supplies the new page title for the application. Inside the `div` element, the `h2` element provides a header, whereas the `fieldset` element, which is commonly used as a container inside of iUI destination pages, is used to house the content. Figure 9-3 displays the results for iPhone and Figure 9-4 shows the same page in iPad.

The `panel` class and `fieldset` styles are shown in the following code. In addition, the default `h2` style is provided:

```
body > .panel {
    padding-left:    10px;
    padding-right:   10px;
    background: #c8c8c8 url(pinstripes.png);
}
body > .panel > *:first-child {
    margin-top: 10px;
}
body > .panel > h2 {
    margin:          0 0 8px 14px;
    font-size:       inherit;
    font-weight:     bold;
    color:           #4d4d70;
    text-shadow:     rgba(255,255,255,.75) 2px 2px 0;
}

body > .panel > ul > li {
    list-style:      none;
    padding:         12px;
}

fieldset > .row {
    min-height:      42px;
}
fieldset > .row > p {
```

```
width:          auto;
height:         auto;
padding:        12px;
margin:         0;
text-align:     left;
} }
```

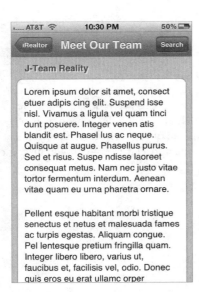

FIGURE 9-3

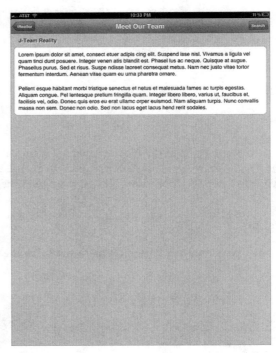

FIGURE 9-4

The `panel` class property displays the vertical pinstripes, which is a standard background for iOS applications. The `fieldset`, used primarily for displaying rows, is used because it provides a white background box around the text content the page displays.

CREATING A SECONDARY NAVIGATION LIST

In iRealtor, tapping the Featured Listings menu item (`<li><a href="#featuredListings">Featured Listings</a></li>`) should display a list of special homes that are being featured by this fictional local realtor. Here's the code:

```
<ul id="featuredListings" title="Featured">
    <li><a href="#406509171">30 Bellview Ave, Bolton</a></li>
    <li><a href="#">21 Milford Ave, Brandon</a></li>
    <li><a href="#">10 Main St, Leominster</a></li>
    <li><a href="#">12 Smuggle Lane, Marlboro</a></li>
```

```
        <li><a href="#">34 Main Ave, Newbury</a></li>
        <li><a href="#">33 Infinite Loop, Princeton</a></li>
        <li><a href="#">233 Melville Road, Rutland</a></li>
        <li><a href="#">320 Muffly, Sliver</a></li>
        <li><a href="#">1 One Road, Zooly</a></li>
    </ul>
```

Code snippet index.html

The result is a basic navigation list, as shown in Figure 9-5 (and, for iPad in Figure 9-6). The first entry specifies a local URL that the app loads when that entry is selected. The MLS listing destination page is in Figure 9-8 later in the chapter.

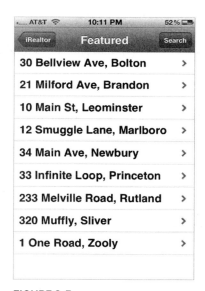

FIGURE 9-5

FIGURE 9-6

DESIGNING FOR LONG NAVIGATION LISTS

In the iRealtor sample app, the sizes of the individual screens contain a limited amount of data so that I can package all of these screens within a single HTML page using internal links.

However, in a real-world situation, this single-page approach could become problematic if you are dealing with large amounts of data. Therefore, you can use Ajax to break up your application into chunks, yet still maintain the same integrated look and feel of a single page app. When you use Ajax, iUI and other frameworks enable you to load content into your application on demand by providing an external URL. However, the document that is retrieved needs to be a document fragment, not a complete HTML page.

iUI fully encapsulates `XMLHttpRequest()` for you. Therefore, when you supply an external URL in a link that does not have `target="_self"` defined, iUI retrieves the document fragment and displays it.

What's more, although a document fragment such as the one shown in the previous section previously works fine for small amounts of data, the performance quickly drags with long lists. To deal with this issue, iUI and other frameworks enable you to break large lists into manageable chunks by loading an initial set of items, and then providing a link to the next set (see Figure 9-7). This design emulates the way the iOS Mail app works with incoming messages.

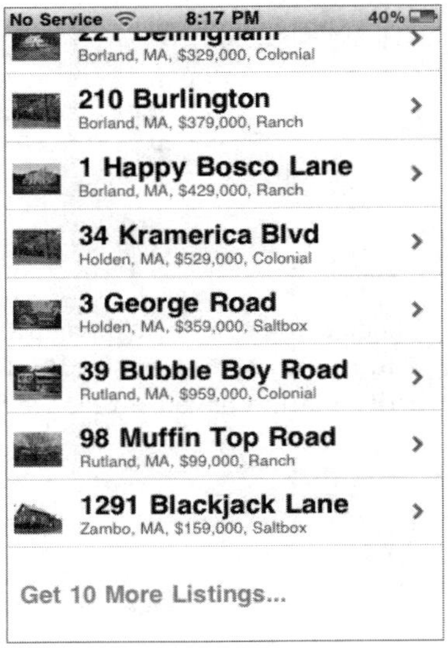

To provide this functionality in your application, create a link and add `target="_replace"` as an attribute. iUI loads the items from the URL replacing the current link. As with other Ajax links, the URL needs to point to a document fragment, not a complete HTML file. Here's the link added to the bottom of the listings `ul` list:

FIGURE 9-7

```
<li><a href="listings1.html" target="_replace">Get 10 More Listings.</a></li>
```

When using the `target="_replace"` attribute, you need to use a fragment of a `ul` element and not a different structure. For example, the following document fragment is valid to use with a `_replace` request:

```
<li>item 1</li>
<li>item 2</li>
<li>item 3</li>
```

However, the following document fragment would not be correct because it is not valid inside a `ul` element:

```
<ul>
<li>item 1</li>
<li>item 2</li>
<li>item 3</li>
</ul>
```

CREATING A DESTINATION PAGE

Each of the MLS listings in iRealtor has its own individual destination page that is accessed by a local URL, such as the following:

```
<a class="listing" href="#406509171">20 May Lane</a>
```

The design goal of the page is to provide a picture and summary details of the house listing. But, taking advantage of iPhone's services, suppose you also want to add a button for looking up the address in the Map app and an external web link to a site providing town information. Figures 9-8 and 9-9 show the end design for this destination page.

The document fragment for this page is as follows:

```html
<div id="406509171" title="20 May Lane" class="panel">
    <div style="text-align: center">
        <img class="panelImage" src="images/406509171.png"/>
    </div>
  <h2>Details</h2>
  <fieldset>
        <div class="row">
            <p>MLS: 406509171</p>
        </div>
        <div class="row">
            <p>Address: 20 May Lane</p>
        </div>
        <div class="row">
            <p>City: Acton</p>
        </div>
        <div class="row">
            <p>Price: $318,000</p>
        </div>
        <div class="row">
            <p>Type: Single Family</p>
        </div>
        <div class="row">
            <p>Acres: 0.27</p>
        </div>
        <div class="row">
            <p>Rooms: 6</p>
        </div>
        <div class="row">
            <p>Bath: 1</p>
        </div>
  </fieldset>
  <br/>
   <a  class="whiteButton" target="_self"
   href="http://maps.google.com/maps?q=20+May+Lane,+Acton,+MA">
   Map To House</a>
  <br/>
   <a  class="whiteButton" target="_self"
   href="http://www.mass.gov/?pageID=mg2localgovccpage&L=3&L0=Home&L1=
   State%20Government&L2=Local%20Government&sid=massgov2&selectCity=Acton">
   View Town Info</a>
   <br/>
</div>
```

Code snippet index.html

Note several things in this code. First, the `div` element is assigned the `panel` class, just as you did for the Meet Our Team page earlier in the chapter. Second, the individual items of the MLS listing data are contained in `div` elements with the `row` class. The set of `div` `row` elements is contained in a `fieldset`. Third, the button links to the map and external web page are assigned a `whiteButton` class. Figures 9-8 and 9-9 shows the page as it looks in iPhone.

FIGURE 9-8

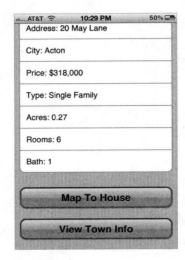

FIGURE 9-9

Yes, it works in iPad, too. Figure 9-10 shows the look.

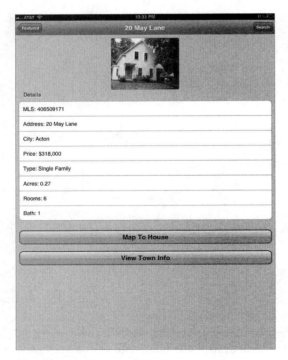

FIGURE 9-10

The styles for this page come from both `iui.css` and from a custom style I added to `index.html`. First, here are the `row class` and `label` styles in `default-theme.css` (if you recall, the `fieldset` is defined earlier in the chapter):

```
fieldset > .row {
    min-height:      42px;
}
fieldset > .row > p {
    width:           auto;
    height:          auto;
    padding:         12px;
    margin:          0;
    text-align:      left;
}
fieldset > .row > label {
    margin:          0 0 0 14px;
    line-height:     42px;
    font-weight:     bold;
}

body > .panel > ul > li:first-child > a,
body > .panel > ul > li:first-child,
fieldset > .row:first-child {
    -webkit-border-top-left-radius:      10px;
    -webkit-border-top-right-radius:     10px;
    -moz-border-radius-topleft:          10px;
    -moz-border-radius-topright:         10px;
    border-top-left-radius:              10px;
    border-top-right-radius:             10px;
}
body > .panel > ul > li:last-child > a,
body > .panel > ul > li:last-child,
fieldset > .row:last-child {
    -webkit-border-bottom-left-radius:   10px;
    -webkit-border-bottom-right-radius:  10px;
    -moz-border-radius-bottomleft:       10px;
    -moz-border-radius-bottomright:      10px;
    border-bottom-left-radius:           10px;
    border-bottom-right-radius:          10px;
    border-bottom:   0;
}
```

The `row` class emulates the general look of an iOS list row found in such locations as the native Settings and Contacts apps. The `.row:first -child.row:` and `last-child` style adds the rounded corners to the top and bottom of the `fieldset`. The `.row > label` style defined in `iui.css` emulates the look of iOS Settings.

What's more, to style the house image I needed to add a custom style in `index.html`:

```
.panelImage
{
    border:                 1px solid #888;
    -webkit-border-radius:  6px;
```

```
-moz-border-radius:        6px;
border-radius:             6px;
}
```

This style rounds the corners of the image and adds a border around it, providing a much more pleasing iOS-looking effect.

However, before leaving this page, notice the two buttons at the bottom of the page:

```
<a  class="whiteButton" target="_self"
href="http://maps.google.com/maps?q=20+May+Lane,
+Acton,+MA">Map To House</a>
<br/>
<a  class="whiteButton" target="_self"
href="http://www.mass.gov/?pageID=mg2localgovccpage&L=3&L0=Home&L1=
State%20Government&L2=Local%20Government&sid=massgov2&selectCity=Acton">
View Town Info</a>
```

The first button, when clicked, sends the user to the Maps app on the iOS device and displays the specified address. Figure 9-11 shows the result in iPhone.

FIGURE 9-11

ADDING A DIALOG

The application pages that have been displayed have either been edge-to-edge navigation lists or destination panels for displaying content. However, you probably have a need to create a modal dialog. When a user is in a dialog, he needs to either perform the intended action (such as a search or submittal) or cancel out. Just as in any desktop environment, a dialog is ideal for form entry.

iRealtor needs dialog boxes for two parts of the application—Search and the Mortgage Calculator. The user can access the Search dialog by tapping the Search button on the top toolbar. Here's the calling link:

```
<a class="button" href="#searchForm">Search</a>
```

The link displays the internal link #searchForm. This references the form element with an id of searchForm:

Available for download on Wrox.com

```
<form id="searchForm" title="Search Listings" class="dialog"
    name="searchForm" action="search.php" method="GET">

    <div class="toolbar">
        <h1>Search Listings</h1>
        <a class="button leftButton" type="cancel">Cancel</a>
        <a class="button blueButton" href="javascript:formname.submit()">Search</a>
    </div>

    <fieldset>
        <div class="row">
        <label for="proptype">Choose</label>
        <select id="proptype" name="proptype" size="1">
            <option value="">Property Type</option>
            <option value="SF">Single-Family</option>
            <option value="CC">Condo</option>
            <option value="MF">Multi-Family</option>
            <option value="LD">Land</option>
            <option value="CI">Commercial</option>
            <option value="MM">Mobile Home</option>
            <option value="RN">Rental</option>
            <option value="BU">Business Opportunity</option>
        </select>
        </div>
        <div class="row">
        <label>Min $:</label>
        <input type="text" name="minPrice"/>
        </div>
        <div class="row">
        <label>Max $:</label>
        <input type="text" name="maxPrice"/>
        </div>
        <div class="row">
        <label>MLS #:</label>
        <input type="text" name="mlsNumber"/>
        </div>
    </fieldset>
</form>
```

Code snippet index.html

The `dialog` class indicates that the form is a dialog. The form elements are wrapped inside a `fieldset`. The action buttons for the dialog are actually defined as links. To be specific, the Cancel and Search links are defined as `button leftButton` and `button blueButton` classes, respectively. These two action buttons are displayed in a toolbar `div` defined inside the form itself. The toolbar `div` also displays the `h1` content as the dialog title.

A `select` list defines the type of properties that the user wants to choose from. Three `input` fields are defined for additional search criteria.

Figure 9-12 shows the form when displayed in the iPhone viewport, and Figure 9-13 shows the same form in iPad. Per iOS guidelines, the bottom part of the form is shaded to obscure the background page. Figure 9-14 displays the iOS-specific selection list that is automatically displayed when the user taps in the `select` element. Finally, Figure 9-15 shows the pop-up keyboard that is displayed when the user taps in the `input` fields.

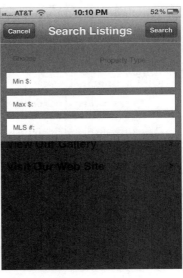

FIGURE 9-12

FIGURE 9-13

FIGURE 9-14

FIGURE 9-15

Consider the CSS styles that are used to display this dialog. From `default-theme.css`, there are several rules to pay attention to:

```css
body > .dialog,
body[orient="landscape"] > .dialog {
    top:        0px;
    z-index:    2;
    background: rgba(0, 0, 0, 0.8);
    padding:    0;
}
body > .dialog > div.toolbar {
    float:      left;
    width:      100%;
}

body > .dialog > fieldset {
    margin:         0;
    border:         none;
    padding:        10px 0 0 0;
    border-top:     1px solid #b3becd;
    background:     #7388a5 repeat-x;
}

body > .dialog > fieldset > div.row {
    padding:            0 10px;
    border:             0px;
    background-color:   transparent;
    -webkit-border-radius:  0;
}
```

```
body > .dialog > fieldset > div.row > label {
    position:            absolute;
    margin:              0;
    padding:             10px 8px 10px 12px;
    font-weight:         normal;
    line-height:         1em;
    font-size:           12px;
    color:               #666;
}
body > .dialog > fieldset > div.row >
    input:not([type|=radio]):not([type|=checkbox]) {
    font-size:           12px;
    font-weight:         bold;
    padding:             8px 0 6px 120px;
    border:              1px solid #47607c;
    -webkit-border-radius:  0px;
    background-color:       #fff;
}
```

The `body > .dialog` rule places the form over the entire application, including the top toolbar. It also defines a black background with .8 opacity. Notice the way in which the `.dialog > fieldset > label` style is defined so that the `label` element appears to be part of the `input` element.

When you submit this form, it is submitted via Ajax to allow the results to slide in from the side to provide a smooth transition.

You may, however, have other uses for dialogs beyond form submissions. For example, suppose I'd like to include a simple JavaScript-based mortgage calculator in iRealtor that is accessible from the top-level navigation menu. Here's the link:

```
<li><a href="#calc">Mortgage Calculator</a></li>
```

The link accesses the document fragment contained in an external URL that contains the following form:

Available for
download on
Wrox.com

```
<form id="calculator" class="dialog">
    <div class="toolbar">
        <h1>Mortgage Calculator</h1>
        <a class="button leftButton" type="cancel">Cancel</a>
        <a class="button blueButton" href="javascript:formname.submit()">Search</a>
    </div>

    <fieldset>
        <div class="row">
            <label for="amt">Loan amount</label>
              <input class="calc" type="text" id="amt" name="amtZip"/>
        </div>
        <div class="row">
            <label for="ir">Interest rate</label>
            <input class="calc" type="text" id="ir" name="irZip"/>
        </div>
        <div class="row">
            <label for="term">Years</label>
            <input class="calc"  type="text" id="term"
```

```
                onblur="calc()"name="termZip"/>
        </div>
        <div class="row">
            <label for="payment">Monthly payment</label>
            <input class="calc" type="text" readonly="true" id="payment"/>
        </div>
        <div class="row">
            <label for="total">Total payment</label>
            <input class="calc" type="text"  readonly="true" id="total"/>
        </div>
    </fieldset>
</form>
```

Code snippet index.html

 NOTE *The first three* input *elements have a dummy* name *attribute that includes* Zip *in it. The* Zip *string prompts the numeric keyboard to display rather than the alphabet keyboard. The last two input elements don't need it because they are read-only.*

The purpose of the form is for the user to enter information in the first three input elements and then call the JavaScript function calc(), which then displays the results in the bottom two input fields. Because the calculation is performed inside a client-side JavaScript, no submittal is needed with the server.

The JavaScript function calc() resides in the document head of the index.html file. Here's the scripting code:

Available for
download on
Wrox.com

```
<script type="application/x-javascript">
function calc() {
    var amt = document.getElementById('amt').value;
    var ir =  document.getElementById('ir').value / 1200;
    var term =  document.getElementById('term').value * 12;
    var total=1;
    for (i=0;i<term;i++) {
       total = total * (1 + ir);
    }
    var mp = amt * ir / ( 1-(1/total));
   document.getElementById('payment').value = Math.round(mp*100)/100;
   document.getElementById('total').value = Math.round(mp * term *100)/100;
}
</script>
```

Code snippet index.html

This routine performs a standard mortgage calculation and returns the results to the `payment` and `total input` fields. Figures 9-16 and 9-17 show the calculator in action on iPhone.

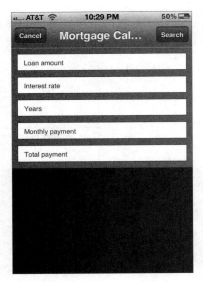

FIGURE 9-16

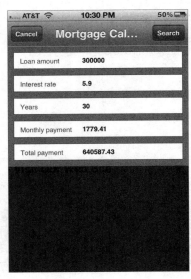

FIGURE 9-17

Listing 9-1 provides a full code view of the `index.html` file.

LISTING 9-1: index.html

```html
<!DOCTYPE html>
<html>
<head>

<title>iRealtor</title>
<meta content="yes" name="apple-mobile-web-app-capable" />
<meta name="viewport"
   content="width=device-width; initial-scale=1.0;
   maximum-scale=1.0; user-scalable=0;"/>
<link rel="stylesheet" href="iui/iui.css" type="text/css" />
<link rel="stylesheet" href="iui/t/default/default-theme.css" type="text/css"/>
<script type="application/x-javascript" src="iui/iui.js"></script>

<script type="application/x-javascript">
function calc()
{
    var amt = document.getElementById('amt').value;
    var ir =  document.getElementById('ir').value / 1200;
    var term =  document.getElementById('term').value * 12;
    var total=1;
    for (i=0;i<term;i++)
```

```
    {
       total = total * (1 + ir);
    }
    var mp = amt * ir / ( 1 - (1/total));
    document.getElementById('payment').value = Math.round(mp*100)/100;
    document.getElementById('total').value = Math.round(mp * term *100)/100 ;
}
</script>

<style>

.panelImage
{
    border:                 1px solid #888;
    -webkit-border-radius:  6px;
    -moz-border-radius:     6px;
    border-radius:          6px;
}

</style>

</head>

<body>

<!-- Top toolbar -->
<div class="toolbar">
    <h1 id="pageTitle"></h1>
    <a id="backButton" class="button" href="#"></a>
    <a class="button" href="#searchForm">Search</a>
</div>

<!-- Home menu -->
<ul id="home" title="iRealtor" selected="true">
    <li><a href="#featuredListings">Featured Listings</a></li>
    <li><a href="#">Buying & Tips</a></li>
    <li><a href="#calculator">Mortgage Calculator</a></li>
    <li><a href="#meetOurTeam">Meet Our Team</a></li>
    <li><a href="#">View Our Gallery</a></li>
    <li><a href="http://www.myirealtor.com"
        target="_self">Visit Our Web Site</a></li>
</ul>

<!-- Featured Listings -->
<ul id="featuredListings" title="Featured">
    <li><a href="#406509171">30 Bellview Ave, Bolton</a></li>
    <li><a href="#">21 Milford Ave, Brandon</a></li>
    <li><a href="#">10 Main St, Leominster</a></li>
    <li><a href="#">12 Smuggle Lane, Marlboro</a></li>
    <li><a href="#">34 Main Ave, Newbury</a></li>
    <li><a href="#">33 Infinite Loop, Princeton</a></li>
    <li><a href="#">233 Melville Road, Rutland</a></li>
    <li><a href="#">320 Muffly, Sliver</a></li>
```

```
    <li><a href="#">1 One Road, Zooly</a></li>
</ul>

<!-- Calculator -->
<form id="calculator" class="dialog">
    <div class="toolbar">
      <h1>Mortgage Calculator</h1>
      <a class="button leftButton" type="cancel">Cancel</a>
      <a class="button blueButton" href="javascript:formname.submit()">Search</a>
    </div>

    <fieldset>
        <div class="row">
            <label for="amt">Loan amount</label>
            <input class="calc" type="text" id="amt"/>
        </div>
        <div class="row">
            <label for="ir">Interest rate</label>
            <input class="calc" type="text" id="ir"/>
        </div>
        <div class="row">
            <label for="term">Years</label>
            <input class="calc"  type="text" id="term"
            onblur="calc()"/>
        </div>
        <div class="row">
            <label for="payment">Monthly payment</label>
            <input class="calc" type="text" readonly="true"
            id="payment"/>
        </div>
        <div class="row">
            <label for="total">Total payment</label>
            <input class="calc" type="text"  readonly="true"
            id="total"/>
        </div>
    </fieldset>
</form>


<!-- Meet Our Team -->
<div id="meetOurTeam" class="panel" title="Meet Our Team">
    <h2>J-Team Reality</h2>
    <fieldset>
        <div class="row">
            <p class="normalText">Lorem ipsum dolor sit amet,
consect etuer adipis cing elit. Suspend isse nisl. Vivamus
a ligula vel quam tinci dunt posuere. Integer venen atis
blandit est. Phasel lus ac neque. Quisque at augue. Phasellus
purus. Sed et risus. Suspe ndisse laoreet consequat metus.
Nam nec justo vitae tortor fermentum interdum. Aenean vitae
quam eu urna pharetra ornare.</p>
            <p class="normalText">Pellent esque habitant morbi
tristique senectus et netus et malesuada fames ac turpis egestas.
Aliquam congue. Pel lentesque pretium fringilla quam. Integer
libero libero, varius ut, faucibus et, facilisis vel, odio.
```

Donec quis eros eu erat ullamc orper euismod. Nam aliquam
turpis. Nunc convallis massa non sem. Donec non odio. Sed
non lacus eget lacus hend rerit sodales.</p>
        </div>
    </fieldset>
</div>

<!-- House Listing -->
<div id="406509171" title="20 May Lane" class="panel">
    <div style="text-align: center">
        <img class="panelImage" src="images/406509171.png"/>
    </div>
  <h2>Details</h2>
    <fieldset>
            <div class="row">
                <p>MLS: 406509171</p>
            </div>
            <div class="row">
                <p>Address: 20 May Lane</p>
            </div>
            <div class="row">
                <p>City: Acton</p>
            </div>
            <div class="row">
                <p>Price: $318,000</p>
            </div>
            <div class="row">
                <p>Type: Single Family</p>
            </div>
            <div class="row">
                <p>Acres: 0.27</p>
            </div>
            <div class="row">
                <p>Rooms: 6</p>
            </div>
            <div class="row">
                <p>Bath: 1</p>
            </div>
    </fieldset>

    <a class="whiteButton" target="_self"
        href="http://maps.google.com/maps?q=
        20+May+Lane,+Acton,+MA">Map To House</a>

    <a class="whiteButton" target="_self"
    href="http://www.mass.gov/?pageID=
    mg2localgovccpage&L=3&L0=Home&L1=State%20
    Government&L2=Local%20Government&sid=massgov2
    &selectCity=Acton">View Town Info</a>

</div>

<!-- Search Form -->
<form id="searchForm" title="Search Listings"

```
class="dialog" name="searchForm" action="search.php"
method="GET">

<div class="toolbar">
   <h1>Search Listings</h1>
   <a class="button leftButton" type="cancel">Cancel</a>
   <a class="button blueButton" href="javascript:formname.submit()">Search</a>
</div>

 <fieldset>
    <div class="row">
    <label for="proptype">Choose</label>
    <select id="proptype" name="proptype" size="1">
        <option value="">Property Type</option>
        <option value="SF">Single-Family</option>
        <option value="CC">Condo</option>
        <option value="MF">Multi-Family</option>
        <option value="LD">Land</option>
        <option value="CI">Commercial</option>
        <option value="MM">Mobile Home</option>
        <option value="RN">Rental</option>
        <option value="BU">Business Opportunity</option>
    </select>
    </div>
    <div class="row">
    <label>Min $:</label>
    <input type="text" name="minPrice"/>
    </div>
    <div class="row">
    <label>Max $:</label>
    <input type="text" name="maxPrice"/>
    </div>
    <div class="row">
    <label>MLS #:</label>
    <input type="text" name="mlsNumber"/>
    </div>
   </fieldset>
</form>

</body>
</html>
```

SCRIPTING UI BEHAVIOR

When you use a framework such as iUI, you have a main JavaScript file (such as iui.js) that powers all of the UI behavior for you when you include it in your document head. However, because the framework takes control over many aspects of the environment, a solid understanding of the library's internals can be invaluable to you.

NOTE *Note that the material in this section is advanced, but you may find it a helpful walkthrough of the scripting underpinnings of an iOS web app.*

The following example is `iui.js`. The `iui.js` consists of the object `window.iui`, three listeners for `load` and `click` events, and several supporting routines. All of the JavaScript code is enclosed in an anonymous function with several constants and variables defined:

```
(function() {
var slideSpeed = 20;
var slideInterval = 0;
var currentPage = null;
var currentDialog = null;
var currentWidth = 0;
var currentHash = location.hash;
var hashPrefix = "#_";
var pageHistory = [];
var newPageCount = 0;
var checkTimer;
// **** REST OF IUI CODE HERE ****
})();
```

The anonymous function creates a local scope to allow private semi-global variables and avoid name conflicts with applications that use `iui.js`.

On Document Load

When the HTML document loads, the following listener function is triggered:

```
addEventListener("load", function(event)
{
    var page = iui.getSelectedPage();
    var locPage = getPageFromLoc();

    if (page)
        iui.showPage(page);

    if (locPage && (locPage != page))
        iui.showPage(locPage);

    setTimeout(preloadImages, 0);
    if (typeof window.onorientationchange == "object")

        window.onorientationchange=orientChangeHandler;
        hasOrientationEvent = true;
        setTimeout(orientChangeHandler, 0);
    }
    setTimeout(checkOrientAndLocation, 0);
    checkTimer = setInterval(checkOrientAndLocation, 300);
}, false);
```

The `getSelectedPage()` method of the JSON object `iui` is called to get the selected page—the block element node that contains a `selected="true"` attribute. This node is then passed to `iui.showPage()`, which is the core routine to display content.

`setTimeout()` is often used when calling certain JavaScript routines to prevent timing inconsistencies. Using `setTimeout()`, iUI calls an image preloader function to load application images.

Getting back to `iui.showPage()`, its code is as follows:

```
showPage: function(page, backwards)
{
    if (page)
    {
        if (page == currentPage)
        {
            console.log("page = currentPage = " + page.id);
            iui.busy = false;
            return;
        }

        if (currentDialog)
        {
            currentDialog.removeAttribute("selected");
            sendEvent("blur", currentDialog);
            currentDialog = null;
        }

        if (hasClass(page, "dialog"))
        {
            iui.busy = false;
            sendEvent("focus", page);
            showDialog(page);
        }
        else
        {
            sendEvent("load", page);
            var fromPage = currentPage;
            sendEvent("blur", currentPage);
            currentPage = page;
            sendEvent("focus", page);

            if (fromPage)
            {
                if (backwards) sendEvent("unload", fromPage);
                setTimeout(slidePages, 0, fromPage, page, backwards);
            }
            else
            {
                updatePage(page, fromPage);
            }
        }
    }
}
```

The `currentDialog` semi-global variable is evaluated to determine whether a dialog is already displayed. (`currentDialog` is set in the `showDialog()` function.) This variable would be `null` when the document initially loads because of the line `var currentDialog = null;` earlier in `iui.js`, which runs every time the document loads.

The node is then evaluated to determine whether it is a dialog (containing `class="dialog"` as an attribute) or a normal page. Although the opening page is usually considered a normal page, you may want to have a login or initial search dialog.

Loading a Standard iUI Page

For normal pages, iUI assigns the value of `currentPage` to the variable `fromPage` and then reassigns `currentPage` to the `page` parameter. If `fromPage` is not null (that is, every page after the initial page), then iUI performs a slide-in animation with a function called `slidePages()`. The `fromPage`, `page`, and `backwards` variables are passed to `slidePages()`.

However, because this is the first time running this routine (and `fromPage` equals `null`), the `updatePage()` function is called:

```
function updatePage(page, fromPage)
{
    if (!page.id)
        page.id = "__" + (++newPageCount) + "__";

    location.hash = currentHash = hashPrefix + page.id;
    pageHistory.push(page.id);

    if(hasTitle) {
        var pageTitle = $("pageTitle");
        if (page.title)
            pageTitle.innerHTML = page.title;
        var ttlClass = page.getAttribute("ttlclass");
        pageTitle.className = ttlClass ? ttlClass : "";
    }

    if (page.localName.toLowerCase() == "form" && !page.target)
        showForm(page);

    var backButton = $("backButton");
    if (backButton)
    {
        var prevPage = $(pageHistory[pageHistory.length-2]);
        if (prevPage && !page.getAttribute("hideBackButton"))
        {
            backButton.style.display = "inline";
            backButton.innerHTML = prevPage.title ? prevPage.title : "Back";
            var bbClass = prevPage.getAttribute("bbclass");
            backButton.className = (bbClass) ? 'button ' + bbClass : 'button';
        }
        else
            backButton.style.display = "none";
    }
    iui.busy = false;
}
```

The updatePage() function is responsible for updating the pageHistory array, which is required for enabling the Safari Back button to work even in single-page web apps, such as iRealtor. The value of the node's title attribute is then assigned to be the innerHTML of the top toolbar's h1 pageTitle.

If the page name contains the string form in it then the showForm() function is called. Otherwise, the routine continues on, looking to see if a backButton element is defined in the toolbar. If so, then the page history is updated and button title is updated.

Subsequent pages always bypass the direct call to updatePage() and use the slidePages() function instead. Here is the code:

```
function slidePages(fromPage, toPage, backwards)
{
    var axis = (backwards ? fromPage : toPage).getAttribute("axis");

    clearInterval(checkTimer);

    sendEvent("beforetransition", fromPage, {out:true});
    sendEvent("beforetransition", toPage, {out:false});
    if (canDoSlideAnim() && axis != 'y')
    {
        slide2(fromPage, toPage, backwards, slideDone);
    }
    else
    {
        slide1(fromPage, toPage, backwards, axis, slideDone);
    }

    function slideDone()
    {
        if (!hasClass(toPage, "dialog"))
            fromPage.removeAttribute("selected");
        checkTimer = setInterval(checkOrientAndLocation, 300);
        setTimeout(updatePage, 0, toPage, fromPage);
        fromPage.removeEventListener('webkitTransitionEnd', slideDone, false);
        sendEvent("aftertransition", fromPage, {out:true});
        sendEvent("aftertransition", toPage, {out:false});
        var linkObj = document.getElementsByTagName('a');
        for (var i = 0; i <= (linkObj.length-1); i++) {
            linkObj[i].removeAttribute('selected');
        }
    }
}
```

The primary purpose of slidePages() is to emulate the standard iOS slide animation effect when you move between pages. It achieves this by using JavaScript timer routines to incrementally update the style.left property of the fromPage and the toPage. The updatePage() function (discussed previously) is called inside a setTimeout routine.

Handling Link Clicks

Because most of the user interaction with an iOS web app is tapping the interface to navigate the application, the event listener for link clicks is, in many ways, the "mission control center" for iui.jss. Check out the code:

```
addEventListener("click", function(event)
{
    var link = findParent(event.target, "a");
    if (link)
    {
        link.setAttribute("selected", "true");
        setTimeout(function(){ link.removeAttribute("selected");}, 100);

        if (link.href && link.hash && link.hash != "#" && !link.target)
        {
            followAnchor(link);
        }
        else if (link == $("backButton"))
        {
            if(window.history)
                history.go(-1);
            else
                iui.goBack();
        }
        else if (link.getAttribute("type") == "submit")
        {
            var form = findParent(link, "form");
            if (form.target == "_self")
            {
                // Note: this will not call any onsubmit handlers!
                form.submit();
                return;  // allow default
            }
            submitForm(form);
        }
        else if (link.getAttribute("type") == "cancel")
        {
            cancelDialog(findParent(link, "form"));
        }
        else if (link.target == "_replace")
        {
            followAjax(link, link);
        }
        else if (iui.isNativeUrl(link.href))
        {
            return;
        }
        else if (link.target == "_webapp")
        {
            location.href = link.href;
        }
        else if (!link.target)
        {
```

```
            followAjax(link, null);
        }
        else
            return;

        event.preventDefault();
    }

    var div = findParent(event.target, "div");
    if (div && hasClass(div, "toggle"))
    {
        div.setAttribute("toggled", div.getAttribute("toggled") != "true");
        event.preventDefault();
    }

}, true);
```

This routine evaluates the type of link:

➤ If it is an internal URL then the page is passed to `followAnchor()`, which, among other things, calls `iui.showPage()`.

➤ If the `backButton` is tapped then `history.back()` is triggered.

➤ Dialog forms typically contain Submit and Cancel buttons. If a Submit button is tapped then `submitForm()` is called. If a Cancel button is tapped then `cancelDialog()` is called.

➤ External URLs that have `target="_replace"` or that do not have target defined are Ajax links. Both of these call the `followAjax()` method.

➤ If it is none of these, then it is an external link with a `target="_self"` attribute defined and the default iUI behavior is suspended and the link is treated as normal.

Loading a Dialog

If the node that is passed into the main `showPage()` function is a dialog (`class="dialog"`), then the `showDialog()` function is called, which in turn calls `showForm()`. These two functions are shown in the following code:

```
function showDialog(page)
{
    currentDialog = page;
    iui.addClass(page, "show");

    if (hasClass(page, "dialog"))
        showForm(page);
}

function showForm(form)
{
    form.onsubmit = function(event)
    {
        event.preventDefault();
```

```
            submitForm(form);
        };

    form.onclick = function(event)
    {

        if (event.target == form && hasClass(form, "dialog"))
            cancelDialog(form);
    };
}
```

The showForm() function assigns event handlers to the onsubmit and onclick events of the form. When a form is submitted, the submitForm() function submits the form data via Ajax. When an element on the form is clicked, then the dialog is closed. The following code shows the routines that are called from a typical dialog box:

```
function submitForm(form)
{
    if (!iui.busy)
    {
        iui.busy = true;
        iui.addClass(form, "progress");
        iui.showPageByHref(form.action, encodeForm(form), form.method || "GET",
          null, clear);
    }
    function clear() {   iui.removeClass(form, "progress"); }
}


function encodeForm(form)
{
    function encode(inputs)
    {
        for (var i = 0; i < inputs.length; ++i)
        {
            if (inputs[i].name)
                args[inputs[i].name] = inputs[i].value;
        }
    }

    var args = {};
    encode(form.getElementsByTagName("input"));
    encode(form.getElementsByTagName("textarea"));
    encode(form.getElementsByTagName("select"));
    encode(form.getElementsByTagName("button"));
    return args;
}

function cancelDialog(form)
{
    return iui.removeClass(form, "show");
}
```

EXERCISES

1.   Using iUI, how do you define multiple screens inside the same HTML page?

2.   How do you define a navigation list that is replaced by new data coming from an Ajax source?

3.   When evaluating frameworks, such as iUI, how important is it to consider support for iPad as well as other mobile platforms?

Answers to the Exercises can be found in the Appendix.

▶ **WHAT YOU LEARNED IN THIS CHAPTER**

TOPIC	KEY CONCEPTS
Defining a multi-screen, single page web app	Frameworks like iUI and jQuery Mobile enable you to define full apps inside a single HTML file
Using iUI framework	Creating your UI and logic in HTML and linking in the framework's CSS and JS files for styling and functionality

10

Handling Touch Interactions and Events

An essential part of any web application is the ability to respond to events triggered by the user or by a condition that occurs on the client: the clicking of a button, the pressing of a key, the scrolling of a window. Although the user interacts with an HTML element, the entire document, or the browser window, JavaScript serves as the watchful eye behind the scenes that monitors all of this activity taking place and fires off events as they occur.

With its touch interface, iPhone and iPad devices are all about direct interactivity with the user. As a result, it is not surprising that any iOS web app you create can handle the variety of *gestures* — finger taps, flicks, swipes, and pinches — that a user naturally performs as they interact with your app on their mobile device.

THREE TYPES OF TOUCH EVENTS

There are three primary types of touch-related events to consider when developing an iOS web app:

➤ **Mouse emulation events:** Events in which a one- or two-finger action simulates a mouse.

➤ **Touch events:** Events that dispatch when one or more fingers touch the screen. You can trap touch events and work with multiple finger touches that occur at different points on the screen at the same time.

➤ **Gesture events:** Gesture events are combinations of touch events that also support scaling and rotation information.

The mouse emulation events are the ones that you'll likely be working with for most typical interactions inside your web app. I begin with exploring the mouse emulation events and then later move on to talking about the multitouch and gesture events.

MOUSE-EMULATION EVENTS

When working with touch interactions and events for iOS devices, keep in mind that several of the gestures that a user performs are designed to emulate mouse events. At the same time, I need to make one thing very clear: *The finger is not the same as a mouse.* As a result, the traditional event model that web developers are so used to working with on desktop computers does not always apply as you may expect in this new context. The new ground rules are described in the following sections.

Many Events Handled by Default

By default, many of the events are handled automatically by iOS and Safari on iOS. As a result, you do not need to write any code to handle the basic touch interactions of the user. Flick-scrolling, zoom pinching and unpinching, and one-finger panning (or scrolling) are those sorts of user inputs that come free, so to speak. You can, however, trap for many of these events with touch or gesture events.

Conditional Events

The way in which Safari events are handled depends on two key variables:

➤ **Number of fingers:** Different events fire depending upon whether a one-finger or two-finger gesture is performed. Tables 10-1 and 10-2 list the common iOS one- and two-finger gestures and the ability to trap these events.

➤ **Event target:** Events are also handled differently depending upon the HTML element being selected. In particular, the event flow varies depending on whether the target element is clickable or scrollable. A clickable target is one that supports standard mouse events (for example, mousemove, mousedown, mouseup, click), whereas a scrollable target is one equipped to deal with overflow, scrollbars, and so on. (However, as I'll discuss later in the chapter, you can make any element clickable by registering an event handler for it.)

TABLE 10-1: One-Finger Gestures

GESTURE	EVENT(S) FIRED	DESCRIPTION
Panning	onscroll fired when gesture ends	No events triggered until user stops panning motion.
Touch and hold	None	Some native iPhone apps support this gesture. For example, touch and hold on an image displays a Save dialog.

GESTURE	EVENT(S) FIRED	DESCRIPTION
Double-tap	None	
Tap	*Clickable element:* mouseover, mousemove, mousedown, mouseup, click *Non-clickable element:* None	If mouseover or mousemove changes page content then the remaining events in the sequence are canceled.

TABLE 10-2: Two-Finger Gestures

GESTURE	EVENT(S) FIRED	DESCRIPTION
Pinch/unpinch zoom	None	The gesture used to zoom and unzoom on a web page or image.
Two-finger panning	*Scrollable element:* mouseevent *Non-scrollable element:* None	If it's a non-scrollable element, then the event is treated as a page-level scroll (which fires an onscroll when the gesture stops).

Mouse Events: Think "Click," Not "Move"

The general rule of thumb for iPhone event handling is that no events trigger *until* the user's finger leaves the touch screen. As a result, the normal flow of mouse events is radically altered over the traditional browser event model because mouse events now depend on the actual selection (or clicking) of an element, not simply when a finger passes over it. Said differently, the focus or selection of an element is what matters, not the movement of the mouse.

Take the example of a page that consists of two links, Link A and Link B. Suppose a user glides his finger from Link A, passes over top the Link B, and then clicks on Link B. Here's how the events are handled:

➤ The mouseover, mousemove, mousedown event handlers of B are fired only *after* a mouseup event occurs (but before mouseup is triggered). As a result, from a practical standpoint, these preliminary mouse events are rendered useless.

➤ Because you can't perform a mousedown and mouseup without a click, they all refer to the same event.

➤ The mouseout event of A is fired only after the user clicks on B, not when the finger moved off A itself.

➤ The CSS pseudo-style :hover is applied to B only when the user selects it and is removed from A only when B is actually selected, not before.

Therefore, for most purposes, you should design your app to respond to click events rather than the other mouse events.

Click-Enabling Elements

If the element you are working with is not considered "clickable" by Safari on iOS then all mouse-related events for it are ignored. However, there are certain situations in which this can be problematic, such as if you are using span or div elements in a cascading menu and want to change the menu display based on the context of the user.

To override Safari's default behavior, you need to force the element to be considered "clickable" by Safari on iOS. To do so, you assign an empty click handler to the element (click="void(0)"). For example:

```
<span mousemove="displayMenu(event)" click="void(0)">Run Lola Run</span>
```

After you add the empty click handler, the other mouse-related events begin to fire.

Event Flow

Besides the anomaly of the timing of the mousedown event, the rest of the supported mouse and key events fire in Safari on iOS in the same sequence as a standard web browser. Table 10-3 shows the event sequences that occur when both a block-level element and a form element are clicked. The form element column also displays the order of key events if the user types in the on-screen keyboard.

TABLE 10-3: Event Sequencing

CLICKABLE BLOCK-LEVEL ELEMENTS (E.G., LINK)	FORM ELEMENT (E.G., TEXTAREA, INPUT)
mouseover	mouseover
mousedown	mousedown
mouseup	focus
click	mouseup
mouseout (only after the next element receives focus)	click
	keydown
	keypress
	keyup
	change
	blur (only after the next element receives focus)
	mouseout (only after the next element receives focus)

Unsupported Events

You cannot trap for all events inside of Safari on iOS. For example, you cannot trap for events associated with a user switching between pages in Safari. The focus and blur events of the window object are not triggered when the focus moves off or on a page. Additionally, when another page becomes the active page, JavaScript events (including polling events created with `setInterval()`) are not fired. However, the `unload` event of the `window` object is triggered when the user loads a new page in the current window.

Table 10-4 lists the events that are fully supported and unsupported.

TABLE 10-4: Event Compatibility

SUPPORTED EVENTS	UNSUPPORTED EVENTS
click	cut
mouseout*	copy
mouseover*	paste
mouseup*	drag
mousedown*	drop
mouseout*	dblclick
blur	selection
change	formfield.onmouseenter
focus	formfield.onmouseleave
load	formfield.onmousemove
unload	formfield.onselect
reset	contextmenu
mousewheel	error
submit	resize
abort	scroll
orientationchange	
touchstart	
touchmove	
touchend	
touchcancel	
gesturestart	
gesturechange	
gestureend	

*Different behavior than in a desktop browser. (See the "Mouse Events: Think 'Click,' Not 'Move'" section earlier in this chapter.)

TOUCH EVENTS

In addition to the mouse-emulation events, Safari on iOS also captures additional touch-related sequences of events for each finger that touches the screen surface. A touch event begins when a finger touches the screen surface, continues when the finger moves, and ends when the finger leaves it. The four touch events are shown in Table 10-5.

TABLE 10-5: Touch Events

EVENT	DESCRIPTION
touchstart	Fires when a finger touches the screen surface
touchmove	Fires when the same finger moves across the surface
touchend	Fires when a finger leaves the surface of the screen
touchcancel	Fires when the touch is cancelled by the operating system

Each of these touch events have properties that enable you to get information about the touch:

➤ event.touches returns an array of all of the touches on a page. For example, if there were four fingers on the surface, then the touches property would return four Touch objects.

➤ event.targetTouches returns just the touches that were started from the same element on a page.

➤ event.changedTouches returns all of the touches involved in the event.

The information contained in each of these properties varies depending on what multitouch event is performed. Table 10-6 shows several example scenarios.

TABLE 10-6: Touch Scenarios

TOUCH SCENARIO	TOUCHES	TARGETTOUCHES	CHANGEDTOUCHES
One finger touches surface	1 item	1 item	1 item
Two fingers down on same target at the same time	2 items	2 items	2 items
Two fingers touching different targets at different times	2 items	1 item	1 item
Moving one finger across the surface			1 item
Moving two fingers across the surface			2 items
Lift up a finger from the surface	(Removed from list)	(Removed from list)	1 item

The items inside these arrays are `Touch` objects (shown in Table 10-7) that provide the information related to the touch events.

TABLE 10-7: Touch Object Properties

PROPERTY	DESCRIPTION
clientX	x coordinate of the object relative to the full viewport (not including scroll offset)
clientY	y coordinate relative to the full viewport (not including scroll offset)
identifier	Unique integer of the touch event
pageX	x coordinate relative to the page
pageY	y coordinate relative to the page
screenX	x coordinate relative to the screen
screenY	y coordinate relative to the screen
target	Originating element (node) that dispatched the touch event

Unlike mouse-emulated events, you can trap for multiple touches to occur on screen at the same time and then have your app respond to them.

For example, if you want to do a test to determine how these events are fired, you could add event handlers and then take different actions when these events occur. Here's the JavaScript code:

```
function init()
{
document.addEventListener("touchstart", touchEventHandler, false);
document.addEventListener("touchmove", touchEventHandler, false);
document.addEventListener("touchcancel", touchEventHandler, false);
document.addEventListener("touchend", touchEventHandler, false);
}

function touchEventHandler(event)
{
    // Gather basic touch info
    var numTouch = event.touches.length;
    var numTargetTouches = event.targetTouches.length;
    var numChangedTouches = event.changedTouches.length;

    // Get first touch object
if (numTouch > 0)
    {
var touchObj = event.touches[0];
        var x = touchObj.screenX;
        var y = touchObj.screenY;
    }

    if (event.type == "touchstart")
```

```
        {
            // do something to begin
        }
        else if (event.type == "touchmove")
        {
            // do something on move
        }
        else if (event.type == "touchend")
        {
            // do something to end
        }
        else
        {
            // do something when cancelled
        }
    }
```

GESTURE EVENTS

During a multitouch sequence, touch events are dispatched through `touchstart`, `touchmove`, `touchend`, and `touchcancel`. However, Safari on iOS also dispatches gesture events when multiple fingers are touching the surface of the screen. The three gesture events are shown in Table 10-8.

TABLE 10-8: Gesture Events

EVENT	DESCRIPTION
gesturestart	Fires when two or more fingers touch the screen surface
gesturechange	Fires when the these fingers move across the surface or perform another change
gestureend	Fires when one of the fingers involved in the gesture leaves the surface of the screen

The two key properties associated with gesture events are the following:

➤ `scale` returns the multiplier of the pinch or push since the gesture started. (`1.0` is the baseline value.)

➤ `rotation` returns the rotation value since the gesture began.

DETECTING AN ORIENTATION CHANGE

One of the unique events that an iPhone web application developer needs to be able to trap for is the change between vertical and horizontal orientation. Safari on iOS provides support for the `orientationchange` event handler of the `window` object. This event is triggered each time the device is rotated by the user.

TRY IT OUT   Detecting an Orientation Change

For a demonstration of how to detect an orientation change in your app, follow the steps below.

1. Create the following HTML document in your text editor and then save the document as *BIDHJ-Ch10-Ex2.html*.

Available for
download on
Wrox.com

```
<!DOCTYPE html PUBLIC "-//W3C//DTD XHTML 1.0 Strict//EN"
          "http://www.w3.org/TR/xhtml1/DTD/xhtml1-strict.dtd">
<html xmlns="http://www.w3.org/1999/xhtml">
<head>
<title>Orientation Change Example</title>
<meta name="viewport" content="width=320; initial-scale=1.0;
   maximum-scale=1.0; user-scalable=0;">
</head>
<body onload="orientationChangeHandler();"
   onorientationchange="orientationChangeHandler();">
<h4 id="mode">Ras sed nibh.</h4>
<p>
Donec semper lorem ac dolor ornare interdum. Praesent condimentum.
Suspendisse lacinia interdum augue. Nunc venenatis ipsum sed ligula.
Aenean vitae lacus. Sed sit amet neque. Vestibulum ante ipsum primis
in faucibus orci luctus et ultrices posuere cubilia Curae; Duis
laoreet lorem quis nulla. Curabitur enim erat, gravida ac,
posuere sed, nonummy in, tortor. Donec id orci id lectus
convallis egestas. Duis ut dui. Aliquam dignissim dictum metus.
</p>
</body>
</html>
```

Code snippet BIDHJ-Ch10-Ex2.html

2. Add the following script code in the document head and then save the file:

Available for
download on
Wrox.com

```
<script type="application/x-javascript">
    function orientationChangeHandler()
    {
      var str = "Orientation: ";
      switch(window.orientation)
      {
          case 0:
              str += "Portrait";
          break;

          case -90:
              str += "Landscape (right, screen turned clockwise)";
          break;

          case 90:
              str += "Landscape (left, screen turned counterclockwise)";
          break;

          case 180:
            str += "Portrait (upside-down portrait)";
```

```
            break;
        }
        document.getElementById("mode").innerHTML = str;
    }


    </script>
```

Code snippet BIDHJ-Ch10-Ex2.html

How It Works

An `onorientationchange` attribute is added to the `body` element and assigned the JavaScript function `orientationChangeHandler()`. The `orientationChangehandler()` function evaluates the `window.orientation` property to determine the current state: `0` (Portrait), `-90` (Landscape, clockwise), `90` (Landscape counterclockwise), or `180` (Portrait, upside down). The current state string is then output to the document. Figure 10-1 shows the result in Portrait mode, and Figure 10-2 shows the page displayed in Landscape mode.

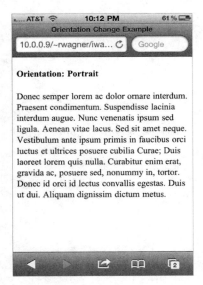

FIGURE 10–1

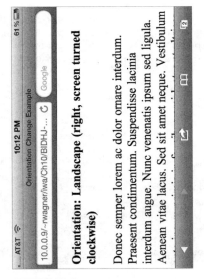

FIGURE 10–2

However, note that the `onorientationchange` event is not triggered when the document loads. Therefore, in order to evaluate the document orientation at this time, assign the `orientationChangeHandler()` function to the `onload` event.

Changing a Style Sheet When Orientation Changes

The most common procedure in which you will use an `onorientationchange` event is to specify a style sheet based on the current viewport orientation. To do so, you can expand upon the previous orientationChangeHandler() function by updating the orient attribute of the body element based on the current orientation and then updating the active CSS styles off of that attribute value.

TRY IT OUT   Changing a Style Sheet When Orientation Changes

For a demonstration of how to change a style sheet when the orientation changes in your app, use the following steps.

1.   Create the following HTML document in your text editor and then save the document as *BIDHJ-Ch10-Ex3.html*.

Available for download on Wrox.com

```
<!DOCTYPE html PUBLIC "-//W3C//DTD XHTML 1.0 Strict//EN"
        "http://www.w3.org/TR/xhtml1/DTD/xhtml1-strict.dtd">

<html xmlns="http://www.w3.org/1999/xhtml">
<head>
<title>orientationChange: Change CSS Stylesheet</title>
<meta name="viewport" content="width=320; initial-scale=1.0;
  maximum-scale=1.0; user-scalable=0;">

</head>

<body>
    <div id="canvasMain" class="container">
        <div class="toolbar anchorTop">
            <div class="main">
                <div class="header">AppTop</div>
            </div>
        </div>
        <div class="center">
    <p>Orientation mode:<span id="iMode"></span></p>
        <p>Width:<span id="iWidth"></span></p>
        <p>Height:<span id="iHeight"></span></p>
        <p>Bottom toolbar height:<span id="iToolbarHeight"></span></p>
        <p>Bottom toolbar top:<span id="iToolbarTop"></span></p>
        </div>
        <div id="bottomToolbar" class="toolbar anchorBottom">
            <div class="main">
                <div class="header">
                    AppBottom
                </div>
            </div>
        </div>
    </div>
</body>
</html>
```

Code snippet BIDHJ-Ch10-Ex3.html

2.   Add the following style code inside the document head:

Available for download on Wrox.com

```
Insert IconMargin  [download]
    <!-- Portions based on iUI -->
<style type="text/css" media="screen">

    body {
```

```
        margin: 0;
        padding: 0;
        width: 320px;
        height: 416px;
        font-family: Helvetica;
        -webkit-user-select: none;
        cursor: default;
        -webkit-text-size-adjust: none;
        background: #000000;
        color: #FFFFFF;
    }

.container {
        position: absolute;
        width: 100%;
    }

.toolbar {
        position: absolute;
        width: 100%;
        height: 60px;
        font-size: 28pt;
    }

.anchorTop {
        top: 0;
    }

.anchorBottom {
        bottom: 0;
    }

.center {
        position: absolute;
        top: 60px;
        bottom: 60px;
    }


.main {
        overflow: hidden;
        position: relative;
    }

.header {
        position: relative;
        height: 44px;
        -webkit-box-sizing: border-box;
        box-sizing: border-box;
        background-color: rgb(111, 135, 168);
        border-top: 1px solid rgb(179, 186, 201);
        border-bottom: 1px solid rgb(73, 95, 144);
        color: white;
        font-size: 20px;
        text-shadow: rgba(0, 0, 0, 0.6) 0 -1px 0;
        font-weight: bold;
```

```
        text-align: center;
        line-height: 42px;
    }

    /* Styles adjusted based on orientation  */
    body[orient='portrait'] .container {
        height: 436px;
    }

    body[orient='landscape'] .container {
        height: 258px;
    }

    body[orient='landscape'] .toolbar {
        height: 30px;
        font-size: 16pt;
    }

    body[orient='landscape'] .center {
        top: 50px;
        bottom: 30px;
    }

</style>
```

Code snippet BIDHJ-Ch10-Ex3.html

3.   Add the following script code in the document head and then save the file:

```
<script type="application/x-javascript">

    addEventListener('load', function() {
        setTimeout(orientationChange, 0);
    }, false);

    var currentWidth = 0;

    function orientationChange() {
        if (window.innerWidth != currentWidth) {
    currentWidth = window.innerWidth;
        var orient = currentWidth == 320 ? 'portrait' : 'landscape';
        document.body.setAttribute('orient', orient);

        setTimeout(function() {
                    document.getElementById('iMode').innerHTML = orient;
                    document.getElementById('iWidth').innerHTML = currentWidth
                      + 'px';
                    document.getElementById('iHeight').innerHTML =
                     document.getElementById('canvasMain').offsetHeight
                      + 'px';
                    document.getElementById('iToolbarHeight').innerHTML =
                        document.getElementById('bottomToolbar').offsetHeight
                          + 'px';
                    document.getElementById('iToolbarTop').innerHTML =
```

```
                        document.getElementById('bottomToolbar').offsetTop
                        +'px'; }, 100);

        setTimeout(function() {
           window.scrollTo(0, 1);
        }, 100);
      }
    }

    setInterval(orientationChange, 400);

</script>
```

Code snippet BIDHJ-Ch10-Ex3.html

How It Works

In this example, a series of div elements is used to imitate a basic iPhone interface, consisting of a top toolbar, content area, and bottom toolbar.

In the CSS styles, notice the selector for the final four rules are dependent upon the state of the orient attribute of body. Based on the body element's orient value, the container CSS class changes its height, the top and bottom toolbars adjust their height and font-size, and the main content area (the center class) is repositioned to fit with the sizing changes around it.

In the JavaScript code, the orientationChangeHandler() function is called when the window loads or changes orientation. It updates the body element's orient attribute to either portrait or landscape.

Figures 10-3 and 10-4 show the document loaded in both portrait and landscape modes, respectively.

FIGURE 10-3

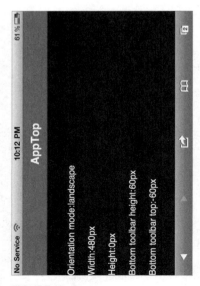

FIGURE 10-4

CHANGING ELEMENT POSITIONING BASED ON ORIENTATION CHANGE

When you begin to understand the basic interaction between an `orientationChangeHandler()` function and orientation-dependent styles, you can begin to dynamically position elements of the UI based on whether the current viewport is in portrait or landscape mode. Suppose, for example, you would like to align an arrow image to the bottom left of a page. Here's the `img` declaration:

```
<img id="pushBtn" src="bottombarknobgray.png"/>
```

To align the graphic in portrait mode, you could specify the CSS rule as the following:

```
#pushbtn
{
    position: absolute;
    left: 10px;
    top: 360px;
}
```

However, if you leave the positioning as is, the button goes off screen when the user tilts the viewport to landscape mode. Therefore, a second landscape-specific rule with an adjusted `top` value is needed for the button image:

```
body[orient="landscape"] #pushBtn
{
    left: 10px;
    top: 212px;
}
```

The `orientationChangeHandler()` function is as follows:

Available for
download on
Wrox.com

```
function orientationChangeHandler()
{
    if (window.orientation == 0 || window.orientation == 180)
        document.body.setAttribute('orient', 'portrait')
    else
        document.body.setAttribute('orient', 'landscape');
}
```

Code snippet BIDHJ-Ch10-Ex4.html

As Figures 10-5 and 10-6 show, the button image aligns to the bottom left of the page document in both portrait and landscape modes respectively.

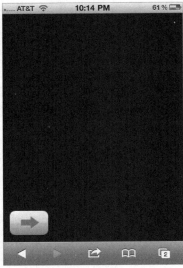

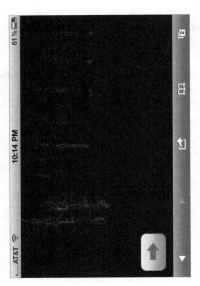

FIGURE 10-5   **FIGURE 10-6**

TRAPPING FOR KEY EVENTS
WITH THE ON-SCREEN KEYBOARD

As with an ordinary web page, you can validate keyboard input by trapping the keydown event. To illustrate, suppose you have an input field in which you want to prevent the user from entering a numeric value. To trap for this, begin by adding a keydown handler to the input element:

```
<input onkeydown="return validate(event)" />
```

In the document header, add a script element with the following code inside of it:

```
function validate(e) {
    var keynum = e.which;
    var keychar = String.fromCharCode(keynum);
    var chk = /\d/;
    return !chk.test(keychar)
}
```

As a standard JavaScript validation routine, this function tests the current character code value to determine whether it is a number. If a non-number is found, then true is returned to the input field. Otherwise, a false is sent back and the character is disallowed.

EXERCISES

1. What are the three major types of touch events?

2. Do you need to code all touch events in your web app?

3. What event do you trap to handle screen orientation changes?

Answers to the Exercises can be found in the Appendix.

▶ **WHAT YOU LEARNED IN THIS CHAPTER**

TOPIC	KEY CONCEPTS
Handling mouse-like events	No events trigger *until* the user's finger leaves the touch screen. Design your app to respond to click events rather than the other mouse events.
Responding to multitouch events	Trap for multiple touches to occur on screen at the same time and then have your app respond to them.
Dealing with screen orientation changes	Add a handler for the `body` element's `onorientationchange` event.
Trapping for key events	Add a `keydown` handler to the appropriate writable element.

11

Special Effects and Animation

WHAT YOU WILL LEARN IN THIS CHAPTER:

➤ Creating gradients using CSS and JavaScript

➤ Adding shadows and reflections

➤ Creating animations with JavaScript

The strengths of Safari on iOS as a development platform are evident when you begin to explore the capabilities you have with advanced graphics, animation, and other special effects. You can utilize some of the more advanced capabilities of JavaScript, HTML 5, and CSS to create cool effects in your web apps. In this chapter, I explore how to work with effects and animation.

GRADIENTS

A gradient is a coloring effect you can add to your web page in which a color gradually changes to another color over the surface of a canvas or other element. A *linear gradient* is applied to a rectangular block surface whereas a *radial gradient* is displayed as a circle. You can specify the start and end colors as well as color values in between (known as *color stops*). You can create gradients in both CSS and JavaScript. Read on to find out how.

Creating CSS Gradients

You can use the Safari-supported function `-webkit-gradient()` to create a "virtual" gradient image and define it as an image URL parameter. Here's the syntax for a linear gradient:

```
-webkit-gradient(linear, startPoint, endPoint, from(color),
    color-stop(percent, color), to(color))
```

The `linear` parameter defines the type of gradient. The `startPoint` and `endPoint` parameters define the start and end points of the gradient and are typically represented by constants: `left top`, `left bottom`, `right top`, `right bottom`.

The `from()` and `to()` functions indicate the starting and ending colors, and the `color-stop()` function defines a color at a particular point on the gradient.

For example, the following style can be added to a `div` or other block element to create a gradient that starts with light green at the top left and ends with black on the lower left. A color stop of dark green is added at the 50% mark. Here's the style:

```
.simpleLinear
{
  width:100px;
  height:100px;
  border:1px solid black;
  background: -webkit-gradient( linear, left top, left bottom,
    from(#a1f436), color-stop(0.5, #668241), to(rgb(0, 0, 0)));
}
```

As you can see, the color can be defined using a hex value or using the `rgb()` function.

The results are shown in Figure 11-1.

You can add multiple `color-stop()` functions to a gradient to have more complex effect. The following style begins with maroon and ends with white, but also has green and blue color stops defined at the 30% and 80% points along the gradient (see Figure 11-2):

```
.complexLinear
{
  width:100px;
  height:100px;
  border:1px solid black;
  background: -webkit-gradient(linear, left top, left bottom,
    from(#a21c47), to(#f9f9f9), color-stop(0.3, #564fb5),color-stop(0.8, #66cc00));
}
```

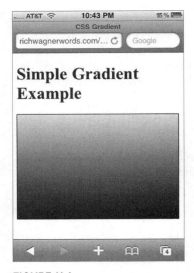

FIGURE 11-1

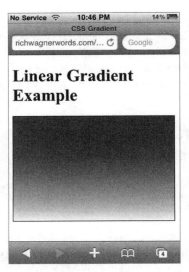

FIGURE 11-2

To create a radial gradient, you use the following syntax:

```
-webkit-gradient(radial, innerCenter, innerRadius, outerCenter,
    outerRadius, from(color), color-stop(percent, color), to(color));
```

The `innerCenter` defines the x, y coordinate of the center of the inner circle that starts the gradient. The `innerRadius` defines the width of the radius for the inner circle. The `outerCenter` and `outerRadius` define the same thing for the outer circle that ends the gradient. The `from()`, `to()`, and `color-stop()` functions work the same way as the linear gradient.

The following style example defines a small gradient 10-radial circle starting at coordinates 30, 30 and ending with a 30-radial circle at coordinates 50, 50. It has one color stop, midway through the gradient (see Figure 11-3):

```
.radial
{
  width:100px;
  height:100px;
  border:1px solid black;
  background: -webkit-gradient(radial, 30 30, 10, 50 50, 30,
    from(#a1f436), to(rgba(1,0,0,0)), color-stop(50%, #668241));
}
```

You can also combine multiple gradients onto a single surface simply by listing one after the other. The following style example defines two radial gradients for a 200×200-sized div:

```
.radial2
{
  width:200px;
  height:200px;
  border:1px solid black;
  background: -webkit-gradient(radial, 20 20, 10, 25 25, 40, from(#a1f436),
    to(rgba(1,0,0,0)), color-stop(50%, #668241)),
    -webkit-gradient(radial, 100 100, 20, 20 20, 40,
      from(#a21c47), to(#f9f9f9), color-stop(50%, #66cc00));
}
```

The result is a cone-like object as shown in Figure 11-4.

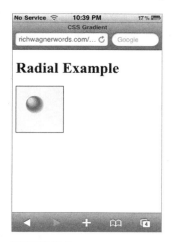

FIGURE 11-3   **FIGURE 11-4**

Creating Gradients with JavaScript

If you prefer scripting, you can also create both linear and radial gradients by using the following methods of the context object:

➤ createLinearGradient(x1,y1,x2,y2) creates a gradient from the starting point (x1,y1) to the end point (x2, y2).

➤ createRadialGradient(x1,y1,r1,x2,y2,r2) creates a gradient circle. The first circle is based on the x1, y1, and r1 values and the second circle based on the x2, y2, and r2 values.

Both of these methods return a canvasGradient object that can have colors assigned to it with the addColorStop(position, color) method. The position argument is a float number between 0.0 and 1.0 that indicates the position of the color in the gradient. The color argument is any CSS color.

TRY IT OUT   Creating a JavaScript Gradient

The following is an example of creating a gradient using JavaScript.

1. Create the following HTML document in your text editor and then save the document as *BIDHJ-Ch11-Ex1.html*.

```
<!DOCTYPE html PUBLIC "-//W3C//DTD XHTML 1.0 Strict//EN"
        "http://www.w3.org/TR/xhtml1/DTD/xhtml1-strict.dtd">
<html xmlns="http://www.w3.org/1999/xhtml">
<head>
<title>Draw Gradient</title>
<meta name="viewport" content="width=320; initial-scale=1.0;
    maximum-scale=1.0; user-scalable=0;">
</head>
<body>
<canvas id="myCanvas" width="300" height="300"
    style="position:absolute; left:0px; top:0px; z-index:1"/>
</body>
</html>
```

Code snippet BIDHJ-Ch11-Ex1.html

2. Add the following JavaScript code inside the document head:

```
<script type="application/x-javascript">
function drawGradient()
{
    var canvas = document.getElementById('myCanvas');
    var context = canvas.getContext('2d');
    var lg = context.createLinearGradient(0,125,250,125);
    context.globalAlpha="0.8";
    lg.addColorStop(0,'white');
    lg.addColorStop(0.75,'blue');
    lg.addColorStop(1,'red');
```

```
    context.fillStyle = lg;
    context.strokeStyle="#666666";
    context.lineWidth=".5";
    context.fillRect(10,10,250,250);
    context.strokeRect(10,10,250,250);
}
</script>
```

Code snippet BIDHJ-Ch11-Ex1.html

3. Add an `onload` event handler to the `body` tag and save the file:

```
<body onload="drawGradient ()">
```

Code snippet BIDHJ-Ch11-Ex1.html

How It Works

A linear gradient is added to a square box on the canvas. The gradient starts on the left side, transitions to blue, and ends on the right in red. The first color stop is set to white, the second is set to blue, and the third is red. After you assign the color stops using the `addColorStop()` method, you assign the `lglinearGradient` object as the `fillStyle` for the context. You then call the `fillRect()` method to paint the block and add a gray border using the `strokeRect()` method. Figure 11-5 shows the results.

Now that you have linear gradients under your belt, you can create radial gradients using a similar methodology. You create a radial gradient by using the `createRadialGradient()` method and then adding color stops at the appropriate positions. For example:

```
function drawRadialGradient()
{
    var canvas = document.getElementById('myCanvas');
    var context = canvas.getContext('2d');
    var rg = context.
createRadialGradient(45,45,10,52,50,35);
    rg.addColorStop(0, '#95b800');
    rg.addColorStop(0.9, '#428800');
    rg.addColorStop(1, 'rgba(220,246,196,0)');
    context.fillStyle = rg;
    context.fillRect(0,0,250,250);
}
```

FIGURE 11-5

The `createRadialGradient()` method defines two circles, one with a 10px radius and the second with a 35px radius. You add three color stops using `addColorStop()`, and then you assign the `rg radialGradient` object to the `fillStyle` property. See Figure 11-6.

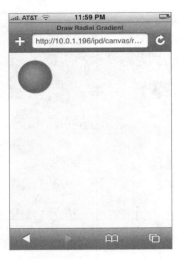

FIGURE 11-6

ADDING SHADOWS

Shadow effects are a common visual technique you can use to enhance the look of your page element. Using JavaScript, the context object provides four properties that you can use for defining shadows on the canvas:

➤ shadowColor defines the CSS color of the shadow.

➤ shadowBlur specifies the width of the shadow blur.

➤ shadowOffsetX defines the horizontal offset of the shadow.

➤ shadowOffsetY specifies the vertical offset of the shadow.

Let me show you how to use them. The following code uses these properties to define a blurred shadow for an image:

```
function drawImg(){
  var canvas = document.getElementById('myCanvas');
  var context = canvas.getContext('2d');
  context.shadowColor = "black";
  context.shadowBlur = "10";
  context.shadowOffsetX = "5";
  context.shadowOffsetY = "5";
  var img3 = new Image();
```

```
        img3.src = 'images/nola.jpg';
        img3.onload = function()
    {
        context.drawImage( img3, 20, 30 );
    }
    }
```

The four bold lines of code define a blurred black shadow that is offset 5px from the canvas. Figure 11-7 shows the result.

ADDING REFLECTIONS

If you have used the CoverFlow view in the Music app, you may have noticed the use of reflections. In fact, image reflections are an increasingly popular effect for images. Using CSS techniques, you can add reflections to your images or block elements.

FIGURE 11-7

To create a reflection, use the -webkit-box-reflect property:

```
-webkit-box-reflect : directionoffsetmaskImage|-webkit-gradient;
```
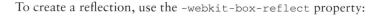

The direction parameter specifies the direction of the reflection relative to the object: above, below, left, or right. The offset parameter defines the offset distance (in pixels or as a percentage) that the reflection should be offset from the block. The maskImage parameter specifies a mask image. Or, as shown, you can also use a -webkit-gradient() function instead. For example, suppose you want to add a bottom reflection to an image using a gradient, you could use the following style rule:

```
<style>

  .reflectedImage
  {
    border:1px solid black;
    -webkit-box-reflect:below 3px -webkit-gradient(linear, left top,
      left bottom, from(transparent), color-stop(0.5, transparent), to(white));
  }

</style>
</head>
<body>

<img src="images/nola.jpg" class="reflectedImage"/>

</body>
```

Notice that the `-webkit-gradient()` function defines a linear gradient as the reflection. It begins fully transparent and ends fully white to blend into the background. Figure 11-8 shows the result.

FIGURE 11-8

Reflections on black backgrounds can be especially visually compelling on an iOS viewport. The following example shows a reflection on black (see Figure 11-9):

```
<!DOCTYPE html PUBLIC "-//W3C//DTD XHTML 1.0 Strict//EN"
        "http://www.w3.org/TR/xhtml1/DTD/xhtml1-strict.dtd">

<html xmlns="http://www.w3.org/1999/xhtml">
<head>
<title>CSS Reflections</title>
<meta name="viewport" content="width=320; initial-scale=1.0;
   maximum-scale=1.0; user-scalable=0;">

<style>

  .reflectedImage
  {
    -webkit-box-reflect:below 3px -webkit-gradient(linear, left top,
     left bottom, from(transparent), color-stop(0.5, transparent), to(black));
  }

  body
  {
    background-color:#000000;
  }

</style>
</head>
```

```
<body>

<img src="images/nola.jpg" class="reflectedImage"/>

</body>
</html>
```

If you want to add reflections using JavaScript, I recommend checking out several open source libraries that use canvas programming to create sophisticated charts and image effects, such as reflections. Two particularly noteworthy libraries are PlotKit and Reflection.js. PlotKit is a JavaScript Chart Plotting library (available at www.liquidx.net/plotkit), and Reflection.js (available at http://cow.neondragon .net/stuff/reflection) enables you to add reflections to your images. The Reflection.js library uses canvas to render the reflection, but it enables you to use it simply by adding a reflect class to an image.

FIGURE 11-9

WORKING WITH MASKS

Masks are a common designer technique used to hide parts of an image. Typically you use a mask to create a blurred border around an image. You can use the CSS property -webkit-mask-image to add masks to images. Its syntax is shown below:

```
-webkit-mask-box-image: uritop right bottom left xRepeat yRepeat;
```

The uri is used to specify the mask image, such as one shown in Figure 11-10. The top, right, bottom, and left parameters are used to define the distance the mask is from the edge of the image. The repeat parameters specify x, y repeat styles. You can also use the constants as well: repeat (tiled), stretch, or round (which stretches all parts of the image slightly so that there are no partial tiles at any end).

For example, to create a vignette mask around an image that uses the mask image shown in Figure 11-10, you could use the following style definition:

FIGURE 11-10

```
.vignetteMask
{
  -webkit-mask-box-image: url(images/mask.png) 25 stretch;
}
```

The 25 parameter specifies a 25 pixel distance around the full image, and stretch stretches the mask (which is smaller than the image it is applied to) to equally match the size of the image it is applied to. Figure 11-11 shows the results.

You are not limited to using a masked image, however. You can also use a `-webkit-gradient()` function to achieve a faded mask effect. For example, consider this style:

```
.fadeToWhite
{
  -webkit-mask-image:-webkit-gradient(linear, left top,
    left bottom, from(rgba(0,0,0,1)), to(rgba(0,0,0,0)));
}
```

A linear gradient provides a masking effect for the image that uses this style. Notice how the bottom of the image in Figure 11-12 fades into the background.

FIGURE 11-11

FIGURE 11-12

Or, to achieve a rounded masking effect, you can combine the use of a `-webkit-border-radius` declaration with a `-webkit-mask-image` property. Consider the following:

```
.roundedImage
{
  -webkit-border-radius: 12px;
  -webkit-mask-image:-webkit-gradient(linear, left top,
    left bottom, from(rgba(0,0,0,1)), to(rgba(0,0,0,0)));
}
```

The mask is applied to an image with rounded corners.

CREATING TRANSFORM EFFECTS

You can use three methods of a canvas `context` object to transform the state of a canvas:

➤ `translate(x, y)` changes the origin coordinate (0, 0) of the canvas.

➤ `rotate(angle)` rotates the canvas around the current origin of a specified number of radians.

➤ `scale(x, y)` adjusts the scale of the canvas. The x parameter is a positive number that scales horizontally, and the y parameter scales vertically.

The following example uses `translate()` and `scale()` as it draws a circle successive times onto the canvas. Each time these methods are called, their parameters are adjusted:

```
function transform()
{
  var canvas = document.getElementById('myCanvas');
  var context = canvas.getContext('2d');
  var s=1;
  for (i=1;i<6;i++)
  {
    var t=i*8;
    context.translate(t,t);
    context.scale(s,s);
    context.fillStyle = "rgba(" + t*4 + ","+ t*6 + "," + t*8 + ", 0.3)";
    context.beginPath();
    context.arc(50,50,40,0,2*pi, false);
    context.fill();
    s=s-0.05;
  }
}
```

The t variable is eight times the current iteration of the `for` loop, and then is used as the parameter for `translate()`. The `scale()` method uses the s variable, which is decremented by 0.05 after each pass. The `fillStyle()` method also uses the t variable to adjust the rgb color values for each circle drawn. Figure 11-13 shows the result of the transformation.

The `rotate()` method rotates the canvas based on the specified angle. For example, in the following code, an image is drawn on the canvas three times, and each time the `translate()` and `rotate()` parameter's values and the `globalAlpha` property are changed:

```
function rotateImg(){
  var canvas = document.getElementById('myCanvas');
  var context = canvas.getContext('2d');
  context.globalAlpha="0.5";
    var r=1;
  var img = new Image();
  img.src = 'images/jared.jpg';
  img.onload = function() {
    for (i=1;i<4;i++) {
      context.translate(50,-15);
```

```
        context.rotate(.15*r);
        context.globalAlpha=i*.33;
        context.drawImage(img, 20, 20);
        r+=1;
      }
    }
  }
```

Figure 11-14 shows the layered result. Note the difference in transparency of the bottommost image to the topmost.

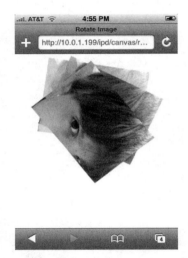

FIGURE 11-13   **FIGURE 11-14**

Note that as you begin to work with more advanced drawings on the canvas, you need to manage the drawing state. A drawing state includes the current path, the values of the major context properties (such as `fillStyle` and `globalAlpha`), and any transformations (such as rotating) that have been applied. To this end, you can use the `save()` and `restore()` methods. The `save()` method saves a snapshot of the canvas, which can then be retrieved later using the `restore()` method. The `save()` and `restore()` methods enable you to return to a default drawing state with minimal additional code and without needing to painstakingly re-create every setting.

CREATING ANIMATIONS

You can use the context drawing capabilities discussed earlier in combination with JavaScript timer routines to create animations on the canvas. On first take, the potential for creating canvas-based animation sounds like a perfect light-weight substitute for Flash animation. For some purposes, it can be ideal. However, any such excitement needs to be kept in check. Perhaps the chief shortcoming of canvas drawing in JavaScript is that you need to repaint the entire canvas for each frame of your animation. As a result, complex animations are at risk for being jerky on the mobile device. That being said, canvas animation can be a powerful tool to add to your development toolbox.

Like a motion picture or video clip, an animation is a series of frames that, when viewed one after the other, gives the appearance of movement. Therefore, when you code, your job is to show a drawing, clear it, draw the next frame in the series, clear it, and so on until your animation is completed or it loops back to the start. If you are changing any context settings and need to reset them for each new frame, you need to use the save() and restore() methods.

TRY IT OUT   **Creating a JavaScript-based Animation**

The following example shows how to animate an object using JavaScript.

1. Create the following HTML document in your text editor and then save the document as *BIDHJ-Ch11-Ex2.html*.

```
<!DOCTYPE html PUBLIC "-//W3C//DTD XHTML 1.0 Strict//EN"
        "http://www.w3.org/TR/xhtml1/DTD/xhtml1-strict.dtd">
<html xmlns="http://www.w3.org/1999/xhtml">
<head>
<title>Animate</title>
<meta name="viewport" content="width=320; initial-scale=1.0;
    maximum-scale=1.0; user-scalable=0;">
</head>
<body bgcolor="black">
<canvas id="myCanvas" width="300" height="300"
    style="position:absolute; left:0px; top:0px"/>
</body>
</html>
```

Code snippet BIDHJ-Ch11-Ex2.html

2. Add the following script code inside the document head:

```
<script type="application/x-javascript">

function init() {
  setInterval( animate, 1 );
}

var p = 0;

function animate(){
  var canvas = document.getElementById('myCanvas');
  var context = canvas.getContext('2d');
  context.globalCompositeOperation = "copy";
  context.fillStyle = "rgba(0,0,255, 0.3)";
```

```
    context.beginPath();
    context.arc(50+p,50+p,30,0, 360, false);
    context.fill();
    p+=1;
    }
    </script>
```

Code snippet BIDHJ-Ch11-Ex2.html

3. Add an `onload` event handler to the `body` tag and save the file:

Available for download on Wrox.com

```
onload="init()"
```

Code snippet BIDHJ-Ch11-Ex2.html

How It Works

The HTML page shows a simple animation program in which a circle moves diagonally from the top left to the bottom right part of the canvas. The `init()` function is called when the document is loaded, which sets off a timer to call `animate()` every 100 milliseconds. The `animate()` function clears the canvas, moves the orientation point, and draws a filled circle. The `p` variable is then incremented by one before repeating.

FIGURE 11-15   **FIGURE 11-16**

Figures 11-15 and 11-16 show the start and finish of the animation effect.

EXERCISES

1. When you draw onto a canvas, what is the key object that you work with?

2. What CSS property do you use to create a reflection?

3. What do the `context` object's `save()` and `restore()` methods do?

Answers to the Exercises can be found in the Appendix.

▶ WHAT YOU LEARNED IN THIS CHAPTER

TOPIC	KEY CONCEPTS
Creating gradients	With CSS, use `-webkit-gradient()` function
	With JavaScript, use `createLinearGradient()` or `createRadialGradient()`
Adding shadows	Use the following context object properties: `shadowColor`, `shadowBlur`, `shadowOffsetX`, `shadowOffsetY`
Creating reflections	Use CSS property `-webkit-box-reflect`
Adding a mask to an image	Use CSS property `-webkit-mask-image`

12

Integrating with iOS Services

WHAT YOU WILL LEARN IN THIS CHAPTER:

➤ Tapping into iOS services and built-in apps within your app

➤ Sending email and SMS text messages

➤ Mapping `href` links to iOS services

One of the most intriguing ideas when creating a web app for iOS is integrating the application with core mobile services, such as dialing phone numbers or sending e-mails. After all, when you break through those inside-the-browser barriers, the application becomes more than just a web app and extends its functionality across the mobile device.

However, iOS service integration is a mixed bag; it's a "good news, bad news" situation. On the upside, four of the most important mobile functions (Phone, Mail, SMS Messaging, and Google Maps) are accessible to the developer. On the downside, there are no means of tapping into other core services, such as Calendar, Address Book, Camera, Clock, Music, and Settings.

Also, the exact types of services available vary according to iOS device. iPhone includes all of these features, whereas iPad and iPod touch are both limited based on their device hardware capabilities (that is, neither offer phone or SMS capabilities).

MAKING PHONE CALLS FROM YOUR APP

Here's a basic example to get your feet wet in the waters of iOS service integration. You can make a phone call from your application simply through a special telephone link. A telephone link is specified through the `tel:` protocol. The basic syntax is the following:

```
<a href="tel:1-507-555-5555">1-507-555-5555</a>
```

When a user clicks the link, the phone does not automatically dial. Instead, iPhone displays a confirmation box (see Figure 12-1) that enables the user to click Call or Cancel.

FIGURE 12-1

PHONE NUMBERS

Telephone links can go beyond ordinary numbers. iPhone provides partial support for the RFC 2086 protocol (`www.ietf.org/rfc/rfc2806.txt`), which enables you to develop some sophisticated telephone-based URLs. For example, the following link calls the U.S. Postal Service, pauses for two seconds, and then presses 2 to get a Spanish version:

```
<a href="tel:+1-800-ASK-USPS;pp2">USPS (Espanol)</a>
```

Note that p creates a 1-second pause, so pp causes a 2-second pause before continuing. Safari also automatically creates telephone links for you in your pages. Any number that takes the form of a phone number is displayed as a link. Therefore, if you ever have a situation in which you do not want to link a telephone number (or a number that could be interpreted as a phone number) then add the `format-detection` meta tag to the document head:

```
<meta name = "format-detection" content = "telephone=no">
```

For legacy support, you can also break up the number sequence using a `span` element. For example:

```
<p>Your ID is 5083212202.</p>
```

would become:

```
<p>Your ID is <span>5083</span>212202.</p>
```

TRY IT OUT Creating a Call Link

For a demonstration of how to call from inside of your web app, use the following steps.

1. Create the following HTML document in your text editor and then save the document as *BIDHJ-Ch12-Ex1.html*.

Available for download on Wrox.com

```
<!DOCTYPE html PUBLIC "-//W3C//DTD XHTML 1.0 Strict//EN"
    "http://www.w3.org/TR/xhtml1/DTD/xhtml1-strict.dtd">
<html xmlns='http://www.w3.org/1999/xhtml' xml:lang='en'>
    <head>
        <meta http-equiv='content-type' content='text/html; charset=utf-8' />
        <meta http-equiv='content-language' content='en-us' />
        <title>BIDHJ Example</title>
    </head>
    <body>
        <h2>
            Let's make a call.
        </h2>
    </body>
</html>
```

Code snippet Elements.xml

2. Add the following HTML code inside of the document body and then save the file:

Available for download on Wrox.com

```
<p>Apple: <a target="_self" href="tel:800-692-7753"
onclick="return (navigator.userAgent.indexOf('iPhone') != -1)">1-800-MY-APPLE</a>
</p>

    <p>No one in particular: <a target="_self" href="tel:(765) 555-1212"
onclick="return (navigator.userAgent.indexOf('iPhone') != -1)">(765) 555-1212</a>
    </p>
```

Code snippet Elements.xml

Figure 12-2 shows the page that displays.

How It Works

The `a` links use the `tel:` protocol in the `href` value. To degrade gracefully when running on iPod touch or iPad, the `onclick` handler ensures that the link works only if running on iPhone by evaluating the browser's user agent string and checking to make sure that the string `iPhone` is located.

Then when the user presses the link, the telephone-enabled device launches the device's Phone app, as shown in Figure 12-3.

FIGURE 12-2

FIGURE 12-3

SENDING EMAILS

Emails can also be sent from your application through links using the familiar `mailto:` protocol, as shown in the following example:

```
<a href="mailto:jack@ibmcorp.com">Jack Armitage</a>
```

If you've worked with HTML pages at all before, you are probably quite familiar with mail links. However, here's what happens when an email link is clicked on an iOS device.

When the user presses this link, Mail opens and a new message window is displayed, as shown in Figure 12-4. The user can then fill out the subject and body of the message and send it. As you might expect, you cannot automatically send an email message using the `mailto:` protocol without user intervention. The `mailto:` protocol always takes the user to a new message window.

Following the `mailto:` protocol, you can also include parameters to specify the subject, cc address, bcc address, and message body. Table 12-1 lists these options.

FIGURE 12-4

TABLE 12-1: Optional mailto: Attributes

OPTION	SYNTAX
Multiple recipients	, (comma separating email addresses)
Message subject	`subject=Subject Text`
Cc recipients	`cc=name@address.com`
Bcc recipients	`bcc=name@address.com`
Message text	`body=Message text`

 NOTE *Per HTTP conventions, precede the initial parameter with a* ? *(such as* `?subject=`*) and precede any additional parameters with an* &.

The `mailto:` protocol normally allows line breaks in the `body` attribute value using `%0A` for a line break and `%0A%0A` for a line break followed by a blank line. However, iOS devices ignore the `%0A` codes and put all the text on one line. iOS has a workaround, though, which is actually a pretty cool alternative. Read about the workaround in the following activity.

Creating a Preformatted Email

For a demonstration of how to create your own predefined email in your web app, follow these steps.

1. Create the following HTML document in your text editor and then save the document as *BIDHJ-Ch12-Ex2.html*.

Available for
download on
Wrox.com

```
<!DOCTYPE html PUBLIC "-//W3C//DTD XHTML 1.0 Strict//EN"
    "http://www.w3.org/TR/xhtml1/DTD/xhtml1-strict.dtd">
<html xmlns='http://www.w3.org/1999/xhtml' xml:lang='en'>
  <head>
    <meta http-equiv='content-type' content='text/html; charset=utf-8' />
    <meta http-equiv='content-language' content='en-us' />
    <title>BIDHJ Example</title>
  </head>
  <body>
    <h2>
        I am shy. I'd rather send an email than call anyone.
    </h2>
  </body>
</html>
```

Code snippet Elements.xml

2. Add the following HTML code inside of the document body and then save the file:

Available for
download on
Wrox.com

```
<p><a href="mailto:jack@ibmcorp.com">Blank Email to Jack</a></p>

<p><a href="mailto:jack@ibmcorp.com?subject=Meeting&body=Dear Jack,<br/>
I look forward to our upcoming meeting together
<strong>this Friday at  8am.</strong><br/>
Sincerely,<br/>Jason Malone&cc=jason@iphogcorp.com">Reminder Email</a>
</p>
```

Code snippet Elements.xml

How It Works

iOS enables you to embed HTML in your message body, therefore enabling you to add br tags for line breaks and even other tags (such as strong) for formatting. Combining several parameters, you can actually create your own canned email right inside the code.

When the page displays and the user clicks the Reminder Email link, an email page displays with all of the text and message settings. All the user needs to do is press the Send button. (See Figure 12-5.)

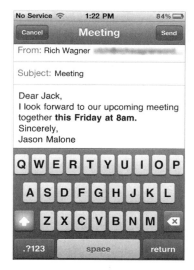

FIGURE 12-5

SENDING SMS MESSAGES

You can send SMS messages using the `sms` protocol in much the same way as you integrate email. For example, the following code launches the SMS application, addressing a text message to `765-545-1212`:

```
<a href="sms:765-545-1212" onclick="return
  (navigator.userAgent.indexOf('iPhone') != -1)">(765) 545-1212</a>
```

As Figure 12-6 shows, the user can enter the message using the keyboard and send it when finished.

Note, that as I did with Phone dial links, I added a check in the `onclick` handler to only jump to the SMS `href` link if the device running is an iPhone, not an iPod touch or iPad.

Alternatively, if you just want to launch the SMS app without a specific number to text, simply use a blank `sms:`.

```
<a href="sms:">Send SMS Message</a>
```

As you can see, with Phone, Email, and SMS support, your iOS web apps can support the normal capabilities of a contact management app. For example, suppose you combine each of these links into one page (*BIDHJ-Ch12-Ex3.html*):

FIGURE 12-6

```
<!DOCTYPE html PUBLIC "-//W3C//DTD XHTML 1.0 Strict//EN"
    "http://www.w3.org/TR/xhtml1/DTD/xhtml1-strict.dtd">
<html xmlns='http://www.w3.org/1999/xhtml' xml:lang='en'>
  <head>
    <meta http-equiv='content-type' content='text/html; charset=utf-8' />
    <meta http-equiv='content-language' content='en-us' />
    <title>BIDHJ Example</title>
  </head>
  <body>
    <h2>
        James Armitage.
    </h2>

    <p><a href="tel:(765) 555-1212"
onclick="return (navigator.userAgent.indexOf('iPhone') != -1)">Call on phone</a>
    </p>

    <p><a href="mailto:jack@ibmcorp.com">Email message</a></p>

    <p><a href="sms:765-555-1212" onclick="return
      (navigator.userAgent.indexOf('iPhone') != -1)">SMS text</a></p>

  </body>
</html>
```

Code snippet Elements.xml

POINTING ON GOOGLE MAPS

Although Google Maps does not have its own custom `href` protocol, Safari on iPhone and iPad devices is smart enough to reroute any request to `maps.google.com` to the built-in Maps application rather than going to the public Google website. (On iPod touch, Safari links directly to the public Google website.) As a result, you can create a link to specify either a specific location or driving directions between two geographical points.

 NOTE *You cannot specify whether to display the map in Map or Satellite view. The location you specify displays in the last selected view of the user.*

Keep in mind the basic syntax conventions when composing a Google Maps URL:

➤ For normal destinations, start with the `q=` parameter, and then type the location as you would a normal address, substituting + signs for blank spaces.

➤ For clarity, include commas between address fields.

Here's a basic URL to find a location based on city and state:

```
<a href="http://maps.google.com/maps?q=Boston,+MA">Boston</a>
```

Here's the syntax used for a full street address:

```
<a href="http://maps.google.com/maps?q=1000+Massachusetts+Ave,+Boston,+MA">
   Jack Armitage's Office</a>
```

TRY IT OUT   Linking to the Maps App

How about rolling up your sleeves and diving further into the Maps integration? To do so, follow these steps.

1.   Create the following HTML document in your text editor and then save the document as *BIDHJ-Ch12-Ex4.html*.

Available for
download on
Wrox.com

```
<!DOCTYPE html PUBLIC "-//W3C//DTD XHTML 1.0 Strict//EN"
    "http://www.w3.org/TR/xhtml1/DTD/xhtml1-strict.dtd">
<html xmlns='http://www.w3.org/1999/xhtml' xml:lang='en'>
   <head>
      <meta http-equiv='content-type' content='text/html; charset=utf-8' />
      <meta http-equiv='content-language' content='en-us' />
      <title>BIDHJ Example</title>
   </head>
   <body>
      <h2>
           Route trip anyone? Let's go!
      </h2>
   </body>
</html>
```

Code snippet Elements.xml

2.   Add the following Maps-related HTML code inside the document body and then save the file:

Available for
download on
Wrox.com

```
<p><a
   href="http://maps.google.com/maps?q=1000+Massachusetts+Ave,+Boston,+MA+
   (Jack+Armitage's+Office)">
   Jack Armitage's Office</a></p>

 <p><a
  href="http://maps.google.com/maps?q=52.123N,2.456W">
  Jack's Summer Retreat</a></p>

 <p><a
  href="http://maps.google.com/maps?saddr=
   Holden+MA&daddr=1000+Massachusetts+Ave,+Boston,+MA">Directions To Office</a>
 </p>
```

Code snippet Elements.xml

How It Works

As you can see, the example shows three different ways in which you can use Google Maps links in your web app.

When the address shown previously is located in Google Maps, the marker is generically labeled `1000 Massachusetts Ave Boston MA`. However, as the first Maps link shows, you can specify a custom label by appending the URL with `+(Label+Text)`. Figure 12-7 shows the updated label in the Maps app.

What's more, instead of providing a street address, you can also get geeky with your GPS and specify a location using latitude and longitude coordinates as the second link demonstrates.

Finally, if you want to get directions rather than point to a spot on the map, you can use the `saddr=` parameter to indicate the starting address and `daddr=` parameter to specify the destination address, as shown in the third link.

Figure 12-8 shows the directions in the Maps app when that link is clicked.

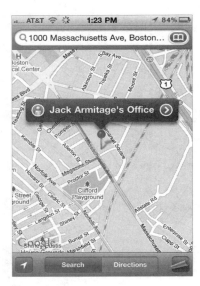

FIGURE 12-7

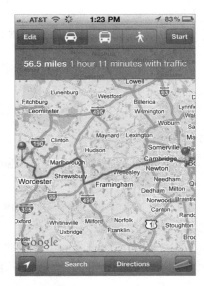

FIGURE 12-8

 NOTE *Google Maps on its public website has an extensive set of parameters. However, except where noted previously, none of these are supported at this time. You cannot, for example, use the* `t=` *parameter to specify the Satellite map, the* `z=` *parameter to indicate the map zoom level, or even* `layer=t` *to turn on the Traffic display. The user needs to perform those steps interactively.*

EXERCISES

1. When creating a web app that accesses iOS services, why would you want to identify the type of iOS device that is running the app?

2. What URL protocols should you use for the following links: a phone number, email message, and SMS message?

3. Do iPhone and iPod touch respond differently when a `maps.google.com` link is clicked in Safari? Explain.

Answers to the Exercises can be found in Appendix A.

▶ **WHAT YOU LEARNED IN THIS CHAPTER**

TOPIC	KEY CONCEPTS
Making phone calls from your app	Use the `tel:` protocol for making phone calls.
Sending emails	Use the `mailto:` protocol for creating an email message and displaying the Mail app. Add optional attributes to your call to add a message subject, additional recipients (to, cc, or bcc), and message text.
Sending SMS messages	Use the `sms:` protocol for creating an SMS message and displaying the SMS app. Degrade gracefully on iPad and iPod touch.
Pointing on Google Maps	Plot an address or GPS location on a map and display it in a Google Map.

13

Packaging Apps as Bookmarks: Bookmarklets and Data URLs

WHAT YOU WILL LEARN IN THIS CHAPTER:

➤ Discovering what bookmarklets are

➤ Creating offline apps using bookmarklets

➤ Encoding your images and source code

Because iOS web apps function inside the Safari environment, there are two seemingly obvious restrictions for the web developer: You must live with the built-in capabilities of the Safari on iOS browser; and you need a constant Wi-Fi (or, for iPhone/iPad, 3G) connection in order to run any application.

As you will discover in Chapter 15, you can use HTML5 offline storage capabilities to get around the dependency on a live connection. However, there are also two lesser-known technologies — bookmarklets and data URLs — that can provide similar results. These technologies have actually been around for years, but they have tended to exist on the periphery of mainstream web development. Developers are now reexamining these two technologies to maximize the potential of the iOS web application platform.

Bookmarklets (short for *bookmark applets*) are mini JavaScript "applets" that can be stored as a bookmark inside Safari. A data URL is a technique for storing an entire web page or application (pages, styles, images, data, and scripts) inside a single URL, which can then be saved as a bookmark inside Safari. This application-in-a-bookmark can then be accessed in offline mode. You probably won't want to package heavy-duty enterprise-level apps in a bookmarklet, but for smaller apps, it could be something to consider.

WORKING WITH BOOKMARKLETS

A *bookmarklet* is JavaScript stored as a URL and saved as a bookmark in the browser. It is typically used as a one-click applet that performs a very specific task or performs an action on the current web page. A bookmarklet uses the `javascript:` protocol followed by script code. For instance, here's the simplest of examples:

```
javascript:alert('iPhone')
```

Because the scripting code for a bookmarklet is housed inside a URL, the script must be condensed into one long string of code. Therefore, to enter multiple statements, separate each line with a semicolon:

```
javascript:alert('Bookmarklet 1');alert('Bookmarklet 2')
```

In this case, I added spaces inside each of the strings. You can either substitute %20 for a blank space or let Safari do the conversion for you.

If the script returns a value, be sure to enclose it inside of `void()` to ensure that the JavaScript code runs as expected. For example, the following WikiSearch bookmarklet displays a JavaScript prompt dialog box (see Figure 13-1), and then calls a Wikipedia search URL using the user's value as the search term:

FIGURE 13-1

```
javascript:t=prompt('Search Wikipedia:',getSelection());
    if(t)void(location.href=
    'http://en.wikipedia.org/w/wiki.phtml?search='+escape(t))
```

Here's a second example that provides a front-end onto Google's define service:

```
javascript:d=
    prompt('Define:',getSelection());
    if(d)void(location.href='http://www.google.com/search?q=define:'+
    escape(d))
```

Adding a Bookmarklet to Safari on iOS

Bookmarklets are normally added in a standard browser through a drag-and-drop action. However, because that user input is not available on your iOS device, one way to add to your bookmarklet is through the following process:

1. On your main computer, create your bookmarklet script and test it by pasting it into the Address box of Safari.

2. When the functionality works as expected, drag the `javascript:` URL from your Address box onto your Bookmarks bar in Safari. If you are going to have a set of bookmarklets, you may wish to create a special Bookmarklets folder to store these scripts. Or, if your bookmarklet is contained within the `href` of an a link, drag the link onto the Bookmarks bar instead.

3. Sync the bookmarks of your iOS device and main computer through iTunes or iCloud.

4. Access the bookmarklet in the Bookmarks inside Safari.

Although this process is convenient enough for you while you are developing your bookmarklet app, you'll probably want to provide a solution directly on the device itself if you intend to distribute the app to others. Here's one way to do so:

1. Create a web page and place your bookmarklet code in a `Textarea` element on the page, making it easy to select and copy to a device's clipboard.

2. Add a new bookmark by tapping the + button.

3. Go to the bookmark you just saved in Safari's bookmarks list and click Edit.

4. Remove the default URL that is shown in the Bookmark dialog box.

5. Paste the JavaScript bookmarklet code into the URL box.

6. Edit the name as desired.

7. Click Done to complete.

Exploring How Bookmarklets Can Be Used

Although you can use bookmarklets for these sorts of general purposes, their real usefulness to iOS web app developers is turning JavaScript into a macro language for Safari to extend the functionality of the browser. For example, Safari always opens normal links in the existing window, replacing the existing page. Richard Herrera from doctyper.com wrote a bookmarklet that transforms the links of a page and forces them to open in a new tab. Here is the script, which is tricky to read because it is contained within a one-line, encoded URL:

```
javascript:(function(){var%20a=document.getElementsByTagName('a');for(var%20i=0,
j=a.length;i%3Cj;i++){a[i].setAttribute('target','_blank');var%20img=document.
createElement('img');img.setAttribute('class',%20'new-window');img.setAttribute
('src','data:image/gif;base64,'+'R0lGODlhEAAMALMLAL66tBISEjExMdTQyBoaGjs7OyUlJ
WZmZgAAAMzMzP//////wAAAAAAAAAAAAA'+'ACH5BAEAAAsALAAAAAAQAAwAAAQ/cMlZqr2Tps13
yVJBjOT4gYairqohCTDMsu4iHHgwr7UA/LqdopZS'+'DBBIpGG5lBQH0GgtU9xNJ9XZ1cnsNicRADs
=');img.setAttribute('style','width:16px!important;height:12px!important;
border:none!important;');a[i].appendChild(img);}})();
```

When executed, the script adds a `target="_blank"` attribute to all links on the page and adds a small "new window" icon after the link (see Figure 13-2).

An iOS user can then use this self-contained "applet" on any page in which he wishes to transform the links. Notice that the icon image used in the script is encoded inside of a data URL, so that the script is not dependent on any external files.

Although the entire script needs to be condensed into a single string of commands, Safari is actually smart enough to convert the hard breaks for you when a multiline script is pasted into the URL box. Just make sure each statement is separated by a semicolon. Therefore, the following code, which is much easier to work with and debug, would still execute properly when pasted directly into the URL box:

Available for
download on
Wrox.com

```javascript
javascript:(
  function(){
        var a=document.getElementsByTagName('a');
        for(var i=0,j=a.length;i%3Cj;i++) {
                a[i].setAttribute('target','_blank');
                var img=document.createElement('img');
                img.setAttribute('class','new-window');
 img.setAttribute('src','data:image/gif;base64,'+'R0lGODlhEAAMALMLAL66tBISEjExMdTQ
yBoaGjs7OyUlJWZmZgAAAMzMzP///////wAAAAAAAAAAAA'+'ACH5BAEAAAsALAAAAAAQAAwAAAQ/cMl
Zqr2Tps13yVVJBjOT4gYairqohCTDMsu4iHHgwr7UA/LqdopZS'+'DBBIpGG5lBQH0GgtU9xNJ9XZ1cnsNi
cRADs=');
                img.setAttribute('style','width:16px!important;
                height:12px!important;
                border:none!important;');
                a[i].appendChild(img);
        }
  })();
```

Code snippet BookmarkletSample.js

Bookmarklets can be handy developer tools to assist in testing and debugging on iOS. For example, the following bookmarklet, based on a script created at `iPhoneWebDev.com`, gives you View Source functionality (see Figure 13-3) on the device itself:

Available for
download on
Wrox.com

```javascript
javascript:
var sourceWindow = window.open("about:blank");
var newDoc = sourceWindow.document;
newDoc.open();
newDoc.write(
"<html><head><title>Source of " + document.location.href +
"</title><meta name=\"viewport\" id=\"viewport\" content=\"initial-scale=1.0;" +
"user-scalable=0;maximum-scale=0.6667;width=480\"/><script>function do_onload()"
+ "{setTimeout(function(){window.scrollTo(0,1);},100);}if(navigator.userAgent.
indexOf" + "(\"iPhone\")!=-1)window.onload=do_onload;</script></head><body>
```

```
</body></html>");
newDoc.close();
var pre = newDoc.body.appendChild(newDoc.createElement("pre"));
pre.appendChild(newDoc.createTextNode(document.documentElement.innerHTML));
```

Code snippet ViewSource.js

FIGURE 13-3

STORING AN APPLICATION IN A DATA URL

In addition to JavaScript functionality, you can also store a web page or even a complete application inside a bookmark. The `data:` protocol enables you to encode an entire page's content — HTML, CSS, JavaScript, and images — inside a single URL. To be clear, data URLs store the actual contents of the page itself, not just a simple link to a remote page. You can save this data URL as a bookmark. When users access this bookmark in Safari, they can interact with the page whether or not they have Internet access. The implications are significant — you can use data URLs to package certain types of web apps and get around the live Internet connection requirement.

Constraints and Issues with Using Data URLs

Although the potential of data URLs is exciting for the developer, make sure you keep the following constraints and issues in mind before working with them:

➤ You can store client-side technologies — such as HTML, CSS, JavaScript, and XML — inside a data URL. However, you *cannot* package PHP, MySQL, or any server-side applications in a bookmark.

➤ Any web application that requires server access for data or application functionality needs to have a way to pack and go: (1) Use client-side JavaScript for application functionality, and

(2) package up a snapshot of the data and put it in a form accessible from a client script. However, in most cases in which you need to use cached data, you should use HTML5 offline storage instead (see Chapter 15).

➤ The Web application must be *entirely* self-contained. Therefore, every external resource the application needs, such as images, style sheets, and .js libraries, must be encoded inside the main HTML file.

➤ External resources that are referenced multiple times cannot be cached. Therefore, each separate reference must be encoded and embedded in the file.

➤ Images must be encoded as Base64, though the conversion increases their size by approximately 33 percent. (*Base64* is a process of encoding binary data so it can be represented with normal character set characters. Encoded Base64 data must then be decoded before it can be used.)

➤ The maximum size of a data URL in Safari for iOS is technically 128KB, though in actual practice you can work with URLs much larger — at least up to several megabytes. However, performance of the Safari Bookmark manager suffers significantly when large amounts of data are stored inside a bookmark. Therefore, think thin for data URL-based applications.

➤ Safari has issues working with complex JavaScript routines embedded in a data URL application.

➤ If your development computer is a Mac then you should be okay working with data URLs. However, if you are working with the Windows version of Safari and trying to sync the bookmark with Safari on iOS, please note that Safari on Windows has limitations in the size of data it can store inside of a bookmark.

DEVELOPING A DATA URL APP

After examining these constraints, it is clear that the best candidates for data URL apps are those that are relatively small in both scope and overall code base. A tip calculator, for example, is a good example applet because its UI would be simple and its programming logic would be straightforward and would not require accessing complex JavaScript libraries. I walk you through the steps needed to create a data URL application in this section.

After reviewing the constraints and making sure that your application will likely work in an offline mode, begin designing and programming as if it were a normal iOS web app. For this sample applet, the interface of the tip calculator is based on a subset of a legacy version of the iUI framework. (To limit the size of the app, I am not including any references to the framework itself.)

The following Try It Out shows how to create a data URL app.

TRY IT OUT | **Creating a Data URL App**

For a demonstration of how to create your own data URL app, follow these steps.

1. Create the following HTML document in your text editor and then save the document as *BIDHJ-Ch13-Ex1.html*.

Available for
download on
Wrox.com

```html
<!DOCTYPE html PUBLIC "-//W3C//DTD XHTML 1.0 Strict//EN"
        "http://www.w3.org/TR/xhtml1/DTD/xhtml1-strict.dtd">
<html xmlns="http://www.w3.org/1999/xhtml">
<head>
<head>
<title>Tipster</title>
<meta name="viewport" content="width=320; initial-scale=1.0;
   maximum-scale=1.0; user-scalable=0;"/>
</head>
<body>
<div class="toolbar">
<h1 id="pageTitle">The Tipster</h1>
<a id="backButton" class="button" href="#"></a>
</div>
<div id="main" title="Tipster" class="panel" selected="true">
<h2 class="tip">Let the Tipster ease your pain and calculate the tip for you.</h2>
<fieldset>
<div class="row">
<label>Bill amount:</label>
<input type="text" id="fldBillTotal" value="20.00" tabindex="1"
   onfocus="clearTotal(this)" onchange="checkTotal(this)"/>
</div>
<div class="row">
<label>Rating:</label>
<select id="fldTipPercent" onchange="getRec()"
tabindex="2">
<option value="0">(Rate service)</option>
<option value="10">Very poor</option>
<option value="12.5">Poor</option>
<option value="15">
   Just as expected</option>
<option value="17.5">
   Above average</option>
<option value="20">Exceptional</option>
<option value="25">Wow!</option>
</select>
</div>
</fieldset>
<fieldset>
<div class="row">
<label>Tip: </label>
<input type="text" id="fldTipRec" value="0.00" readonly="true" disabled="true"/>
</div>
<div class="row">
<label>Final total:</label>
<input type="text" id="fldFinalTotal" value="0.00" readonly="true"
   disabled="true"/>
</div>
</fieldset>
</div>
</body>
</html>
</html>
```

Code snippet BIDHJ-Ch13-Ex1.html

2. Add the following JavaScript code in the page's header:

```
<script type="application/x-javascript">
addEventListener('load', function()
{
  setTimeout(function() {
      window.scrollTo(0, 1);
  }, 100);
 }, false);

function checkTotal(fld)
{
    var x=fld.value;
    var n=/(^\d+$)|(^\d+\.\d+$)/;
    if (n.test(x))
    {
        if (fldTipPercent.selectedIndex != 0) getRec();
    }
    else
    {
        alert('Please enter a valid total')
        clearTotal(fld);
    }
}

function clearTotal(fld)
{
  fld.value = '';
}

function getRec()
{
    if (fldTipPercent.selectedIndex == 0)
    {
        alert('Please rate the service first.'); return;
    }
    var selPercent = Number( eval( fldTipPercent.
    var billAmount = Number( eval( fldBillTotal.value));
    var tipAmount = (selPercent*billAmount);
    var finalP = tipAmount + billAmount;
    fldTipRec.value = '$' + tipAmount.toFixed(2);
    fldFinalTotal.value = '$' + finalP.toFixed(2);
}
</script>
```

Code snippet BIDHJ-Ch13-Ex1.html

3. Add the following <style> element into the document header:

```
<style>
body > .toolbar
{
    box-sizing: border-box;
    -moz-box-sizing: border-box;
```

```
        border-bottom: 1px solid #2d3642;
        border-top: 1px solid #6d84a2;
        padding: 10px;
        height: 45px;
        background: url(
    "data:image/png;base64,iVBORw0KGgoAAAANSUhEUgAAAEAAAArCAIAAAA2QHWOAAAAGXRFWHRTb2Z0
    d2FyZQBBZG9iZSBJbWFnZVJlYWR5ccllPAAAAE1JREFUCNddjDEOgEAQAgn//5qltYWFnb1GB4vdSy4WBAY
    StKyb9+O0FJMYyjMyMWCC35lJM71r6vF1P07/lFSfPx6ZxNLcy1HtihzpA/RWcOj0zlDhAAAAAElFTkSuQm
    CC"
        ) #6d84a2 repeat-x;
}
body > .panel
{
        box-sizing: border-box;
        padding: 10px;
        background: #c8c8c8
    url('data:image/png;base64,iVBORw0KGgoAAAANSUhEUgAAAcAAAABCAIAAACdaSOZAAAAGXRFWHRT
    b2Z0d2FyZQBBZG9iZSBJbWFnZVJlYWR5ccllPAAAABdJREFUeNpiPHrmCgMC/GNjYwNSAAEGADdNA3dnzPl
    QAAAAAElFTkSuQmCC');
}
</style>
```

Code snippet BIDHJ-Ch13-Ex1.html

4. Save your HTML file.

5. Go to the data: URI Kitchen (see Figure 13-4) at `http://software.hixie.ch/utilities/cgi/data/data`.

FIGURE 13-4

6. Upload BIDHJ-Ch13-Ex1.html and then click Generate to create an encoded URL, which is displayed in the URL box of Safari (see Figure 13-5).

FIGURE 13-5

7. Drag the URL onto your Bookmarks bar.

8. Sync up with your iOS device and your application is now ready to run in offline mode.

How It Works

When you look at the app itself, the `fldBillTotal` input field captures the total before the tip. The `fldTipPercent` select list displays a set of ratings for the service, each corresponding with a percentage value. These two factors are then calculated to generate the output values in the `fldTipRec` and `fldFinalTotal` input fields.

Two of the styles reference external images for backgrounds. Therefore, in order to use them, you need to encode these images first. The easiest way to do this is to use an online converter, such as the data: URI Image Encoder (see Figure 13-6) at www.scalora.org/projects/uriencoder. This service performs a Base64 encoding of a local file or a URL. You can then replace the image file reference with the attached encoded string. Now that all external resources are embedded, the application is fully standalone.

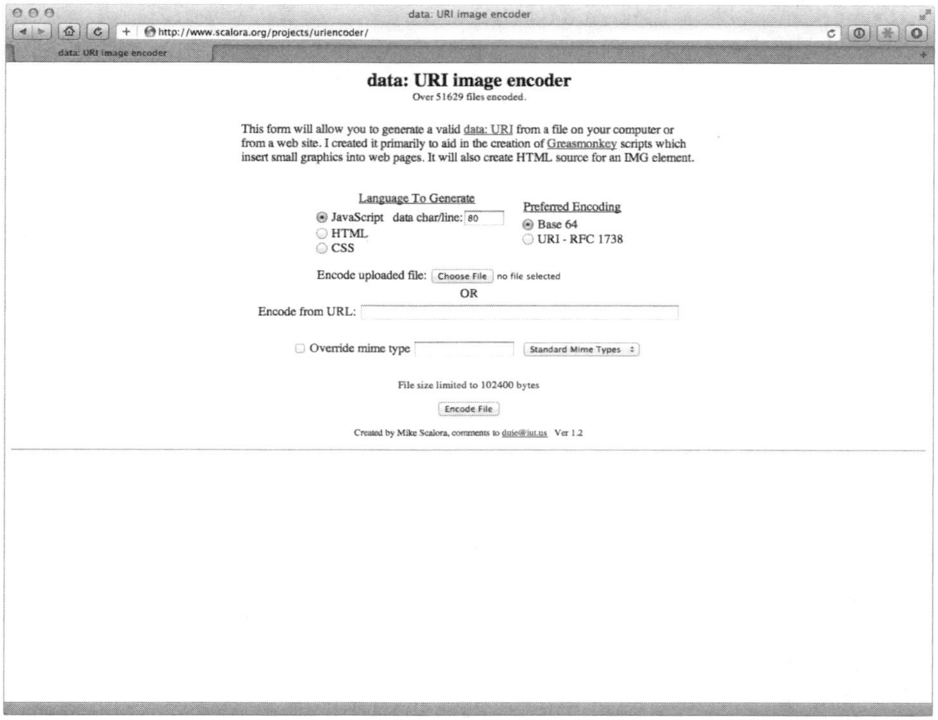

FIGURE 13-6

The final steps involve getting the self-contained app into a form that is accessible when the browser is offline. In the example, I used the data: URI Kitchen to do the conversion, but there are several ways to automate this process for you:

➤ **Url2iphone** (www.somewhere.com/url2iphone.html): This enables you to convert a URL into a bookmark. The most powerful aspect of this tool is that it looks for images, style sheets, and other files that are referenced and encode these as well.

➤ **data: URI image encoder** (www.scalora.org/projects/uriencoder): This tool is great for encoding images into Base64 format. You can specify a URL or upload a local file.

➤ **Filemark Maker** (http://mac.softpedia.com/get/Utilities/Filemark-Maker.shtml): This is a free Mac-based utility that is oriented toward storing Word, Excel, and PDF documents as data URLs. However, it can also be used for HTML pages.

➤ **Encoding bookmarklet:** Developer David Lindquist developed a handy bookmarklet that grabs the current page's source, generates a data: URL, and loads the URL. You can then drag the generated URL onto your Bookmarks bar. Here's the JavaScript code:

```
javascript:x=new XMLHttpRequest();x.onreadystatechange=function()
 {if(x.readyState==4)location='data:text/html;charset=utf-
8;base64,'+btoa(x.responseText)};x.open('GET',location);x.send('');
```

➤ The following Perl syntax turns HTML into a data URL:

```
perl -0777 -e 'use MIME::Base64; $text = <>; $text = encode_base64($text);
   $text =~ s/\s+//g; print "data:text/html;charset=utf-8;base64,$text\n";'
```

➤ In PHP, you could create a function to do the same thing:

```php
<?php
function data_url($file)
{
  $contents = file_get_contents($file);
  $base64   = base64_encode($contents);
  return ('data:text/html;charset=utf-8;base64,' . $base64);
}
?>
```

Figure 13-7 shows a fully functional tip calculator called The Tipster.

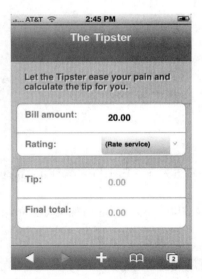

FIGURE 13-7

EXERCISES

1. What protocol is used to execute a bookmarklet?

2. What is the use of the `data:` protocol?

3. How can you reference images in a data URL?

Answers to the Exercises can be found in the Appendix.

▶ **WHAT YOU LEARNED IN THIS CHAPTER**

TOPIC	KEY CONCEPTS
What is a bookmarklet?	A *bookmarklet* is JavaScript stored as a URL and saved as a bookmark in the browser.
Storing an app in a data URL	You can store the contents of a page and its assets inside an encoded data URL.

PART IV
Advanced Programming Techniques

14

Programming the Canvas

WHAT YOU WILL LEARN IN THIS CHAPTER:

➤ Identifying the iOS user agent

➤ Drawing rectangles and other shapes

➤ Drawing images onto a canvas

The unique platform capabilities of the iOS enable developers to create innovative applications inside Safari that go beyond the normal "web app" fare. Safari's support for the canvas element opens drawing and animation capabilities in an ordinary HTML page that were previously available only by using Flash or Java. The canvas element is part of the Web Hypertext Application Technology Working Group (WHATWG) specification for HTML 5.0 (or HTML5).

However, after you begin to open up these capabilities you need to be sure that you are working with an iOS device rather than a standard desktop browser that may not provide HTML5 support. Consequently, you need to be able to identify the user agent for iOS devices.

IDENTIFYING THE USER AGENT

When you are trying to identify the capabilities of the browser requesting your website or application, you generally should avoid detecting the user agent; instead you should use object detection. However, if you are developing an application designed exclusively for iPhone or need to be certain of the browser being used then user agent detection is a valid option. Therefore, this chapter assumes you are creating a Safari-specific application.

The Safari user agent string for iPhone closely resembles the user agent for Safari on other platforms. However, it contains an iPhone platform name and the mobile version number. Depending on the version of Safari on iOS, it looks something like this:

```
Mozilla/5.0 (iPhone; U; CPU OS 3_2 like Mac OS X; en-us)
    AppleWebKit/531.21.10 (KHTML, like Gecko)
    Version/4.0.4 Mobile/7B334b Safari/531.21.10
```

Here's a breakdown of the various components of the user agent:

➤ **The platform string** (iPhone; U; CPU like Mac OS X; en-us): Notice the like Mac OS X line, which reveals some of the underpinnings of the iPhone.

➤ **The WebKit engine build number:** AppleWebKit/420+. This Safari version number is provided on all platforms (including Mac and Windows).

➤ **The marketing version:** (Version/4.0.4). This Safari version number is provided on all platforms (including Mac and Windows).

➤ **OS X build number:** Mobile/7B334b.

➤ **Safari build number:** Safari/531.21.10.

The iPad and iPod touch user agents are similar, but distinct with iPad or iPod as the platform. For example:

```
Mozilla/5.0 (iPad; U; CPU OS 3_2 like Mac OS X; en-us)
    AppleWebKit/531.21.10 (KHTML, like Gecko) Version/4.0.4 Mobile/7B334b
    Safari/531.21.10

Mozila/5.0 (iPod; U; CPU like Mac OS X; en)
    AppleWebKit/420.1 (KHTML, like Geckto)
    Version/3.0 Mobile/3A101a Safari/419.3
```

The version numbers change, obviously, when Apple updates Safari, but the string structure stays the same.

To test whether the device is an iPhone or iPod touch, you need to perform a string search on iPad, iPhone, and iPod. The following function returns true if the user agent is an iOS device:

```
function isAppleMobile() {
  result ((navigator.platform.indexOf("iPhone") != -1) ||
          (navigator.userAgent.indexOf("iPod") != -1)  ||
          ((navigator.userAgent.indexOf("iPad") != -1))
}
```

Be sure not to test for the string Mobile within the user agent, because a non-Apple mobile device (such as Nokia) might be based on the WebKit-based browser.

If you need to do anything beyond basic user agent detection and test for specific devices or browser versions, however, consider using WebKit's own user agent detection script available for download at trac.webkit.org/projects/webkit/wiki/DetectingWebKit. By linking WebKitDetect.js to your page, you can test for specific devices (iPhone and iPod touch) as well as software versions. Here's a sample detection script:

```
<!DOCTYPE html PUBLIC "-//W3C//DTD XHTML 1.0 Strict//EN"
        "http://www.w3.org/TR/xhtml1/DTD/xhtml1-strict.dtd">
<html xmlns="http://www.w3.org/1999/xhtml">
<head>
<title>User Agent Detection via WebKit Script</title>
<meta name="viewport" content="width=320; initial-scale=1.0;
  maximum-scale=1.0; user-scalable=0;">
<script type="application/x-javascript" src="WebKitDetect.js"></script>
</head>
<body>
<p id="log"></p>
</body>
<script type="application/x-javascript">
function addTextNode(str) {
  var t = document.createTextNode(str);
  var p = document.getElementById("log");
  p.appendChild(t);
}
if ( WebKitDetect.isMobile() ) {
  var device = WebKitDetect.mobileDevice();
  // String found in Settings/General/About/Version
  var minSupport = WebKitDetect.mobileVersionIsAtLeast("1C28");
  switch( device ) {
    case 'iPhone':
      if ( minSupport ) {
        addTextNode('If this were a real app, I launch its URL right now.');
        break;
      }
      else {
        addTextNode('Please upgrade your iPhone to the latest update before
running this application.');
        break;
      }
    case 'iPod':
    addTextNode('If this were a real app, I would launch its iPod touch version.');
      default:
      addTextNode( 'This mobile device is not supported by this application.
Go to your nearest Apple store and get an iPhone.');
      case 'iPad:
        addTextNode('If this were a real app, I would launch its iPad version.');
      default:
      addTextNode( 'This mobile device is not supported by this application.
Go to your nearest Apple store and get an iPad.');
  }
}
else {
  addTextNode( 'Desktop computers are so 1990s. Go get an iOS device.' );
}
</script>
</html>
```

With the WebKitDetect.js script included, the WebKitDetect object is accessible. Begin by calling its isMobile() method to determine whether the device is or is not a mobile device. Next, check to ensure that the mobile version is the latest release and save that result in the minSupport variable.

The `switch` statement then evaluates the mobile devices. If it is an iPhone, then it checks to see if `minSupport` is true. If it is true then a real application would begin here. If `minSupport` is false then the user is notified to update his or her iPhone to the latest software version. The remaining two `case` statements evaluate for an iPhone or an unknown mobile device. The final `else` statement is called if the device is not a mobile computer.

PROGRAMMING THE IOS CANVAS

C++ and other traditional software programmers have long worked with a *canvas* on which they could draw graphics. In contrast, web developers typically program the presentation layer using HTML and CSS. Unless they used Flash or Java, developers had no real way to actually draw graphical content on a web page. However, both desktop and mobile versions of Safari support the `canvas` element to provide a resolution-dependent bitmap region for drawing arbitrary content. The `canvas` element defines a drawing region on your web page that you then draw on using a corresponding JavaScript `canvas` object.

The canvas frees you as an application developer to not only draw anything you want to but also to use canvas as a way to render graphs, program games, or add special effects. On Mac OS X, the canvas is often used for creating Dashboard widgets. On iOS, Apple makes use of the canvas for both the Clock and Stocks built-in applications.

Canvas programming can be a mindset difference for web developers who are used to manipulating existing graphics rather than creating them from scratch. It is the loose equivalent of a Photoshop expert beginning to create content using an Adobe Illustrator-like program in which all of the graphics are created in a non-visual manner.

DEFINING THE CANVAS ELEMENT

Think of a canvas as a rectangular block region of a page in which you have full control over what is drawn on it. The canvas is defined using the `canvas` element:

```
<canvas id="theCanvas" width="300" height="300"/>
```

Except for the `src` and `alt` attributes, the `canvas` element supports all the same attributes as the `img` tag. Although the `id`, `width`, and `height` attributes are not required, they should be defined as a sound programming practice. The `width` and `height` are usually defined in pixels, although they can also be defined as a percentage of the viewport.

You can place multiple `canvas` elements on a page, just as long as each one has its own unique ID.

GETTING A CONTEXT

After a canvas region is defined on your web page, you can then draw inside of the flat two-dimensional surface using JavaScript. Just like a web page, the canvas has an origin (0,0) in the top-left corner. By default, all of the x,y coordinates you specify are relative to this position.

As the first step in working with the canvas, you first need to get a 2d context object. This object, which is responsible for managing the canvas' graphics state, is obtained by calling the getContext() method of the canvas object:

```
var canvas = document.GetElementById("theCanvas");
var context = canvas.getContext("2d");
```

Or, because you don't normally work directly with the canvas object, you can also combine the two lines:

```
var context = document.GetElementById("theCanvas").getContext("2d");
```

All of the drawing properties and methods you work with are called from the context object. The context object has many properties (see Table 14-1) that determine how the drawing looks on the page.

TABLE 14-1: Context Properties

PROPERTY	DESCRIPTION
fillStyle	Provides CSS color or style (gradient, pattern) of the fill of a path.
font	Specifies the font used.
globalAlpha	Specifies the level of transparency of content drawn on the canvas. Floating-point value is between 0.0 (fully transparent) and 1.0 (fully opaque).
globalCompositeOperation	Specifies the compositing mode to determine how the canvas is displayed relative to background content. Values include copy, darker, destination-atop, destination-in, destination-out, destination-over, lighten, source-atop, source-in, source-out, source-over, and xor.
lineCap	Defines the end style of a line. String values include butt for flat edge, round for rounded edge, square for square ends. (Defaults to butt.)
lineJoin	Specifies the way lines are joined together. String values include round, bevel, miter. (Defaults to miter.)
lineWidth	Specifies the line width. Floating-point value is greater than 0.
miterLimit	Specifies the miter limit for drawing a juncture between line segments.
shadowBlur	Defines the width that a shadow covers.
shadowColor	Provides CSS color for the shadow.
shadowOffsetX	Specifies the horizontal distance of the shadow from the source.

continues

TABLE 14-1 *(continued)*

PROPERTY	DESCRIPTION
shadowOffsetY	Specifies the vertical distance of the shadow from the source.
strokeStyle	Defines the CSS color or style (gradient, pattern) when stroking paths.
textAlign	Determines the text alignment.
textBaseline	Specifies the baseline of the text (top, hanging, middle, alphabetic, ideographic, or bottom).

DRAWING A SIMPLE RECTANGLE

There are several techniques for drawing on the canvas. Perhaps the most straightforward is by drawing a rectangle. To do so, you work with three context methods:

➤ context.fillRect(x,y,w,h) draws a filled rectangle.

➤ context.strokeRect(x,y,w,h) draws a rectangular outline.

➤ context.clearRect(x,y,w,h) clears the specified rectangle and makes it transparent.

For example, suppose you would like to draw a rectangular box with a set of squares inside of it and a rectangular outline on the outside. Here's a JavaScript function that draws that shape:

```
function draw()
{
var context = document.getElementById('myCanvas').getContext('2d');
    context.strokeRect(10,10,150,140);
    context.fillRect(15,15,140,130);
    context.clearRect(30,30,30,30);
    context.clearRect(70,30,30,30);
    context.clearRect(110,30,30,30);
    context.clearRect(30,100,30,30);
    context.clearRect(70,100,30,30);
    context.clearRect(110,100,30,30);
}
```

After the context is obtained, strokeRect() creates a rectangular outline starting at the coordinate (10,10) and is 150 × 140 pixels in size. The fillRect() method paints a 140 × 130 rectangle starting at coordinate (15,15). The six clearRect() calls clear areas previously painted by fillRect(). Figure 14-1 shows the result.

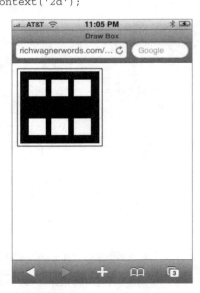

FIGURE 14-1

The full page source is shown in the following code:

```
<!DOCTYPE html PUBLIC "-//W3C//DTD XHTML 1.0 Strict//EN"
        "http://www.w3.org/TR/xhtml1/DTD/xhtml1-strict.dtd">
<html xmlns="http://www.w3.org/1999/xhtml">
<head>
<title>Draw Box</title>
<meta name="viewport" content="width=320; initial-scale=1.0;
    maximum-scale=1.0; user-scalable=0;">
<script type="application/x-javascript">
function draw()
{
    var context = document.getElementById('myCanvas').getContext('2d');
    context.strokeRect(10,10,150,140);
    context.fillRect(15,15,140,130);
    context.clearRect(30,30,30,30);
    context.clearRect(70,30,30,30);
    context.clearRect(110,30,30,30);
    context.clearRect(30,100,30,30);
    context.clearRect(70,100,30,30);
    context.clearRect(110,100,30,30);
}
</script>
</head>
<body onload="draw()">
<canvas id="myCanvas" width="300" height="300" style="position:absolute;
    left:0px; top:0px; z-index:1"/>
</body>
</html>
```

Code snippet BIDHJ-Ch14-Ex1.html

DRAWING OTHER SHAPES

You draw non-rectangular shapes by creating a path for that shape and then either *stroking* (drawing) a line along the specified path or else *filling* (painting) in the area inside of the path. Much like an Etch A Sketch drawing, paths are composed of a series of *subpaths*, such as a straight line or an arc that together form a shape.

When you work with paths, the following methods are used for drawing basic shapes:

➤ beginPath() creates a new path in the canvas and sets the starting point to the coordinate (0,0).

➤ closePath() closes an open path and attempts to draw a straight line from the current point to the starting point of the path. The use of closePath() is optional.

➤ `stroke()` draws a line along the current path.

➤ `fill()` closes the current path and paints the area within it. (Because `fill()` closes the path automatically, you don't need to call `closePath()` when you use it.)

➤ `lineTo(x,y)` adds a line segment from the current point to the specified coordinate.

➤ `moveTo(x,y)` moves the starting point to a new coordinate specified by the *x,y* values.

Using these methods, you can create a list of subpaths to form a shape. For example, the following code creates two triangles next to each other; one is empty and one is filled. An outer rectangle surrounds both triangles. Here's the code:

```
function drawTriangles()
{
var context = document.getElementById('myCanvas').getContext('2d');
// Empty triangle
context.beginPath();
context.moveTo(10,10);
context.lineTo(10,75);
context.lineTo(100,40);
context.lineTo(10,10);
context.stroke();
context.closePath();

// Filled triangle
context.beginPath();
context.moveTo(110,10);
context.lineTo(110,75);
context.lineTo(200,40);
context.lineTo(110,10);
context.fill();

// Outer rectangle
context.strokeRect(3,3,205,80);
}
```

Figure 14-2 shows the results.

 NOTE *If you are new to canvas programming, drawing complex shapes on the canvas can take some getting used to. You may find it helpful initially to go low tech and use a piece of graph paper to sketch out the shapes you are trying to draw and calculate the x,y coordinates using the paper grid.*

The JavaScript canvas enables you to go well beyond drawing with straight lines, however. You can use the following methods to create more advanced curves and shapes:

➤ `arc(x, y, radius, startAngle, endAngle, clockwise)` adds an arc to the current subpath using a radius and specified angles (measured in radians).

➤ `arcTo(x1, y1, x2, y2, radius)` adds an arc of a circle to the current subpath by using a radius and tangent points.

➤ `quadratricCurveTo(cpx, cpy, x, y)` adds a quadratic Bézier curve to the current subpath. It has a single control point (the point outside of the circle that the line curves toward) represented by cpx, cpy. The *x,y* values represent the new ending point.

➤ `bezierCurveTo(cp1x, cp1y, cp2x, cp2y, x, y)` adds a cubic Bézier curve to the current subpath using two control points.

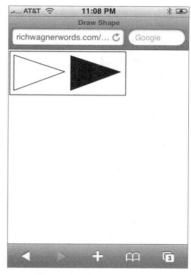

FIGURE 14-2

Using `arc()`, I can create a filled circle inside of an empty circle using the following code:

```
function drawCircles()
{
var context = document.getElementById('myCanvas').getContext('2d');

// Create filled circle
context.beginPath();
context.arc(125,65,30,0, 2*pi, 0);
context.fill();

// Create empty circle
context.beginPath();
context.arc(125,65,35,0, 2*pi, 0);
context.stroke();
context.endPath();
}
```

The `arc()` method starts the arc shape at coordinate (125,65) and draws a 30px radius starting at 0 degrees and ending at 360 degrees at a counterclockwise path.

Figure 14-3 displays the circle shapes that are created when this script is run.

DRAWING AN IMAGE

FIGURE 14-3

In addition to lines and other shapes, you can also draw an image onto your canvas by using the `drawImage()` method. The image can reference either an external image or another canvas element on the page. There are actually three ways in which you can call this method. The first variant simply draws an image at the specified coordinates using the size of the image:

```
context.drawImage(image, x, y)
```

The second method enables you to specify the dimensions of the image with the w and h arguments:

```
context.drawImage(image, x, y, width, height)
```

TRY IT OUT   Drawing an Image onto the Canvas

To draw an image onto the canvas, use the following steps.

1. Create the following HTML document in your text editor and then save the document as *BIDHJ-Ch14-Ex2.html*.

Available for
download on
Wrox.com

```
<!DOCTYPE html PUBLIC "-//W3C//DTD XHTML 1.0 Strict//EN"
          "http://www.w3.org/TR/xhtml1/DTD/xhtml1-strict.dtd">
<html xmlns="http://www.w3.org/1999/xhtml">
<head>
<title>Draw Image</title>
<meta name="viewport" ccntent="width=320; initial-scale=1.0;
   maximum-scale=1.0; user-scalable=0;">
</head>
<body>
<canvas id="myCanvas" width="300" height="300"
   style="position:absolute; left:0px; top:0px; z-index:1"/>
</body>
</html>
```

Code snippet BIDHJ-Ch14-Ex2.html

2. Add the following JavaScript code inside the document:

Available for
download on
Wrox.com

```
<script type="application/x-javascript">
function drawImg()
{
var context = document.getElementById('myCanvas').getContext('2d');
var img = new Image();
img.src = 'images/beach.jpg';
img.onload = function()
{
context.drawImage( img, 0, 0 );
}
}
</script>
```

Code snippet BIDHJ-Ch14-Ex2.html

3. Add an onload event handler to the body element and then save the file:

Available for
download on
Wrox.com

```
<body onload="drawImg()">
```

Code snippet BIDHJ-Ch14-Ex2.html

How It Works

When the document is loaded, it calls the `drawImg()` function. In the function, `context` and `img` objects are created. However, the `drawImage()` method of the `context` object is not called until after the image is loaded.

Figure 14-4 shows the image displayed inside of the canvas. Keep in mind that this is not an HTML `img` element, but the external image file drawn onto the context of the canvas.

FIGURE 14-4

Advanced Drawing

There is a variation of the `drawImage()` method that is slightly more complex. Here's the syntax:

```
context.drawImage(image, sourcex, sourcey, sourceWidth, sourceHeight,
    destx, desty, destWidth, destHeight)
```

In this variant, the method draws a subsection of the image specified by the source rectangle (`sourcex`, `sourcey`, `sourceWidth`, `sourceHeight`) onto a destination rectangle specified by the final arguments (`destx`, `desty`, `destWidth`, `destHeight`). For example, suppose you just want to display the rock thrower in Figure 14-4 rather than the entire picture. Using this expanded syntax of `drawImage()`, you extract a 79 × 131px rectangle from the original picture starting at the coordinate (151, 63). You then paint the same sized rectangle at coordinate (10, 10) on the canvas. Here is the updated code:

```
function drawImg(){
  var canvas = document.getElementById('myCanvas');
  var context = canvas.getContext('2d');
  var img = new Image();
  img.src = 'images/beach.jpg';
  img.onload = function() {
    context.drawImage( img, 151, 63, 79, 131, 10, 10, 79, 131 );
  }
}
```

Figure 14-5 shows the result.

FIGURE 14-5

Drawing with Encoded Images

You can also use a `data:` URI encoded image to eliminate the need for an external image file for canvas painting. For example, start with an online image encoder, such as the one available at `www.scalora.org/projects/uriencoder`. Using this tool, you encode the image, as shown in Figure 14-6.

FIGURE 14-6

You can then integrate the outputted encoded string into the script code as the image object's source (much of the encoded text for this example has been removed for space reasons):

```
function drawImg(){
var img_src = 'data:image/jpeg;base64,'+
'/9j/4AAQSkZJRgABAgAAZABkAAD/7AARRHVja3kAAQAEAAAAMAAA/+4ADkFkb2JlAGTAAAAAf/bAIQA'+
'CQYGBgcGCQcHCQ0IBwgNDwsJCQsPEQ4ODw4OERENDg4ODg0RERQUFhQUERoaHBwaHBgwGiYmYKysrKysr'+
'KysrKwEJCAgJCgkMCgoMDwwODA8TDg4ODhMVDg4PDg4VGhMRERExoXGhYWFhoXHR0aGh0dJCQjJCQr'+
'KysrKysr/8AAEQgA4AEsAwEiAAIRAQMRAf/EAJ8AAAEFAQEBAAAAAAAAAAAAIBAwQFBgAHCAEA'+
'AwEBAQAAAAAAAAAAAAAECAwQFEAABAwIEAwUFBQcEAQUAAAAABAAIDEQQQhMRIFQVETYXGBIgaRoTIj'+
'FLFCUnIzwdFiQyQ0B+GCkhWy0lODNRcRAAICAQMCBAUDBAMAAAAAAAABEQIhMRIDQVFhcYEikaGxExB'+
'MkLw4VIj0WKC/9oADAMBAAIRAxEAPwDyO2t5TdRAvJbqqHFaWRkETzCMzia8VSMEocxw+HVg5WgIke0vq'+
'ZKLmtk6Ke0tYmgRNAyypglK6MUiaOQXEKCgSkSlImIRWcA+U3uVaFaQj5be5AMKi6iVcgQKSiJlgBKLkq'+
'5ACLkq5ACLkq5ACJEq5ACJKJCVyABXFKKQAiQhKUiAEKSIiKIIAhCQjSEIAoSEZQlAgaLqJaJQEDGbg'+
'VhcOYTOOA9N/IHBPXf6Du5DtbKQuPBxr7kpyOMD9x+i/8pWQ/m+P7VsLr+3k/KVj/wCZ4p9GLsT/APp9'+
'OmIIzR8p0jsHErPNY1jQxowbgpW5TOudxkfm2LyN7z5R8u5IlvIJAPYhPvRHNDkfsTEXnpOlt1XXXcu4X'+
'rOpY7TC671j0T3g6YYj+Z5CsLL1B61vpUTTdyPmmma18IPyg2vnb08tLW1Xendsu7v08+K2idI7cdwg'+
'hl0jAQwMMMz9R4CrhmrqTO7centnvNyaz6neJ2O1Ob8NvHJ+oWfiIriV2cfHfZV1lJe+zX0+BwcvLx77q'+
'0Ws/9dE/r4Z1M5u8zX7aQwnRbwuj6IpgOrKZtQH+9Qt7AG87g0ClLmAYf8AyOVptdp1vU9iJcI7SOG4'+
'm1cGQRN1d/4qpguDcbg64lo8zPkmdq/FR0gPtWPIPtnG6+PRf3N+PDUZ28cv/wBP+wF8a3cnGDHDa9rQG'+
'n7FHfknnwyCBk7h7h5JXODXE4E4ktqqq8V3Z23MQToTK3qMsKtOFfaFg02248fidCaSSnw+AwE5FHJK'+
'8MYKuOPIADMk8AOKft7a7EzIxZOn1kAfHG5j6uacjpbQlpVlJuh28fTRWVtb3rD/AFFB6OsUFCI/nl3eV'+
'VeNRNnCXgTbkcxVbm/H5kaBn09jNcwQNuomPZFdPJDWudiGRsqCa0zPsUKW7nlFCQxnFjAGtFewLZv9'+
'Y3EOxWt4yxtRNPM+Jw0DSTG0fM0tpj51RyerdzeySLo2jYpfijFtHT3hbcleNKqXI9JhV7mPFfls7N8S'+
```

```
'w4127YfQoySSTmTxS0XONXF1AKmtAKDwCTCq5TqDM0jm6SQRliATQDTnRABRKEqG2wwhF3euK5AAkJT7'+
'1yrACJOK4lCD5jjkgQYxNEkhp5R4pNWkVGaCpOJzKcBIuCRKkOaBirqmlOGdF1SuwSGenAp+U/IPco4K'+
'duHhls9xya0krZHP0Kbc7k9Nlow4yCslPw8vFdZQgDLioUTnTSumdm817hwVrbUHgsnlnVVbak6BoACl'+
'tywUWM44J8O9ipCZz60VLvc/Tt3mvBWssoaM1nN3c65kZA3OV7WD/caIYkZ6/wBpvdvbFJcN8l03qxyD'+
'I6vNpPaFDIBHby5r1q9261vLF1jcN1RaQ0c2loo1ze0LzDddtn2y8fazCtMWP4PacnBJCsoK84Yc8ihJ'+
'4HNE7t45psk6gDmEyGeibFul7snoqO7tdIDhcyOLhUdR0sUMOHZ5lVbDvO4Xd/fyXtw+461lOJNZqMhS'+
'jchSvBO31yGf4422AHGa5fXuY6R32kLP7XeiyuxM8F0T2vilAz0SN0mnaM12X5HW3Cpaqq1b7ZOKnErU'+
'57bU7O9kn1wzf7fBt9pDPudwDNdbna6YoWsLi2GFjWSup/E6lexQrR8M/pq93G7gbd3AdNBFduYGOdEG'+
'1zHUAwAJIw7lQWPq7dba4MshbdQuPmhkGAYRpc2NwoWVbhhgrrbmnfrXc4LS5kc6b6ZvSdGyJsMQkNWM'+
'axxaaCuQFfFaU5aAxxTWLe3u9ZMr8N+NbrvE19yelU4jwKpkcMVtbXWirLG0bcVPGaSWRsbSPzmvc1X+3'+
'emYtw2fZru9A0NdNeX9w8+YxF3Uax1eD8yqrcd22yz3C92qe1N3tzGQWvy39N4NsDVzTjm5xVZuXqndL'+
'xs9tFK6322UgMtGkUaxrQxrNVK0o3FZ7+Ljb3e6Ft2r/ACX6YNdnNyJbfZL3bn/jZaefuZ6BZ+p9svLG'+
'43Nhi+rtnTR2keHUERLWMcWA6tJzPYsp61sWTGHeLZ8cwlAivei7W1k1ARjn5gciskCpdhul/t7nus5j'+
'D1BpkAALXDhVrgRUcCov+WuSuy9YT6rv3gvj/D+1ffx2yuj0jtJO3d4isLHbqaZbQPM7eIllDZHA9orp'+
'8FUpQ/W8ulJLnnU5+bqnEnE41SEAU0mtQCcKUPJc17bnPTReSwdVK7axq8tvxeWcVyTilUFnLly5AHJC'+
'lJQlAjkhPtSoCUwEJQB2LkvFNu8rimhMPVq8EtUDCKdiJApCqhOaXguSKOCVCi4I6h0P/9k=';
```

```
    var canvas = document.getElementById('myCanvas');
    var context = canvas.getContext('2d');
    var img = new Image();
    img.src = img_src;
    img.onload = function() {
      context.drawImage( img, 10, 10 );
    }
  }
```

Figure 14-7 shows the rendered image.

ADDING COLOR AND TRANSPARENCY

The `fillStyle` and `strokeStyle` properties of the `context`
object provide a way for you to set the color, alpha value, or style
of the shape or line you are drawing. (Refer to Table 14-1 for
a list of all context properties.) If you would like to set a color
value, you can use any CSS color, such as the following:

FIGURE 14-7

```
context.fillStyle="#666666";
context.strokeStyle=rgb(125,125,125);
```

After you set `fillStyle` or `strokeStyle`, it becomes the default value for all new shapes in the
canvas until you reassign it.

You can also use `rgba(r,g,b,a)` to assign an alpha value to the shape you are filling in. The `r`, `g`,
and `b` parameters take an integer value between 0–255, whereas `a` is a float value between 0.0 and
1.0 (0.0 being fully transparent, and 1.0 being fully opaque). For example, the following code draws
two circles in the canvas. The large circle has a 90 percent transparency value, and the smaller circle
has a 30 percent transparency value:

```
function drawTransCircles()
{
var context = document.getElementById('myCanvas').getContext('2d');
// Large circle—90% transparency
context.fillStyle = "rgba(13,44,50, 0.9)";
context.beginPath();
```

```
context.arc(95,90,60,0, 2*pi, 0);
context.fill();
// Smaller circle—30% transparency
context.fillStyle = "rgba(0,0,255, 0.3)";
context.beginPath();
context.arc(135,120,40,0, 2*pi, 0);
context.fill();
}
```

Alternatively, you can set the `context.globalAlpha` property to set a default transparency value for all stroke or fill styles. Remember, the value should be a float number between 0.0 and 1.0.

CREATING AN IMAGE PATTERN

You can use an external image to create an image pattern on the back of a canvas element using the `createPattern()` method. The syntax is the following:

```
patternObject = context.createPattern(image, type)
```

The `image` argument references an `Image` object or a different `canvas` element. The `type` argument is one of the familiar CSS pattern types: `repeat`, `repeat-x`, `repeat-y`, and `no-repeat`. The method returns a `Pattern` object.

TRY IT OUT   Drawing an Image Pattern

Use the following steps to create an image pattern on the canvas.

1. Create the following HTML document in your text editor and then save the document as *BIDHJ-Ch14-Ex2.html*.

Available for
download on
Wrox.com

```
<!DOCTYPE html PUBLIC "-//W3C//DTD XHTML 1.0 Strict//EN"
          "http://www.w3.org/TR/xhtml1/DTD/xhtml1-strict.dtd">
<html xmlns="http://www.w3.org/1999/xhtml">
<head>
<title>Draw Image</title>
<meta name="viewport" content="width=320; initial-scale=1.0;
   maximum-scale=1.0; user-scalable=0;">
</head>
<body>
<canvas id="myCanvas" width="300" height="300"
   style="position:absolute; left:0px; top:0px; z-index:1"/>
</body>
</html>
```

Code snippet BIDHJ-Ch14-Ex3.html

2. Add the following JavaScript code inside the document:

Available for
download on
Wrox.com

```
<script type="application/x-javascript">
function drawPattern()
{
    var context = document.getElementById('myCanvas').getContext('2d');
```

```
        var pImg = new Image();
        pImg.src = 'images/tech.jpg';
        // call when image is fully loaded
        pImg.onload = function() {
          var pat = context.createPattern(pImg,'repeat');
          context.fillStyle = pat;
          context.fillRect(0,0,300,300)
        }
      }
    </script>
```

Code snippet BIDHJ-Ch14-Ex3.html

3. Add an `onload` event handler to the `body` element and then save the file:

Available for download on Wrox.com

```
<body onload="drawPattern()">
```

Code snippet BIDHJ-Ch14-Ex3.html

How It Works

When the document is loaded, it calls the `drawPattern()` function. In the function, an `Image` object is created and assigned a source. However, before this image can be used in the pattern, you need to ensure it is loaded. Therefore, you place the rest of the drawing code inside the `Image` object's `onload` event handler. Much like the gradient examples shown earlier, the `Pattern` object that is created with `createPattern()` is then assigned to `fillStyle`. Figure 14-8 shows the results.

FIGURE 14-8

EXERCISES

1. How can you identify the user agent of an iPad?

2. What is the difference between stroking and filling?

3. What is a drawing path composed of?

4. Why would you consider drawing an encoded image onto a canvas?

Answers to the Exercises can be found in the Appendix.

▶ **WHAT YOU LEARNED IN THIS CHAPTER**

TOPIC	KEY CONCEPTS
Identifying an iOS device in the user agent	iOS devices have similar user agent strings, but distinctively identify whether it is an iPhone, iPad, or iPod touch.
Creating a canvas on an HTML page	A `canvas` element defines a rectangular block region on a page that gives you full control via JavaScript over what gets drawn on it.
Drawing shapes	Rectangular shapes are drawn using the `context` object's `fillRect()`, `strokeRect()`, and `clearRect()` methods. Non-rectangular shapes are drawn by creating a path for that shape and then either *stroking* (drawing) a line along the specified path or else *filling* (painting) in the area inside of the path.
Drawing images	Use the `context` object's `drawImage()` method to draw an image. The image can reference either an external image or another canvas element on the page.

15

Offline Applications

WHAT YOU WILL LEARN IN THIS CHAPTER:

➤ Storing files locally in an offline cache

➤ Storing data on the client using key-value storage

➤ Accessing a local SQL database with JavaScript

In the past, one of the key differences between native iOS apps and web apps was the ability of native apps to work with local and remote data, whereas web apps were limited to working only when a live connection was available. However, Safari on iOS has embraced support for HTML 5's offline capabilities, enabling you to create web apps that work even when the user has no access to the Internet.

In this chapter, I walk you through these offline capabilities.

HTML 5 OFFLINE APPLICATION CACHE

Safari on iOS takes advantage of HTML 5's offline application cache to enable you to pull down remote files from a web server and store them in a local cache. Consequently, when the device is not connected to the Internet, either through 3G or Wi-Fi access, users can continue to work with your web app in offline mode.

You can include any file in the manifest that can be displayed locally without server-side processing — images (.jpg, .png, and .gif), HTML files, CSS style sheets, and JavaScript scripts.

Safari then attempts to download files in the manifest. If successful, Safari on iOS looks for these files in the cache first before going to the server. However, in the event of a missing file, incorrect URL, or other error, the update process fails and no further files are downloaded. Then, the next time the manifest is loaded, Safari attempts to download all files once again.

After Safari downloads the files in a manifest file, the cache is only updated in the future if the manifest file changes. (Note that the content of the manifest file is what is evaluated to determine whether or not to update the cache, not its last-saved date or other file attribute.) However, if you want to force an update, you can do so programmatically through JavaScript.

Create a Manifest File

To enable the offline cache, you need to create a manifest file that lists each of the files you want to have available offline. The manifest file is an ordinary text file, without any HTML or XML markup at all, that includes two parts:

➤ **Declaration:** The manifest is declared by typing the following on the first line of the file:

```
CACHE MANIFEST
```

➤ **URL Listings:** The subsequent lines list the URLs for each file that you want to cache. The paths must be relative to the path of the manifest file.

You can also add comments to the file by adding a # to the start of each line.

Here's an example manifest file used for a small web app.

Available for download on Wrox.com

```
CACHE MANIFEST

# images
jackarmitage.png

# in-use assets
../assets/global.css
../assets/cui.css
../assets/assets.js
../assets/whiteButton.png
../assets/toolButton.png
../assets/toolbar.png
../assets/toggleOn.png
../assets/toggle.png
../assets/thumb.png
../assets/selection.png
../assets/prev.png
../assets/pinstripes.png
../assets/next.png
../assets/loading.gif
../assets/listGroup.png
../assets/listArrowSel.png
../assets/listArrow.png
../assets/grayrow.png
../assets/grayButton.png
../assets/cancel.png
../assets/blueButton.png
../assets/blackToolButton.png
../assets/blackToolbar.png
../assets/blackButton.png
../assets/backButton.png
```

Code snippet example.manifest

After you have created the manifest file, you need to save it with a `.manifest` extension.

In order for offline cache to work correctly, you need to be sure that your web server serves up the manifest file correctly. Because HTML 5 offline cache is still an "emerging" technology, many ISPs do not provide built-in support for it. Therefore, check to make sure your server assigns the MIME type text/cache-manifest to the `manifest` extension. In my case, I had to add it as a custom MIME type.

Reference the Manifest File

When you have created the manifest file and uploaded it to your server, you need to link it into your web app by adding the `manifest` attribute to the root `html` tag of your web file:

```
<html manifest="prospector.manifest"xmlns="http://www.w3.org/1999/xhtml">
```

In this case, the `prosector.manifest` file is in the same directory as the `index.html` file.

Programmatically Control the Cache

You have access to the cache using the JavaScript `window.applicationCache` object from inside your web app. To force a cache update, you can use the `update()` method. When the update is complete, you can swap out the old cache with the new cache using the `swapCache()` method.

However, before you begin this update process, you need to check first to make sure that the application cache is ready for updating by checking the `status` property of the `applicationCache` object. This property returns one of the values shown in Table 15-1.

TABLE 15-1: applicationCache.status Values

CONSTANT	NUMBER	DESCRIPTION
window.applicationCache.UNCACHED	0	No cache is available
window.applicationCache.IDLE	1	Local cache is up to date
window.applicationCache.CHECKING	2	Manifest file is being checked for changes
window.applicationCache.DOWNLOADING	3	Safari is downloading changed files and added them to the cache
window.applicationCache.UPDATEREADY	4	New cache is ready for updates and overrides your existing cache
window.applicationCache.OBSOLETE	5	Cache is obsolete and is therefore being deleted

For example:

```
if (window.applicationCache.status == window.applicationCache.UNCACHED)
{
    alert("Houston, we have a cache problem");
```

```
    }
    else if (window.applicationCache.status == window.applicationCache.IDLE)
    {
        alert("No changes are necessary.");
    }
    else
    {
        alert("Let's do something with the cache.");
    }
```

You can assign event handlers to the applicationCache object based on the results of the update process. For example:

```
    var localCache = window.applicationCache;
    localCache.addEventListener("updateready", cacheUpdateReadyHandler, false);
    localCache.addEventListener("error", cacheErrorHandler, false);
```

The applicationCache events that are supported include the following:

- ➤ checking
- ➤ error
- ➤ noupdate
- ➤ downloading
- ➤ updateready
- ➤ cached
- ➤ obsolete

Because I am focused on programmatically performing an update, I just listen for the updateready and error events:

```
    // Handler when local cache is ready for updates
    function cacheUpdateReadyHandler()
    {
    }

    // Handler for cache update errors
    function cacheErrorHandler()
    {
    alert("Houston, we have a cache problem");
    }
```

After these event handlers are defined, you are ready to start the update and swap process.

```
    // Handler when local cache is ready for updates
    function cacheUpdateReadyHandler()
    {
        localeCache.update();
        localeCache.swapUpdate();
    }
```

The `update()` method updates the cache and then `swapUpdate()` replaces the old cache with the new cache you successfully downloaded.

Checking Connection Status

When you use application cache, you may have some online processing that you want to disable if you are in offline mode. You can check the connection status in your web app by checking the `navigator` objects `onLine` property:

```
if (navigator.onLine)
    alert("Online. All services available.")
else
    alert("Offline. Disabling currency rate updates.");
```

TRY IT OUT   **Creating an Application Cache**

The following example shows the application cache in action.

1. Create the following HTML document in your text editor and then save the document as *BIDHJ-Ch15-Ex1.html*.

Available for
download on
Wrox.com

```
<!DOCTYPE html PUBLIC "-//W3C//DTD XHTML 1.0 Strict//EN"
    "http://www.w3.org/TR/xhtml1/DTD/xhtml1-strict.dtd">
<html xmlns="http://www.w3.org/1999/xhtml">
<head>
<meta http-equiv="Content-Type" content="text/html; charset=utf-8" />
<meta name="viewport" content="width=device-width,
    minimum-scale=1.0, maximum-scale=1.0">
<title>Cache Me If You Can</title>
</head>
<body>
<div id="progressSpinner" style="display:none;">
<p>Loading...<img src="spinner.gif" alt="Loading..." width="16" height="16" /></p>
</div>
<div id="content">
<div id="onlineIndicator">online|offline</div>
<p>This is a test of the Safari on iOS applicationCache.</p>
<img src="boy.png" />
</div>
</body>
</html>
```

Code snippet BIDHJ-Ch15-Ex1.html

2. Add the following script code inside the document head:

Available for
download on
Wrox.com

```
<script type="text/javascript">

    // Assign var to applicationCache
    var localCache = window.applicationCache;

    // Show progress indicator
```

```
localeCache.addEventListener("progress", cacheProgressHandler, false);
// Swap cache
localeCache.addEventListener("updateready", cacheUpdateReadyHandler, false);
// Hide progress indicator
localeCache.addEventListener("cached", cacheNoUpdateHandler, false);
localeCache.addEventListener("noupdate", cacheNoUpdateHandler, false);
// Show error msg
localeCache.addEventListener("error", cacheErrorHandler, false);

// Called on load
function init()
{
  if (navigator.onLine)
      document.getElementById("onlineIndicator").textContent = "online"
  else
      document.getElementById("onlineIndicator").textContent = "offline";

  localeCache.update();

}

// Called when no updates are needed
function cacheNoUpdateHandler()
{
    document.getElementById("progressSpinner").style.display = "none";
}

// Called when a cache upate is in progress
function cacheProgressHandler()
{
  document.getElementById("progressSpinner").style.display = "table";
}

// Called when cache is ready to be updated
function cacheUpdateReadyHandler()
{
  localCache.swapCache();
  document.getElementById("progressSpinner").style.display = "none";
}

// Error handler
function cacheErrorHandler()
{
  document.getElementById("progressSpinner").style.display = "none";
  alert("A problem occurred trying to load the cache.");
}


</script>
```

Code snippet BIDHJ-Ch15-Ex1.html

3. Add an `onload` event handler to the `body` tag:

```
<body onload="init()">
```

Code snippet BIDHJ-Ch15-Ex1.html

4. Add a manifest declaration to the HTML tag and then save the document:

```
<html manifest="BIDHJ-Ch15-Ex1.manifest" xmlns="http://www.w3.org/1999/xhtml">
```

5. Create the following text file and then save the document as *BIDHJ-Ch15-Ex1.manifest*.

```
CACHE MANIFEST

#   images
boy.png
spinner.gif
```

Code snippet BIDHJ-Ch15-Ex1.manifest

How It Works

➤ In the HTML document, the `localeCache` variable is assigned to the `window.application Cache`. Handlers are then assigned to `applicationCache` events, which determine whether or not to show a progress indicator of the cache updating process. If the `updateready` event is triggered, then the `swapUpdate()` method is called to update to cache. Figures 15-1 and 15-2 show this example run in both online and offline modes.

FIGURE 15-1

FIGURE 15-2

USING KEY-VALUE STORAGE

In addition to local cache, Safari on iOS also supports HTML 5 key-value storage as a way to provide persistent storage on the client either permanently or within a given browser session. Key-value storage bears several obvious similarities to cookies in client-side storage. However, although cookies are sent back to the server, saved key-value data is not sent back to the server unless you explicitly do so through JavaScript. You also have greater control over the data persistence and window access to that data using key-value storage.

You can specify whether the key values you are saving should be long term or short term by working with two different JavaScript objects: `localStorage` and `sessionStorage`.

➤ Use `localStorage` when you want to store a key-value pair permanently across browser sessions and windows.

➤ Use `sessionStorage` for storing temporary data within a given browser window and session.

Saving a Key Value

You can save a key value in one of two ways. First, you can call the `setItem()` method on the `localStorage` or `sessionObject` object.

```
localStorage.setItem(keyName, keyValue);
```

For example, to save a user-inputted value as the `firstName` key for long-term storage, use the following:

```
localStorage.setItem("firstName", document.getElementById("first_name").value);
```

Second, a shortcut to save a value is to treat the key-value name as an actual property of the `localStorage` or `sessionStorage` objects. For example, you could also write the previous example as the following:

```
localStorage.firstName = document.getElementById("first_name").value;
```

However, if you use this shortcut method, you need to make sure that the name of your key value is a valid JavaScript token.

Any local database is going to have a maximum capacity, so it is good practice to trap for a possible exception in case the capacity has been reached. To do so, you'll want to trap for QUOTA_EXCEEDED_ERR. For example:

```
try
{
    localStorage.firstName = document.getElementById("first_name").value);
}
catch (error)
{
  if (e == QUOTA_EXCEEDED_ERR)
      alert("Unable to save first name to the database.");
}
```

Whenever you interact with the local storage database, a `storage` event is dispatched from the `body` object. Therefore, to handle this event, you can attach a listener to the `body`:

```
document.body.addEventListener("storage", storageHandler, false);
```

The event object that is passed to the handler enables you to get at various pieces of the transaction (see Table 15-2). For example, the following handler outputs the storage event details to an alert box:

```
function storageHandler(event)
{
    var info = "A storage event occurred [" +
                "url=" + event.url + ", " +
                "key=" + event.key + ", " +
                "new value=" + event.newValue + ", " +
                "old value=" + event.oldValue + ", " +
                "window=" + event.window + "]";

    alert(info);
}
```

TABLE 15-2: `storageevent` Properties

PROPERTY	DESCRIPTION
url	URL of the page that calls the storage object. Returns `null` if the requesting page is not in the same window. Returns `undefined` if calling from a local page.
key	Specifies the key that has been added, changed, or removed.
newValue	Provides the new value for the key.
oldValue	Provides the old value for the key. If no key was previously defined, `null` is returned.
window	Reference to the `window` object that called the storage object. Returns `null` if the requesting page is not in the same window.

Loading Key-value Data

You can load data from the `localStorage` and `sessionStorage` objects by calling the `getItem()` method:

```
var keyValue = sessionStorage.getItem(keyName);
```

For example:

```
var accessCode = sessionStorage.getItem("accessCode");
```

Or, as you would expect, you can also access a key value by calling it as a direct property of the respective object:

```
var accessCode = sessionStorage.accessCode;
```

If the key value that you request is not located, then a `null` value is returned:

```
if (sessionStorage.accessCode != null)
{
    var valid = processCode(sessionStorage.accessCode);
}
```

Deleting Key-value Data

You can remove a specific key-value pair or clear all keys from the local key-value database.

To remove a specific key-value pair, use `removeItem()`:

```
localStorage.removeItem(keyName);
```

To remove all keys, use one or both of the following:

```
// Remove all permanent keys
localStorage.clear()
// Remove all session keys
sessionStorage.clear()
```

TRY IT OUT   Using Key-value Storage

To demonstrate, this example walks you through the steps needed to use HTML 5's key-value storage mechanisms to save permanent and temporary values.

1.   Create the following HTML document in your text editor and then save the document as *BIDHJ-Ch10-Ex2.html*.

```
<!DOCTYPE html PUBLIC "-//W3C//DTD XHTML 1.0 Strict//EN"
    "http://www.w3.org/TR/xhtml1/DTD/xhtml1-strict.dtd">
<html xmlns="http://www.w3.org/1999/xhtml">
<head>
    <meta http-equiv="Content-Type" content="text/html; charset=utf-8" />
    <meta name="viewport" content="width=device-width,
      minimum-scale=1.0, maximum-scale=1.0">
    <title>Value Keys</title>
</head>

<body onload="init()">
<div>
<p>Define a key value in which you want to save permanently:</p>

<input id='localValue' onchange="setLocalKeyValue('localValue')"/>

<p>Define a key value in which you want to save for this session only:<p>

<select id="sessionValue" onchange="setSessionKeyValue('sessionValue')">
<option value="UN">(Select State)</option>
<option value="MA">Massachusetts</option>
<option value="ME">Maine</option>
```

```
<option value="RI">Rhode Island</option>
<option value="VT">Vermont</option>
</select>
</div>

<p>
<button onclick='clearAll()'>Clear All</button><br />
</p>
<div id="statusDiv">Start session</div>
</body>
```

Code snippet BIDHJ-Ch15-Ex2.html

2. Add the following JavaScript code inside the document head and save the file:

Available for
download on
Wrox.com

```
<script language="JavaScript" type="text/javascript">

    // Check to see whether or not key-value storage is available
    var localStorageAvail = typeof(localStorage) != "undefined";
    var sessionStorageAvail = typeof(sessionStorage) != "undefined";

    // Assign event listeners
    window.addEventListener("onload", init, false);
    window.addEventListener("onbeforeunload", beforeUnloadHandler, false);

    // Called on load
    function init()
    {
        // If no storage is available
        if (!localStorageAvail || !sessionStorageAvail)
          setStatus("Key value storage is not supported.");
        // Otherwise, assign handler and retrieve any previously stored values
        else
        {
            document.body.addEventListener("storage", storageHandler, false);
            loadValues();
        }
    }

    // Save local key
    // value = id of the element whose value is being saved
    function setLocalKeyValue(value)
    {
        if (localStorage)
        {
            localStorage.setItem(value, document.getElementById(value).value);
            setStatus(document.getElementById(value).id +
              " saved as a local key.");
        }
    }

    // Save session key
    // value = id of the element whose value is being saved
    function setSessionKeyValue(value)
```

```
{
    if (sessionStorage)
    {
        sessionStorage.setItem(value,
          document.getElementById(value).selectedIndex);
        setStatus(document.getElementById(value).id
          + " saved as a session key.");
    }
}


// Loads key-value pairs from local storage
function loadValues()
{
    // Is localValue defined? If so, then assign its value to the text box.
    if (localStorage.localValue)
        document.getElementById('localValue').value =
          localStorage.localValue;
    // Is sessionValue defined? If so, then assign
    // its value as the index to the sessionValue select.
    if (sessionStorage.sessionValue)
        document.getElementById('sessionValue').selectedIndex =
          sessionStorage.sessionValue;
}

// Clear all key-value pairs
function clearStorage()
{
    // Clear local database
    sessionStorage.clear();
    localStorage.clear();

    // Clear UI as well
    document.getElementById('localValue').value = "";
    document.getElementById('sessionValue').selectedIndex = 0;
}

// Save current state
function saveChanges()
{
    setLocalValue('localValue');
    setSessionKeyValue("sessionValue");
    // Used to return to the window
    return null;
}

// Be sure and save changed before a window is closed
function beforeUnloadHandler()
{
    return saveChanges();
}

// Listener for all storage events. Outputs to the status div.
function storageHandler(event)
{
    var info = "A storage event occurred [" +
```

```
                        "url=" + event.url + ", " +
                        "key=" + event.key + ", " +
                        "new value=" + event.newValue + ", " +
                        "old value=" + event.oldValue + ", " +
                        "window=" + event.window + "]";

            setStatus(info);
        }

        // Utility function that outputs specified text to the status div
        function setStatus(statusText)
        {
            var para = document.createElement("p");
            para.appendChild(document.createTextNode(statusText));
            document.getElementById("statusDiv").appendChild(para);
        }

    </script>
```

Code snippet BIDHJ-Ch15-Ex2.html

How It Works

In this example, an `input` element value is saved as a permanent key-value pair, whereas the selection in a `select` list is saved for the current session only. I want to save the values of these elements each time they change, so I assign `onchange` handlers to both of these elements.

I also want to add a button to clear the key values on demand as well as a status box that acts as a console to output the storage events that are taking place. Figure 15-3 shows the page.

With the HTML markup ready, I can look at the JavaScript code needed to power this example. To begin, I want to confirm that key-value storage is available, so I do a test on the `localStorage` and `sessionStorage` objects.

I can then check one or both of these values prior to attempting to save or load storage data.

To save the value of the input element permanently, I add the `setLocalKeyValue()` function. Next, to save the `selectedIndex` of the `select` element as a session-only key-value pair, I use the `setSessionKeyValue()` function.

FIGURE 15-3

To retrieve the values of these key-value pairs, I use the loading function named `loadValues()`. Next, to clear all of the local values, I define a `clearStorage()` function to remove key-value pairs from both `sessionStorage` and `localStorage` objects as well as the UI fields.

The following figures demonstrate this example when run. Figure 15-4 shows the data being entered on screen. Figure 15-5 is what's shown after pressing the Refresh button within the current session. As you can see, both values are retained. However, after closing out that window and calling the URL again, the session value is cleared, as shown in Figure 15-6.

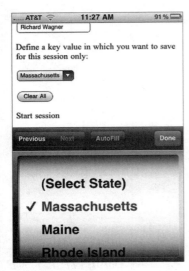

FIGURE 15-4

FIGURE 15-5

FIGURE 15-6

When you are working with key-value storage, I recommend using the Web Inspector that is provided with the Windows and Mac versions of Safari (you can find it on the Develop menu). The Databases panel (see Figure 15-7) enables you to see the current state of the key-value pairs for the page you are working with.

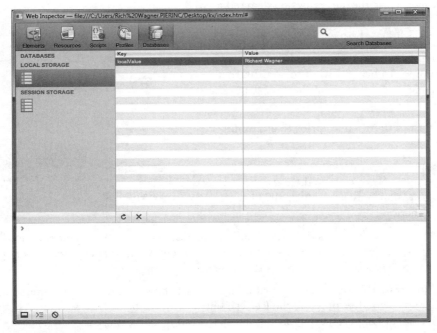

FIGURE 15-7

GOING SQL WITH THE JAVASCRIPT DATABASE

When you begin to develop more substantial web applications, you may easily have local storage needs that go beyond simple caching and key-value pair persistence. Perhaps your app stores application data locally and periodically syncs with a database on a backend server. Or maybe your web app uses a local database as its sole data repository. Using HTML 5's database capabilities, you can access a local SQLite relational database right from JavaScript to create tables, add and remove records, and perform queries.

Open a Database

Your first step is to open a database by calling the `openDatabase()` method of the `window` object:

```
var db = window.openDatabase(dbName, versionNum, displayName, maxSize);
```

The `dbName` parameter is the database name stored locally; `versionNum` is its version number; `displayName` is the display name of the database used by the browser (if needed); and `maxSize` is the maximum size in bytes that the database will be (additional size requires user confirmation). For example:

```
var db = window.openDatabase("customers", "1.0", "Customer database", 65536);
```

After the database is open, you can perform a variety of tasks on the database.

Each task you perform must be part of a transaction. A database transaction can include one or multiple SQL statements and is set up as follows:

```
db.transaction(transactionFunction, successCallbackFunction,
    errorCallbackFunction,);
```

Querying a Table

Suppose you want to perform a simple query on a customer table in your database. You could set up the query inside of a transaction, such as the following:

```
var db = window.openDatabase("customers", "1.0", "Customer database", 65536);

if (db)
{
    var updateSqlStr = "SELECT * FROM customers";
    db.transaction( function(transaction) {
      transaction.executeSql(updateSqlStr) },
        successHandler, errorHandler);
}


function successHandler(result)
{
    if (result.rows.length > 0)
```

```
        {
            for (var i=0; i<result.rows.length; i++)
            {
                var r = results.rows.item(i);
                alert(r["first_name"] + " was retrieved from the database.");
            }
        }
    }

    function errorHandler(error)
    {
        alert("An error occurred when trying to perform a query.");
    }
```

In this example, the db.transaction calls a SQL execute statement to return all of the customers from the database. The successHandler() function is called when the database is successful. The errorHandler() function is called if the operation failed.

The result object returned contains a rows array that contains each record in the returning set. You can access each of the fields by specifying its field name inside the brackets.

EXERCISES

1.   What is the purpose of a manifest file?

2.   Do you need to do anything special on the web server to use a manifest file?

3.   What's the difference between HTML 5 key-value storage and cookies?

Answers to the Exercises can be found in Appendix A.

▶ WHAT YOU LEARNED IN THIS CHAPTER

TOPIC	KEY CONCEPTS
Enabling offline cache	Create a manifest file that lists the files you want to store offline.
Loading local assets	Access your offline cache using the `window.applicationCache` object.
Saving and loading key values	Use the `setItem()` and `getItem()` methods of the `localStorage` or `sessionObject`.

16

Building with Web App Frameworks

WHAT YOU WILL LEARN IN THIS CHAPTER:

➤   Exploring the jQuery Mobile frameworks

➤   Using iWebKit to create a web app

When the iPhone was first introduced, you had few options for creating web apps for Apple's mobile device. You could use the original iUI `.js` library, or you could create everything from scratch. In the words of S.E. Hinton, that was then, and this is now. Today, you have a plethora of options available to you — not only for creating apps for iPhone and iPad, but also for creating them for Android.

In this chapter, I highlight two of the frameworks — jQuery Mobile and iWebKit — both of which provide great alternatives for web developers. I focus on these two for their ease of use, consistency with standard web conventions, and because they offer two different approaches to iOS support. jQueryMobile is focused on providing cross-platform mobile solutions, so it doesn't attempt to emulate the native iOS look and feel with its theming options. (However, I also introduce you to an open-source template that does just that.)

iWebKit, on the other hand, takes an opposite approach. Much like the updated iUI framework covered in Chapter 9, iWebKit focuses on providing a native-looking iOS experience for web apps. Based on your app needs, you can decide which makes the most sense for you.

As part of the comparison, I create a basic navigation-based app with each framework to help illustrate how you can utilize each framework for a common solution.

USING jQUERY MOBILE

If you worked through the Hello World example in Chapter 5, you already have an introduction to jQuery Mobile. jQuery Mobile is built on the popular jQuery framework and makes heavy use of normal HTML mixed with CSS and JavaScript. Although this book focused on jQuery Mobile's support for iOS, it also supports Android, BlackBerry, Windows Phone 7, Kindle, Nook, and other mobile platforms.

One of the advantages to using a platform such as jQuery Mobile is that it enables you to focus more on the business logic of the app and less on the UI and general app functionality. For example, jQuery Mobile supports touch events, animated page transitions, back button history support, and theming.

A jQuery Mobile app begins with an `index.html` page. The typical basic structure consists of core elements in the head and page.

Head:

➤ `viewport` meta tag and any other desired tags for mobile app development.

➤ Links to the jQuery Mobile CSS style sheet. This file can be your own maintained version of the style sheet or else just link to the master library on `code.jquery.com`.

➤ Links to the jQuery and jQuery Mobile JavaScript libraries. As with the style sheet, these can be your own files or else just link to the master libraries on `code.jquery.com`.

Body:

➤ One or more `div` elements with a `data-role="page"` attribute to indicate a mobile "page" of the app.

➤ Within each page `div`, there are usually three nested `div` elements:

> ➤ `<div data-role="header">` defines the header.

> ➤ `<div data-role="content">` defines the content section.

> ➤ `<div data-role="footer">` defines the footer.

The following is the basic template:

```
<!DOCTYPE html>
<html>
    <head>
    <title>Page Title</title>

    <meta name="viewport" content="width=device-width, initial-scale=1">

    <link rel="stylesheet"
     href="http://code.jquery.com/mobile/1.0rc2/jquery.mobile-1.0rc2.min.css" />
    <script
        type="text/javascript" src="http://code.jquery.com/jquery-1.6.4.min.js">
        </script>
    <script type="text/javascript"
        src="http://code.jquery.com/mobile/1.0rc2/jquery.mobile-1.0rc2.min.js">
```

```
        </script>
    </head>
    <body>

    <div data-role="page">

        <div data-role="header">
            <h1>Page Title</h1>
        </div><!-- /header -->

        <div data-role="content">
            <p>Page content goes here.</p>
        </div><!-- /content -->

        <div data-role="footer">
            <h4>Page Footer</h4>
        </div><!-- /footer -->
    </div><!-- /page -->

    </body>
    </html>
```

The preceding template is the starting point for most any app, and the following exercise shows you how to transform that template into a basic app.

TRY IT OUT   Creating a Basic jQuery Mobile App

Use the following steps to create a basic app using the jQuery Mobile framework.

1. Create a new blank HTML file in your text editor and save the document as `BIDHJ-Ch16-Ex1.html`.

2. Add the following code the file:

```
<!DOCTYPE html>
<html>
    <head>
    <title>SL Schools</title>

    <meta name="viewport" content="width=device-width, initial-scale=1">

    <link rel="stylesheet"
     href="http://code.jquery.com/mobile/1.0rc2/jquery.mobile-1.0rc2.min.css" />
    <script type="text/javascript"
      src="http://code.jquery.com/jquery-1.6.4.min.js"></script>
    <script type="text/javascript"
      src="http://code.jquery.com/mobile/1.0rc2/jquery.mobile-1.0rc2.min.js">
      </script>
    </head>
    <body>

    <div data-role="page">

        <div data-role="header">
            <h1>SL Schools</h1>
```

```
    </div><!-- /header -->

    <div data-role="content">
    </div><!-- /content -->

    <div data-role="footer">
        <h4>Operation Classroom</h4>
    </div><!-- /footer -->
</div><!-- /page -->

</body>
</html>
```

Code snippet BIDHJ-Ch16-Ex1.html

3. Add the following bulleted list in the content `div`:

```
<ul data-role="listview" data-theme="g">
    <li><a href="#albert">Albert Academy</a></li>
    <li><a href="#baoma">Baoma Secondary School</a></li>
    <li><a href="#bo">Bo Centenary</a></li>
    <li><a href="#fergusson">Fergusson Memorial Secondary School</a></li>
    <li><a href="#koidu">Koidu Secondary School</a></li>
    <li><a href="#taiama">Taiama Secondary School</a></li>
    <li><a href="#makeni">Makeni Secondary School</a></li>
</ul>
```

Code snippet BIDHJ-Ch16-Ex1.html

4. Add the following page `div` code after the first one, but before the closing body tag:

```
<div data-role="page" id="albert">

    <div data-role="header">
        <h1>Albert Academy</h1>
    </div><!-- /header -->

    <div data-role="content">

        <h2>About the School</h2>

        <p>Albert Academy is located on Berry Street in Freetown. The school began
        on October 4, 1904, and was named after American missionary, Rev. Ira E.
        Albert who was killed in a boating accident.  Rev. Albert was from
        Pennsylvania. The school has grown from 6 students to 2000, and currently
        has a staff of 126. Albert Academy is one of the most successful
        institutions of learning in Sierra Leone. Plans are to renovate
        the boarding house into classrooms for the Junior Secondary School.</p>

        <p><img
          src="http://www.gbgm-umc.org/operationclassroom/images/albert.jpg">
        </p>
```

```
<h2>Priorities</h2>
<ul>
    <li>Renovate the boarding school for the Junior Secondary School.
    The boarding home will container 24 classrooms. This will enable
    the school to move to a single shift instead of a double shift and
    will provide more classroom time.  The renvoation cost is $2500
    per room.</li>
    <li>100 scholarships are needed. </li>
</ul>

</div><!-- /content -->

<div data-role="footer">
    <h4>Operation Classroom</h4>
</div><!-- /footer -->
</div><!-- /page -->
```

Code snippet BIDHJ-Ch16-Ex1.html

5. Add a `data-add-back-btn="true"` attribute to the page `div`:

**Available for
download on
Wrox.com**

```
<div data-role="page" id="albert" data-add-back-btn="true">
```

Code snippet BIDHJ-Ch16-Ex1.html

6. Save your file.

How It Works

In this exercise, you learned how to create a basic navigation style app using jQuery Mobile. After creating the basic structure for the main app file, you added content to the home page of the app using a bulleted list. Because the ul list has `data-role="listview"` defined, jQuery Mobiles styles the element as a full side-to-side navigation list. Each `li` item indicates a row in the list and is linked to an internal link, which links the item with another `div` page in the same file. The `id` attribute of the `div` page is the `href` value, prefixed with a #. For example, the `albert div` page is linked using the `#albert` value. The remaining links are not defined for this example, but could be filled out as needed.

The Albert Academy page provides details about the school. Notice that you just need to use basic HTML styles in the content section of the page. Nothing fancy is needed here.

In order to return to the home page of the app, I need to add a Back button on the top toolbar, which is a basic feature of most every iOS app. Back button support is included with jQuery Mobile, but it is not enabled by default. Therefore, to enable the Back button on a toolbar, you need to add the `data-add-back-btn="true"` attribute to the page `div`.

Figures 16-1 and 16-2 show the results.

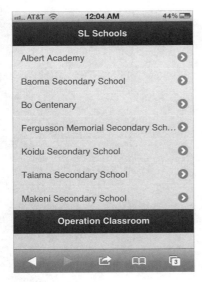

FIGURE 16-1

FIGURE 16-2

Although the look of the app is perfectly acceptable, suppose you want your jQuery Mobile web app to emulate the native look and feel of iOS. Fortunately, there's a Github-based jQuery Mobile theme called iOS-Inspired-jQuery-Mobile-Theme that you can add into your app to make it much more iOS-like.

TRY IT OUT Theming Your jQuery Mobile App

Follow these steps to transform your jQuery Mobile app into a theme that resembles iOS.

1. Go to the following URL:

   `https://github.com/taitems/iOS-Inspired-jQuery-Mobile-Theme`

2. Click the Download button and download a zip file of the theme to your hard drive.

3. Unzip the contents of the zip file.

4. Copy the `ios_inspired` folder to your main app folder.

5. Open the `BIDHJ-Ch16-Ex1.html` file you created in the previous exercise. Save it as `BIDHJ-Ch16-Ex2.html`.

6. Add the following style sheet link below the jQuery Mobile style sheet link:

```
<link rel="stylesheet" href="ios_inspired/styles.css" />
```

Code snippet BIDHJ-Ch16-Ex2.html

7. Save the file.

How It Works

In this exercise, you add a link to the iOS Inspired style sheet, which transforms your jQuery Mobile app into an iOS-looking app. To do so, you download the Github-based style sheet and then link it into your app for usage, adding the entry after the main jQuery Mobile style sheet reference. Figures 16-3 and 16-4 show the updated look.

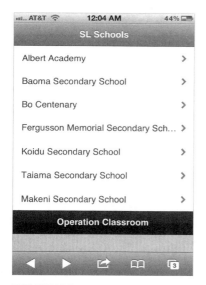

FIGURE 16-3

FIGURE 16-4

USING iWEBKIT

Although jQuery Mobile is designed to provide support to a variety of mobile platforms, iWebKit is a web app framework that is optimized for the iOS platform. Whereas jQuery Mobile provides the basic UI concepts and controls that work well across mobile platforms, iWebKit has support for iOS-specific visual elements, such as different list types as demonstrated in the framework's demo app (see Figures 16-5, 16-6, and 16-7).

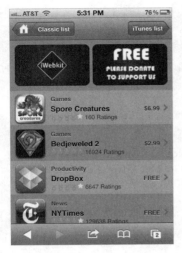

FIGURE 16-5

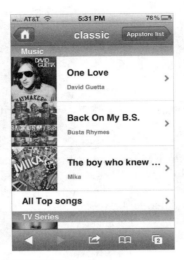

FIGURE 16-6

FIGURE 16-7

An iWebKit web app begins with the following structure.

Head:

➤ `viewport` meta tag and any other desired tags for mobile app development

➤ Links to the iWebKit CSS style sheet inside your folder structure

➤ Links to the iWebKit JavaScript library, also within your folder structure

Body:

➤ `topbar` div to define the top toolbar

➤ `content` div to define the content area

➤ `footer` div to define the page footer

The following is the basic iWebKit template:

```
<!DOCTYPE html PUBLIC "-//W3C//DTD XHTML 1.0 Strict//EN"
    "http://www.w3.org/TR/xhtml1/DTD/xhtml1-strict.dtd">
<html xmlns="http://www.w3.org/1999/xhtml">

<head>
<meta content="yes" name="apple-mobile-web-app-capable" />
<meta content="text/html; charset=utf-8" http-equiv="Content-Type" />
<meta
    content="minimum-scale=1.0,width=device-width, maximum-scale=0.6667,
    user-scalable=no"
    name="viewport" />
<link href="css/style.css" rel="stylesheet" media="screen" type="text/css" />
<script src="javascript/functions.js" type="text/javascript"></script>
<title>Title of your page</title>
```

```
</head>

<body>

<div id="topbar">

</div>
<div id="content">
</div>
<div id="footer">
    <!-- Support iWebKit by sending us traffic; please keep this footer on
     your page, consider it a thank you for my work :-) -->
    <a class="noeffect"
     href="http://snippetspace.com">iPhone site powered by iWebKit</a>
      </div>

</body>

</html>
```

<p><strong>TRY IT OUT</strong>   <strong>Creating a Basic iWebKit App</strong></p>

Using the iWebKit template provided earlier as a starting point, follow the steps to create a basic app using the iWebKit framework.

1. Download the iWebKit framework from http://snippetspace.com/projects/iwebkit.

2. Unzip the contents of the zip file.

3. Copy the Framework folder into your root app folder.

4. Rename the Framework folder to iwebkit.

5. Create a new blank HTML file in your text editor save the document as BIDHJ-Ch16-Ex3.html.

6. Add the following code to the file:

Available for
download on
Wrox.com

```
<!DOCTYPE html PUBLIC "-//W3C//DTD XHTML 1.0 Strict//EN"
    "http://www.w3.org/TR/xhtml1/DTD/xhtml1-strict.dtd">
<html xmlns="http://www.w3.org/1999/xhtml">

<head>
<meta content="yes" name="apple-mobile-web-app-capable" />
<meta content="text/html; charset=utf-8" http-equiv="Content-Type" />
<meta
    content="minimum-scale=1.0, width=device-width, maximum-scale=0.6667,
    user-scalable=no" name="viewport" />
<link href="iwebkit/css/style.css" rel="stylesheet" media="screen"
    type="text/css" />
<script src="iwebkit/javascript/functions.js" type="text/javascript"></script>
<title>Operation Classroom</title>
</head>
<body>
<div id="topbar">

</div-->
```

```
    </div>
<div id="content">
</div>
<div id="footer">
    <!-- Support iWebKit by sending us traffic; please keep this footer
      on your page, consider it a thank you for my work :-) -->
    <a class="noeffect" href="http://snippetspace.com">iPhone site
      powered by iWebKit</a></div>
</body>

</html>
```

Code snippet BIDHJ-Ch16-Ex3.html

7. Add the following code inside the `topbar` div:

Available for
download on
Wrox.com

```
<div id="title">SL Schools</div>
<div id="rightnav"><a href="search.html" >Search</a></div>
```

Code snippet BIDHJ-Ch16-Ex3.html

8. Add the following `ul` list inside the `content` div:

Available for
download on
Wrox.com

```
<ul class="pageitem">
    <li class="menu"><a href="albert.html"><span class="name">Albert Academy</span>
      <span class="arrow"></span></a></li>
    <li class="menu"><a href="baoma.html">
    <span class="name">Baoma Secondary School</span>
      <span class="arrow"></span></a></li>
    <li class="menu"><a href="bo.html">
     <span class="name">Bo Centenary</span><span class="arrow"></span></a></li>
    <li class="menu"><a href="fergusson.html">
      <span class="name">Fergusson Memorial Secondary School</span>
      <span class="arrow"></span></a></li>
    <li class="menu"><a href="koidu.html">
     <span class="name">Koidu Secondary School</span>
     <span class="arrow"></span></a></li>
    <li class="menu"><a href="taiama.html">
     <span class="name">Taiama Secondary School</span>
     <span class="arrow"></span></a></li>
    <li class="menu"><a href="makeni.html">
     <span class="name">Makeni Secondary School</span>
     <span class="arrow"></span></a></li>
</ul>
```

Code snippet BIDHJ-Ch16-Ex3.html

9. Save your main app file.

10. Create a new HTML file and name it `albert.html`. Place it in the same directory as your app.

11. Add the following code into the file:

```
<!DOCTYPE html PUBLIC "-//W3C//DTD XHTML 1.0 Strict//EN"
    "http://www.w3.org/TR/xhtml1/DTD/xhtml1-strict.dtd">
<html xmlns="http://www.w3.org/1999/xhtml">

<head>
<meta content="yes" name="apple-mobile-web-app-capable" />
<meta content="index,follow" name="robots" />
<meta content="text/html; charset=utf-8" http-equiv="Content-Type" />
<meta
    content="minimum-scale=1.0, width=device-width, maximum-scale=0.6667,
        user-scalable=no" name="viewport" />
<link href="iwebkit/css/style.css" rel="stylesheet"
    media="screen" type="text/css" />
<script src="iwebkit/javascript/functions.js" type="text/javascript"></script>
<title>Albert Academy</title>
</head>
<body>
<div id="topbar">
</div>
<div id="content">
</div>
<div id="footer">
    <!-- Support iWebKit by sending us traffic; please keep this footer
    on your page, consider it a thank you for my work :-) -->
    <a class="noeffect" href="http://snippetspace.com">iPhone site
    powered by iWebKit</a></div>

</body>

</html>
```

Code snippet albert.html

12. Add the following code inside the `topbar` div:

```
<div id="title">Albert Academy</div>
<div id="leftnav">
    <a href="BIDHJ-Ch16-Ex3.html">
<img alt="home" src="images/home.png" /></a></div>
```

Code snippet albert.html

13. Add the following code inside the `content` div:

```
<span class="graytitle">About the School</span>
<ul class="pageitem">
    <li class="textbox"><span class="header">Development</span>

    <p>Albert Academy is located on Berry Street in Freetown. The school began
    on October 4, 1904, and was named after American missionary, Rev. Ira E.
    Albert who was killed in a boating accident.  Rev. Albert was from
    Pennsylvania. The school has grown from 6 students to 2000, and currently
    has a staff of 126. Albert Academy is one of the most successful
```

```
        institutions of learning in Sierra Leone. Plans are to renovate
        the boarding house into classrooms for the Junior Secondary School.</p>

        <p>
         <img src="http://www.gbgm-umc.org/operationclassroom/images/albert.jpg">
        </p>

        <li class="textbox"><span class="header">Priorities</span>
            <ul>
                <li>Renovate the boarding school for the Junior Secondary School.
                The boarding home will container 24 classrooms. This will enable
                the school to move to a single shift instead of a double shift
                and will provide more classroom time.  The renvoation cost is
                $2500 per room.</li>
                <li>100 scholarships are needed. </li>
            </ul>
        </li>
    </ul>
```

Code snippet albert.html

14. Save the file.

How It Works

In this exercise, you create the starting point for a basic navigation-style app using iWebKit. You begin by downloading the iWebKit framework and installing it in your application folder. After creating the basic template file for any iWebKit app, you add a title to the top bar and a right button named Search.

The ul list you added serves as the navigation list for the home page. Note that the class="pageitem" attribute is used to indicate that it is a main content area that you'll be filling with content. The pageitem element in your page is considered the most important element in an iWebKit page.

The li items in the bulleted list are defined as list items with the class="menu" attribute. Inside of the links, a span element defines the text to display along with an optional right-align arrow span element.

Notice that the links are to distinct HTML files, not internal links like you defined using jQuery Mobile. Therefore, for a real app, each of these pages that are referenced need to be defined individually, like you do with albert.html.

The albert.html file uses the same general structure as the main app file. You add a back button inside the topbar div using the <div id="leftnav"/> element, which returns the user to the home page.

Inside the content div, the title is defined using a span element. The <ul class="pageitem"/> element contains the text content, which is enclosed in two <li class="text"> elements.

Figures 16-8, 16-9, and 16-10 show the app running in iPhone, and Figure 16-11 shows the app in iPad.

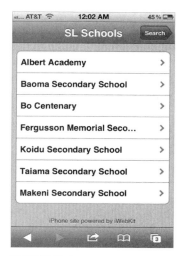

FIGURE 16-8

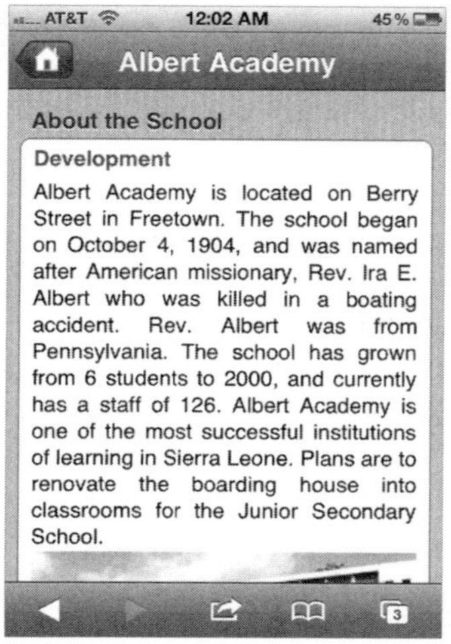

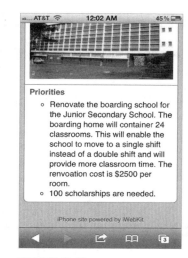

FIGURE 16-9

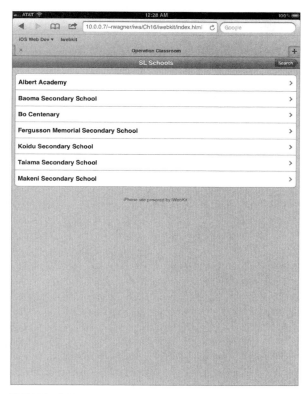

FIGURE 16-10

FIGURE 16-11

EXERCISES

1. Why is cross-platform support an important decision point in terms of which framework you might use?

2. Which of the frameworks enables you to contain multiple pages inside the same HTML file?

Answers to the Exercises can be found in the Appendix.

▶ WHAT YOU LEARNED IN THIS CHAPTER

TOPIC	KEY CONCEPTS
Features of jQuery Mobile	Cross-platform support for iOS, Android, BlackBerry, Windows Phone 7, and more
	Built-in support for touch events, page transitions, back button support, and theming
Features of iWebKit	Dedicated to iOS look and feel
	Support for native-looking UI elements, such as App Store- and iTunes-like lists

17

Bandwidth and Performance Optimizations

WHAT YOU WILL LEARN IN THIS CHAPTER:

➤ Shrinking the size of the assets of your app

➤ Optimizing performance of your JavaScript

➤ Writing efficient code

In a decade where broadband is now the norm, many web developers have allowed their sites and applications to be composed of ill-formed HTML, massive JavaScript libraries, and multiple CSS style sheets.

However, when you are developing applications for iPhone, iPad, and iPod touch, you need to refocus your programming and development efforts toward optimization and efficiency. What makes developing iOS apps different from normal web apps is that the developer can no longer rely on the fact that the user is accessing the application from a broadband connection. iPhone and iPad users may be coming to your application using Wi-Fi or a slower 3G connection.

Therefore, as you develop your applications, you should formulate an optimization strategy that makes the most sense for your context. You need to think about both bandwidth and code performance optimizations.

OPTIMIZATION STRATEGIES

If you spend much time at all researching optimization strategy and techniques, you quickly discover that there are two main schools of thought. I refer to the first camp as *hyper-optimizers*. Hyper-optimizers do almost anything to save a byte or an unneeded call to the web server. They are far more concerned with saving milliseconds than they are about the readability of the code that they are optimizing. The second camp, perhaps best described as *relaxed optimizers,* are interested in optimizing their applications. But they are not interested in sacrificing code readability and manageability in an effort to save a nanosecond here or there.

Decide which camp you fall into. Be careful that don't go through complex optimization hoops unless you are able to prove that your steps are going to make a substantive difference in the usability of your application. Many optimization techniques that people advocate offer nominal performance boosts, but end up making your code much harder to work with and maintain.

BEST PRACTICES TO MINIMIZE BANDWIDTH

Arguably the greatest bottleneck of any iOS web app is the time it takes to transport data from the web server to Safari, especially if your application is running over 3G. You can certainly opt for local offline caching. However, you should also consider the following techniques as you assemble your web application.

General

Consider the following general tips as you develop web apps for iOS as well as mobile-friendly web sites.

➤ Separate your page content into separate .css, .js, and .html files so that Safari on iOS can cache each file.

➤ Studies show that loading additional files takes 60% to 90% of the total load time of a web page. Therefore, be sure to minimize the total number of external style sheets, JavaScript library files, and images you include with your page. Because browsers typically make two to four requests at a given time, every additional file that a browser has to wait on for the request to complete creates latency.

➤ Reduce white space (tabs and spaces) wherever possible. Although this might seem like a nominal issue, the amount of excess white space can add up, particularly on a larger-scale web application with dozens of files.

➤ Remove useless tags and unused styles and JavaScript functions in your HTML, CSS style sheets, and JavaScript library files.

➤ Remove unnecessary comments. However, keep in mind the following caveat: Removing comments can reduce file size, but it can make it harder to manage your code in the future.

➤ Use shorter filenames. For example, it is much more efficient to reference tb2.png than TopBannerAlternate2_980.png.

➤ Write well-formed and XML-complaint XHTML code. Although this is not a bandwidth issue, well-formed XHTML requires fewer passes and parsing by Safari before it renders the page. As a result, you can improve the time from initial request to final display through this coding practice.

➤ Consider using gzip compression when you serve your application. (See the following section for more on compression options.)

➤ Consider using a JavaScript compressor on your JavaScript libraries. You could then work with a normal, unoptimized JavaScript library for development (mylibrary.js) and then output a compressed version for runtime purposes (mylibrary-c.js). (See the "Compressing Your Application" section for more on compression options.)

Images

Images can often be the single greatest bottleneck for performance in many web apps. Pay attention to the following tips to optimize how you use images in your app.

➤ Large image sizes are a traditional bottleneck that you should target for your applications. Be meticulous in optimizing the file size of your images. Shaving off 5KB or so from several images in your application can make a notable performance increase.

➤ Make sure your images are sized appropriately for display on the iPhone, iPad, and iPod touch viewports. Never, ever, rely on browser scaling. Instead, match image size to image presentation.

➤ Image data is more expensive than text data. Therefore, consider using canvas drawing in certain cases.

➤ Instead of using image borders, consider using CSS borders instead, particularly with the enhanced -webkit-border-radius property.

➤ Instead of using one large background image, consider using a small image and tiling it.

➤ Use CSS Sprites to combine multiple image files into a larger one. The overall latency impact is reduced because fewer requests are made to the server.

CSS and JavaScript

The manner in which you structure your CSS style sheets and JavaScript code can impact performance. Consider these tips to optimize an often-overlooked area of your code.

➤ Combine rules to create more efficient style declarations. For example, the second declaration is much more space efficient than the first one:

```
// Less efficient
div #content {
        font-family: Helvetica, Arial, sans-serif;
        font-size: 12px; /* Randy: do we want this as px or pt? */
        line-height: 1.2em; /* Let's try this for now.*/
        font-weight: bold;
}
// More efficient
div #content {font: bold 12px/1.2em Helvetica, Arial, sans-serif};
```

➤ Consider using shorter CSS style names and JavaScript variable and function names. After all, the longer your identifiers are, the more space your files take. At the same time, do not make your identifiers so short that they become hard to work with. For example, consider the trade-offs with the following three declarations:

```
/* Inefficient */
#homepage-blog-subtitle-alternate-version{letter-spacing:.1em;}
/* Efficient, but cryptic */
#hbsa{letter-spacing:.1em;}
/* Happy medium */
#blog-subtitle-alt{letter-spacing:.1em;}
```

As you work through these various strategies and test results, a good way to check the total page size is to save the page as a web archive in a desktop version of Safari. The file size of the archive file indicates the HTML page size with all the external resources (images, style sheets, and script libraries) associated with it.

COMPRESSING YOUR APPLICATION

Normally, an iOS web application is launched when a user types the URL in his Safari browser (or clicks its shortcut icon on the home screen). The web server responds to the HTTP request and serves the HTML file and each of the many supporting files that are used in the display and execution of the web app. Although you might have image files optimized as much as possible to minimize bandwidth, each uncompressed HTML file, CSS style sheet, and JavaScript library file requested always takes up much more space than if it were compressed. Therefore, several options are available to compress files or JavaScript code on the fly on the server.

Gzip File Compression

Safari on iOS provides support for gzip compression, a compression option offered by many web servers. Using gzip compression, you can reduce the size of HTML, CSS, and JavaScript files and reduce the total download size by up to four to five times. However, because Safari must uncompress the resources when it receives them, be sure to test to ensure that this overhead does not eliminate the benefits gained.

For example, if you want to turn on gzip compression in PHP, you could use the following code:

```
<?php
ob_start("ob_gzhandler");
?>
<html>
<body>
<p>This page has been compressed.</p>
</body>
</html>
```

JavaScript Code Compression

In addition to reducing the total file size of your website, another technique is to focus on JavaScript code. These compression strategies go far beyond the manual coding techniques described in this chapter and seek to compress and *minify* — remove all unnecessary characters — your JavaScript code. In fact, using these automated solutions, you can potentially reduce the size of your scripts by 30% to 40%.

There are a variety of open-source solutions for compressing JavaScript code, and they tend to take one of two approaches. The *safe optimizers* remove whitespace and comments from code but do not seek to actually change naming inside of your source code. The *aggressive optimizers* go a step further and seek to crunch variable and function names. Although the aggressive optimizers achieve greater compression ratios, they are not as safe to use in certain situations. For example, if you have eval() or with in your code (even though they're not recommended), these routines will be broken during the compression process. What's more, some of the optimizers, such as Packer, use an eval-based approach to compress and uncompress. However, there is a performance hit in the uncompression process, and in certain conditions your script could be slowed down.

Here are some of the options available (ranked in order of conservatism employed in their algorithms):

➤ JSMin (JavaScript Minifier — www.crockford.com/javascript/jsmin.html) is perhaps the best-known JavaScript optimizer. It is the most conservative of the optimizers, focusing on simply removing whitespace and comments from JavaScript code.

➤ YUI Compressor (www.julienlecomte.net/blog/2007/08/13/introducing-the-yui-compressor) is a recently introduced optimizer that claims to offer a happy medium between the conservative JSMin and the more aggressive ShrinkSafe and Packer.

➤ Dojo ShrinkSafe (www.dojotoolkit.org/docs/shrinksafe) optimizes and crunches local variable names to achieve greater compression ratios.

➤ Dean Edwards's Packer (dean.edwards.name/packer) is an aggressive optimizer that achieves high compression ratios.

Deciding which of these options to use depends on your specific needs and the nature of your source code. I recommend starting on the safe side and moving up as needed.

If you decide to use one of these optimizers, make sure you use semicolons to end your lines in your source code. Besides being good programming practice, most optimizers need them to accurately remove excess whitespace.

Although Packer requires semicolons, Dojo ShrinkSafe does not require them and actually inserts missing semicolons for you. So you can preprocess a JavaScript file through ShrinkSafe before using it in a compressor that requires semicolons such as Packer.

To demonstrate the compression ratios that you can achieve, I ran a sample JavaScript library file through several of these optimizing tools. Table 17-1 includes the results.

TABLE 17-1: Benchmark of JavaScript Library Compression

COMPRESSOR	JAVASCRIPT COMPRESSION (BYTES)	WITH GZIP COMPRESSION (BYTES)
No compression	100% (11284)	26% (2879)
JSMin	65% (7326)	21% (2403)
Dojo ShrinkSafe	58% (6594)	21% (2349)
YUI Compressor	64% (7211)	21% (2377)
YUI Compressor (with Munged)	46% (5199)	18% (2012)
YUI Compressor (with Preserve All Semicolons)	64% (7277)	21% (2389)
YUI Compressor (with Munged and Preserve All Semicolons)	47% (5265)	18% (2020)

One final option worth considering is a PHP-based open-source project called Minify. Minify combines, minifies, and caches JavaScript and CSS files to decrease the number of page requests that a page has to make. To do so, it combines multiple style sheets and script libraries into a single download (`code.google.com/p/minify`).

JAVASCRIPT PERFORMANCE OPTIMIZATIONS

The performance of JavaScript on iOS is slower than on the Safari desktop counterparts, although recent improvements in the iOS shrink this gap considerably. For example, consider the following simple DOM-access performance test:

```
<!DOCTYPE html PUBLIC "-//W3C//DTD XHTML 1.0 Strict//EN"
        "http://www.w3.org/TR/xhtml1/DTD/xhtml1-strict.dtd">
<html xmlns="http://www.w3.org/1999/xhtml">
<head>
<title>Performance Test</title>
</head>
<body>
<form id="form1">
<input id="i1" value="zero" type="text">
</form>
<div id="output"></div>
</body>
<script type="application/x-javascript">
var i = 0;
var start1 = new Date().getTime();
divs = document.getElementsByTagName('div');
for(i = 0; i < 80000; i++)
```

```
{
        var d = divs[0];
}
var start2 = new Date().getTime();
var delta1 = start2 - start1;
document.getElementById("output").innerHTML = "Time: " + delta1;
</script>
</html>
```

Safari for Mac OS X executes this script in 529 milliseconds, while Safari for iOS takes 13,922 milliseconds. That's more than 26 times longer! Therefore, in addition to the optimizations you can make in shrinking the overall file size of your application, you should also give priority to making performance gains in execution based on your coding techniques. The following sections cover several best practices you should consider.

Smart DOM Access

When working with client-side JavaScript, accessing the DOM can be at the heart of almost anything you do. However, as essential as these DOM calls may be, it is important to remember that DOM access is expensive from a performance standpoint and so should be done with forethought.

Cache DOM References

Cache references that you make to avoid multiple lookups on the same object or property. For example, compare the following inefficient and efficient routines:

```
// Ineffecient
var str = document.createTextNode("Farther up, further in");
document.getElementById("para1").appendChild(str);
document.getElementById("para1").className="special";
// More efficient
var str = document.createTextNode("Farther up, further in");
var p = document.getElementById("para1");
p.appendChild(str);
p.className="special";
```

What's more, if you make a sizeable number of references to a document or another common DOM object, cache them, too. For example, compare the following:

```
// Less efficient
var l1=document.createTextNode('Line 1');
var l2=document.createTextNode('Line 2');
// More efficient
var d=document;
var l1=d.createTextNode('Line 1');
var l2=d.createTextNode('Line 2');
```

If you reference document a handful of times then it is probably not practical to go through this trouble. However, if you find yourself writing document a thousand times in your code, the efficiency gains make this practice worth considering.

Offline DOM Manipulation

When you are writing to the DOM, assemble your subtree of nodes outside of the actual DOM and then insert the subtree once at the end of the process. For example, consider the following:

```
var comments=customBlog.getComments('index');
var c=comments.count;
var entry;
var commentDiv = document.createElement('div');
document.body.appendChild(commentDiv);
for (var i=0;i<c;i++) {
  entry=document.createElement('p');
  entry.appendChild( document.createTextNode(comments[i]);
  commentDiv.appendChild( entry );
}
```

Consider the placement of the `document.body.appendChild()` method in the code. Because you add the new `div` element to the DOM before you add children to it, the document must be updated for each new paragraph added. However, you can speed up the routine considerably by moving the offending line to the end:

```
var comments=customBlog.getComments('index');
var c=comments.count;
var entry;
var commentDiv = document.createElement('div');
for (var i=0;i<c;i++) {
  entry=document.createElement('p');
  entry.appendChild( document.createTextNode(comments[i]);
  commentDiv.appendChild( entry );
}
document.body.appendChild(commentDiv);
```

With the restructured code, the document display only needs to be updated once instead of multiple times.

Combining document.write() Calls

Along the same line, you should avoid excessive `document.write()` calls. Each call is a performance hit. Therefore, a much better practice is to assemble a concatenated string variable first. For example, compare the following:

```
// Inefficient
document.write('<div class="row">');
document.write('<label class="cui">office</label>');
document.write('<a class="cuiServiceLink"
    target="_self" href="tel:(765) 555-1212">(765) 555-1212</a>');
document.write('</div>');
// More efficient
var s = '<div class="row">' + '<label class="cui">office</label>' +
'<a class="cuiServiceLink"
    target="_self" href="tel:(765) 555-1212">(765) 555-1212</a>' + '</div>';
document.write(s);
```

Using the Window Object

The window object is faster to use because Safari does not have to navigate the DOM to respond to your call. The last window reference in the following example is more efficient than the first three:

```
// Inefficient
var h=document.location.href;
var h=document.URL;
var h=location.href;
// More efficient
var h=window.location.href
```

LOCAL AND GLOBAL VARIABLES

One of the most important practices JavaScript coders should implement in their code is to use local variables and avoid global variables. When Safari processes a script, local variables are always looked for first in the local scope. If it can't find a match, then it moves up the next level, and the next, and so on, until it hits the global scope. Consequently, global variables are the slowest in a lookup. For example, defining variable a at the global level in the following code is much more expensive than defining it as a local variable inside the for routine:

```
// Inefficient
var a=1;
function myFunction(){
  for(var i=0;i<10;i++) {
    var t = a+i;
    // do something with t
  }
}
//More efficient
function myFunction(){
  for(var i=0,a=1;i<10;i++) {
    var t = a+i;
    // do something with t
  }
}
```

DOT NOTATION AND PROPERTY LOOKUPS

Accessing objects and properties by dot notation is never efficient. Therefore, consider some alternatives.

Avoiding Nested Properties

Aim to keep the levels of dot hierarchy small. Nested properties, such as document.property .property.property, cause the biggest performance problems and you should avoid them or access them as few times as possible.

```
// Inefficient
m.n.o.p.doThis();
```

```
m.n.o.p.doThat();
// More efficient
var d = m.n.o.p;
d.doThis();
d.doThat();
```

Accessing a Named Object

If you access a named object, it is more efficient to use `getElementById()` rather than access it via dot notation. For example, compare the following:

```
// Inefficient
document.form1.addressLine1.value
// More efficient
document.getElementById( 'addressLine1' ).value;
```

Property Lookups Inside Loops

When accessing a property inside a loop, it is much better practice to cache the property reference first, and then access the variable inside the loop. For example, compare the following:

```
// Inefficient
for(i = 0; i <10; i++) {
var v = document.object.property(i);
var y = myCustonObject.property(i);
// do something
}
// More efficient
var p = document.object.property;
var cp = myCustonObject.property(i);
for(i = 0; i <10; i++) {
var v= p(i);
var y=cp(i);
// do something
}
```

Here's another example of using the `length` property of an object in the condition of a `for` loop:

```
// Inefficient
for (i=0;i<myObject.length;i++) {
  // Do something
}
// More efficient
for (i=0,var j=myObject.length;i<j;i++) {
  // Do something
}
```

Similarly, if you are using arrays inside loops and using the `length` of the array as a conditional, you want to assign its length to a variable rather than evaluating at each pass. Check this out:

```
// Inefficient
myArray = new Array();
```

```
for (i=0;i<myArray.length;i++) {
  // Do something
}
// More efficient
myArray = new Array();
len = myArray.length;
for (i=0;i<len;i++) {
  // Do something
}
```

String Concatenation

Another traditional problem area in JavaScript is string concatenation. In general, you should try to avoid an excessive number of concatenations and an excessively large string that you are appending to. For example, suppose you are trying to construct a table in code and then write out the code to the document after you are finished. The stringTable() function in the following code is less efficient than the second function intermStringTable() because the latter uses an intermediate string variable row as a buffer in the for loop.

```
<html>
<script type="text/javascript" language="javascript">
function stringTable() {
  var start = new Date().getTime();
  var buf = "<table>";
  for (var i=0; i<10000;i++){
    buf += "<tr>";
    for (var j=0;j<40;j++){
      buf += "<td><i>" + "content" + "</i></td>";
    }
    buf += "</tr>";
  }
  buf += "</table>";
  var duration = new Date().getTime() - start;
  document.write( 'String concat method: ' + duration + '</br>');
}
function intermStringTable(){
  var start = new Date().getTime();
  var buf = "<table>";
  for (var i=0; i<10000;i++){
    var row = "<tr>";
    for (var j=0;j<40;j++){
      row += "<td><i>" + "content" + "</i></td>";
    }
    row += "</tr>";
    buf += row
  }
  buf += "</table>";
  var duration = new Date().getTime() - start;
  document.write('Intermediate concat method: ' + duration + '</br>');
}
</script>
<body>
```

```
</body>
<script type="text/javascript" language="javascript">
stringTable();
intermStringTable();
</script>
</html>
```

WHAT TO DO AND NOT TO DO

You want to be sure to avoid `with` statements, which slow down the processing of the related code block. In addition to the fact that `with` is inefficient, it has also been deprecated in the JavaScript standard. Second, avoid using `eval()` in your scripts. It is very expensive from a performance standpoint. Besides, you should be able to develop a more efficient solution rather than resorting to `eval()`.

Comments add to readability and manageability, but be wise in using them. For example, use them minimally inside loop routines, functions, and arrays. Instead, place comments before or after a look structure to ensure greater efficiency.

```
// Inefficient
var a=0,c=100;
for (var i=0;i<c;i++) {
  // Assign d the value of the next div in the current document
  var d = document.getElementByTagName('div')[i];
  // Perform some math for a
  a=i*1.2;
  // Perform some math for b
  b=(a+i)/3;
}
// More efficient
// Assign val of d to 100 divs and perform y on them
// based on val of a and b.
var a=0,c=100;
for (var i=0;i<c;i++) {
  var d = document.getElementByTagName('div')[i];
  a=i*1.2;
  b=(a+i)/3;
}
```

EXERCISES

1. Is it important to minimize the number of external files you reference in your web app?

2. Does length of CSS style names and JavaScript variables make much of a difference?

3. Is it more efficient to reference an element in your JavaScript code using dot notation or `getElementById()`?

Answers to the Exercises can be found in Appendix A.

▶ WHAT YOU LEARNED IN THIS CHAPTER

TOPIC	KEY CONCEPTS
Minimizing bandwidth	Minimize the number of external files
	Remove content that doesn't need to be in your files (comments, extra white space, unused code/styles)
	Shrink your images as much as possible without degrading image quality
Compressing your application	Compress your JavaScript code using a compression library
Optimize JavaScript code	Avoid nesting objects
	Use `getElementById()` instead of dot notation
	Limit the number of strings you concatenate

18

Debug and Deploy

Get in, get out. That's the attitude that most developers have in testing and debugging their applications. Few developers look forward to these tasks during the development cycle, and so they want to efficiently get into the code, figure out what's working and what's not, fix any problems, and then move on.

Given the heterogeneous nature of web apps, debugging has always been challenging, particularly when trying to work with client-side JavaScript. To address this need, fairly sophisticated debugging tools have emerged over the past few years among the developer community, most notably Firebug and other add-ons to Firefox. However, the problem is that most of these testing tools that web developers have come to rely on for desktop browsers are not ideal for testing iOS web apps.

Many iOS web app developers, unsure of where else to turn, might be tempted to resort to `alert()` debugging — you know, adding `alert()` throughout the body of the script code to determine programmatic flow and variable values. However, not only is this type of debugging painful, but it can also throw off the timing of your script, making it difficult or impossible to simulate real-world results. Therefore, in this chapter, I walk you through the various debugging options you have that either work on your desktop or directly on your iOS device. You will probably want to incorporate aspects of both as part of your regular debugging and testing process.

SIMULATING THE IPHONE OR IPAD ON YOUR DEVELOPMENT COMPUTER

Because you are coding your iOS web app on a desktop computer, you'll find it helpful to also be able to perform initial testing on the desktop as well. To do so, you need to create a test browser environment that is as close as possible to the iPhone or iPad. iOS device emulation enables you to more easily design and tweak the UI (user interface) as well as test to see how your web application or site responds when it identifies the browser as Safari on iOS.

If you are running Mac OS X, you're in luck as you have the best option — Xcode's iOS Simulator and Safari. However, if you are developing on Windows, your only real desktop-based option is Safari.

Xcode's iOS Simulator

Your best option for simulating an iPhone or iPad on your desktop is to use the iOS Simulator that is included with Xcode, the development environment used to create native iOS apps. (See Chapter 19 for details on downloading Xcode.) Not only does the iOS Simulator simulate the iPhone or iPad for testing native apps, but it also has a built-in Safari browser (see Figure 18-1) that simulates the functionality of Safari on iOS.

You can launch the iOS Simulator from within Xcode, but if you are not an Objective-C developer, you may not want to launch the Xcode

FIGURE 18-1

IDE each time you want to debug your app. Because you won't find an icon for the iOS Simulator in your Applications folder, here's how to get quick access to it:

1. From the Finder window, choose Go from the menu and then choose Go to Folder.

2. In the Go to the Folder dialog box, navigate to the following path: `/Developer/ Platforms/iPhoneSimulator.platform/Developer/Applications/IOS Simulator`

3. Click the iPhone Simulator icon.

4. After the iOS Simulator launches, I recommend moving its Dock icon to the left to keep it on your Dock and make it easy to access.

To use the iOS Simulator for viewing a web app, simply click the Safari icon with your mouse. You can load your app from a bookmark or type a URL in the Address box. Figure 18-2 shows a Web app displayed in the iOS Simulator.

FIGURE 18-2

The iOS Simulator is actually quite powerful. Not only do the controls inside of the Safari browser work as expected, but you can also determine which device to emulate as well as simulate rotation from the Rotate Left and Rotate Right items on the Hardware menu (see Figure 18-3). You can then test your app in landscape mode (see Figure 18-4).

FIGURE 18-3

FIGURE 18-4

Using Safari on Mac or Windows

Because Safari on iOS is closely related to its Mac and Windows desktop counterparts, you can also perform initial testing and debugging right on your desktop. However, before doing so, you need to turn Safari into an iOS simulator by performing two actions — changing the user agent string and resizing the browser window.

Changing Safari's User Agent String

Safari on Mac and Windows enables you to set the user agent provided by the browser through the User Agent list, which you access from the Develop menu.

If you don't have the Develop menu available from the top menu bar, go to the Preferences dialog box and click the Advanced button. You see a checkbox there to enable the Develop menu (see Figure 18-5).

FIGURE 18-5

With the Develop menu enabled, choose the desired iOS user agent string you want to emulate in from the User Agent menu, as shown in Figure 18-6.

FIGURE 18-6

After you have selected an iPhone, iPad, or iPod touch user agent, the desktop version of Safari appears to your web app as Safari on iPhone.

Changing the Window Size

To get the same viewport dimensions in Safari, you need to create a bookmarklet (see Chapter 15) and then add it to your Bookmarks bar. The code for the bookmarklet is as follows for iPhone:

```
javascript:window.resizeTo(320,480) // For iPhone/iPod touch
```

For iPad, use the following:

```
javascript:window.resizeTo(480,640) // For iPad
```

WORKING WITH DESKTOP SAFARI DEBUGGING TOOLS

For years, Firefox was considered the browser of choice for web application developers because of its support for third-party tools and add-ons, such as Firebug. However, when creating an application specifically for iOS, you usually want to work with Safari-specific tools. Fortunately, because Safari on iOS is so closely related to the newer desktop versions of Safari, you can take advantage of the debugging tools that are provided with Safari on Mac and Windows. Because you are working with a close relative to Safari on iOS, you still need to perform a second round of testing and debugging on an iOS device, but these tools help you during initial testing of your code.

Working with the Develop Menu

The Safari debug tools are accessible through the Develop menu, which is hidden by default when you install Safari. (As I mentioned in the last section, you can enable it from Advanced section of the Preferences dialog box.)

Many of the menu items in the Develop menu are not relevant to iPhone web app development, but a few are worth mentioning (see Table 18-1).

TABLE 18-1: Useful Safari Develop Commands for the iPhone Web App Developer

NAME	DESCRIPTION
User Agent	Make your browser appear to your app as Safari on iPhone, iPod touch, or iPad
Show Web Inspector	View and search the DOM and styles
Show Error Console	View error and status info in the Web Inspector
Show Snippet Editor	Get instant rendering of an HTML snippet
Log JavaScript Exceptions	Turn on to log exceptions
Show JavaScript Console	View JavaScript errors occurring on a page
Enable Runaway JavaScript Timer	Toggle the timer that halts long-running scripts

The two Safari developer features worth special attention for your needs are the Web Inspector and JavaScript Console.

Working with Safari's Web Inspector

The best debugging feature available in Safari is certainly the Web Inspector. The Web Inspector, shown in Figure 18-7, enables you to browse and inspect the DOM of the current web page. You can access this feature through the Develop menu. However, the handiest way to use it is to right-click an element in your document and choose the Inspect Element menu item. The Web Inspector is displayed, showing the element in the context that you selected in the browser window.

FIGURE 18-7

Here are the basic functions of the Web Inspector:

➤ **Selecting a node to view:** When you click on a node in the inspector pane, two things happen. First, the bottom pane displays node and attribute details, style hierarchy, style metrics, and property values. Second, if the selected node is a visible element in the browser window, the selected block is highlighted with a red border in Safari.

➤ **Changing the root:** To avoid messing with a massive nested DOM hierarchy, you can change the context of the Web Inspector. Double-clicking a node makes it the hierarchical "root" in the inspector pane. Later, if you want to move back up the document hierarchy, use the up arrow or the drop-down combo box.

➤ **Searching the DOM:** You can use the Search box to look for any node of the DOM — element names, node attributes, even content. Results of the search are shown in the inspector pane, displaying the line on which a match was found. If you want to get a better idea of the exact node you are working with, select it and then look for the red outlined box in the Safari window.

➤ **Viewing node details:** The Node pane provides basic node information, including type, name, namespace, and attribute details.

➤ **Viewing CSS properties:** The Styles pane displays CSS rules that are applied to the selected node. It shows the computed style of the selected element by showing you all of the declarations that are used in determining the final style rendering. The rules are lists in cascade order. Any properties that have been overridden are displayed with strikethrough text.

➤ **Viewing style metrics:** The Metrics pane displays the current element as a rectangular block displaying the width × height dimensions, as well as the padding and margin settings (see Figure 18-8).

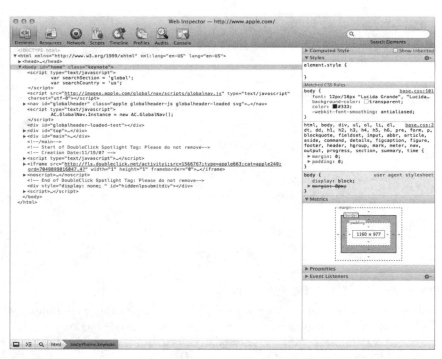

FIGURE 18-8

➤ **Viewing all properties:** The Properties pane displays all of the DOM properties (such as id and innerHTML) for the selected node. Because you cannot drill down on object types, this pane is less useful than the others.

Working with the Scripts Inspector

The Web Inspector also sports a powerful Scripts Inspector, as shown in Figure 18-9. You can use it to inspect variables at point of execution, set breakpoints, step through your code, and view the call stack.

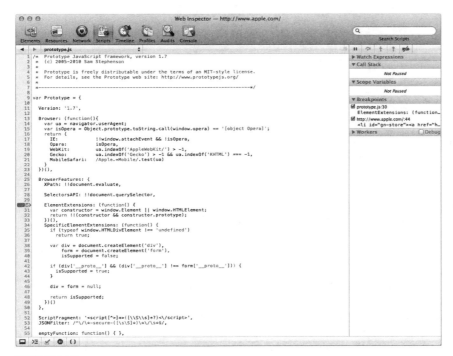

FIGURE 18-9

There are several tasks you can perform in the Script Inspector:

➤ **Setting breakpoints and stepping through code:** You can set a breakpoint in your code by clicking the line number on the left margin of the code window. As Figure 18-10 shows, an arrow is displayed on the breakpoint line. When the line code is executed, then the breakpoint is triggered. You can then step through the script as desired by clicking the Step Into, Step Out, and Step Over buttons. As you step through the code, Script Inspector updates its state for each line executed.

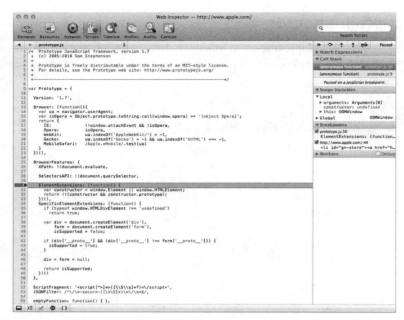

FIGURE 18-10

➤ **Inspecting variables:** The Scope Variables box at the top of the Script Inspector window displays the variables in scope (local, closure, global). You can inspect these variables by right-clicking them and choosing Inspect Element. A new Web Inspector window is displayed on top of the existing window showing the node in its hierarchy along with style, metric, and property details. Close the Web Inspector window to return to the current debugging session.

Although Script Inspector does not work directly with Safari on iOS, it does serve as the most powerful debugging option that iOS web app developers have in their toolkit.

DEBUGGING ON AN IOS DEVICE

So far, you've seen how to test and debug your iOS web apps on your desktop using desktop-based solutions. Although those tools are good for general testing or specific problem-solving, you need to spend some time debugging directly on iOS devices themselves. Unfortunately, no robust debugging tools such as Web Inspector are available, but there are some basic debugging tools that should be a standard part of your Safari on iOS development toolkit.

Debug Console

Safari on iOS includes an integrated Debug Console. If active, the Debug Console displays below the URL bar when an error is encountered or when it has a recommended tip (see Figure 18-11). You can click the right arrow to display a list of console messages (see Figure 18-12). You can filter the errors by JavaScript, HTML, or CSS.

FIGURE 18-11

FIGURE 18-12

You can enable the Debug Console from Settings ➡ Safari ➡ Developer. Inside this menu screen, you can turn on the Debug Console (see Figure 18-13).

DOM Viewer

The DOM Viewer, available from `brainjar.com`, is a web-based DOM viewer that you can work with directly inside of Safari on iOS. The DOM Viewer provides an expandable tree structure that lists all of the properties of a given node. When a property of a node is another node, then you can view its properties by clicking its name. The tree expands to show these details. The DOM Viewer is housed in a separate HTML page that is launched in a separate window from the original page.

Although DOM Viewer does not have the robust capabilities of the desktop Safari's Web Inspector, it does have the assurance that all of the information you are looking at comes directly from Safari on iOS, not its desktop cousin.

FIGURE 18-13

TRY IT OUT   Using the DOM Viewer

To use DOM Viewer, follow these steps:

1. Download the source file at `http://brainjar.com/dhtml/domviewer/domviewer.html`.

2. Save the file in the same directory as your application.

3. Open a page in your app and add a script to the end of your HTML page that you want to inspect:

```
<script type="application/x-javascript">
window.open('domviewer.html');
</script>
```

4. Save the file.

5. Open the page inside Safari. If needed, click the View in DOM Viewer link.

How It Works

The DOM Viewer analyzes the DOM of the current document and displays the full document tree in a new tab inside Safari, as shown in Figure 18-14. You can view DOM node info and interact with it as desired to find the runtime details to track down bugs or missing functionality.

FIGURE 18-14

Specifying a Root Node

One of the things you immediately notice when working with the DOM Viewer inside of the small viewport of the iPhone or iPad is the sheer amount of information you have to scroll through to find what you are looking for. To address this issue, DOM Viewer enables you to specify a particular node (identified by id) as the document root. Here's the code to add that specifies the desired element as the getElementById() parameter:

```
<script type="application/x-javascript">
  var DOMViewerObj = document.getElementById("Jack_Armitage")
  var DOMViewerName = null;
</script>
```

Because it will reference the desired element directly by `getElementById()`, you can add this code in your HTML page *after* the element you want to examine in the body but not before it.

Go to `http://brainjar.com/dhtml/domviewer` for full details on the DOM Viewer.

EXERCISES

1. What is `alert()` debugging, and what are its shortcomings?

2. Help! I want to use Safari's developer tools on my Mac or Windows computer, but there's no Develop menu. What do I do?

3. How can you get debug info on your iOS device?

Answers to the Exercises can be found in Appendix A.

▶ **WHAT YOU LEARNED IN THIS CHAPTER**

TOPIC	KEY CONCEPTS
Preview and interact with your iOS web apps on your Mac computer	Use the Safari app that runs inside Xcode's iOS Simulator
Inspecting a page's DOM and styles	Use the Web Inspector, built into Safari on Mac or Windows
Debug on an iOS Device	Enable the Debug Console in Settings ➪ Safari ➪ Developer

PART V
Next Steps: Developing Native iOS Applications with HTML and JavaScript

19

Preparing for Native iOS Development

Although iOS web apps can perform and even look similar to native apps, many mobile web developers still want to package their web apps inside a native iOS app shell for one reason: real estate in terms of a place in the App Store and a place on the Home screen of the device.

In Chapter 20, I show you how you can transform your web app into a native app without learning a line of Objective-C. However, before doing so, you first need to get the preliminaries out of the way. In order to develop native iOS apps, you need to join the iOS Developer Program and get credentials that you use to install apps on an iOS device. In this chapter, I walk you through all of these initial details.

 NOTE *Although you can develop web apps on a Mac, Windows, or Linux machine, native iOS development is not so platform neutral. You must have a Mac computer in order to build iOS apps.*

DOWNLOADING XCODE

Xcode is the integrated development environment (IDE) for creating native iOS and Mac apps written in Objective-C. Now, before you get queasy thinking about being talked into the idea of programming in Objective-C, don't sweat. Although you need to utilize Xcode to wrap your web apps inside a native wrapper, you don't need to learn Objective-C. I promise!

Xcode is a free download from the Mac App Store. If you can't find it, just search for Xcode and it will be the first app in your search result list.

Figure 19-1 shows Xcode after it has been downloaded and installed onto your machine.

FIGURE 19-1

JOINING THE IOS DEVELOPER PROGRAM

The gateway to native iOS development begins with a membership in the Apple Developer Program. There are two levels: the Standard Program ($99 annually) and the Enterprise Program for developers at companies with more than 500 employees ($299 annually).

The upside to the program is that it enables you to publish apps on the App Store. The downside is that many of the benefits of the Apple Developer Program are specifically for the Objective-C developer, so they are less relevant to you as a web developer.

To join the Apple Developer Program, go to `http://developer.apple.com/programs/ios`. This page is your starting point for registering for and purchasing the program. Click the Enroll Now button to begin.

Complete the steps of enrollment to purchase the Developer Program of your choice. Once you purchased a membership in the Developer Program, you have to be approved by Apple before your developer certificate is awarded. If you're an individual developer, the response time may be only a few hours. If you're a corporation, then it may take a few days before the process is completed.

GETTING AN IOS DEVELOPER CERTIFICATE

After you have been accepted into the iOS Developer Program, you can log in to the iOS Dev Center and download your developer certificate, which is required before you can install native apps onto an iOS device. This certificate links your identity to the validated contact address that you provided to Apple when you registered. You use the developer certificate during testing and debugging and a separate distribution certificate when you submit your app to the App Store.

TRY IT OUT   Obtaining a Developer Certificate

In order to obtain a developer certificate, you need to generate a Certificate Signing Request (CSR). To generate a CSR, do the following on your Mac.

1. Launch the Keychain Access utility.

2. Choose Keychain Access ⇨ Preferences.

3. In the Certificates pane, set the Online Certificate Status Protocol and Certificate Revocation List to Off.

4. Close out the Preferences dialog box.

5. Choose Keychain Access ⇨ Certificate Assistant ⇨ Request a Certificate from a Certificate Authority. The Certificate Assistant opens (see Figure 19-2).

6. In the User Email Address box, type in the email address you used to register for the iOS Developer Program.

7. In the Common Name field, type in your name. Your name will be used as your private key in the Keychain Access utility.

8. Select the Saved to Disk option.

9. Check the Let Me Specify Key Pair Information checkbox.

FIGURE 19-2

10. Click Continue.

11. Save your `.certSigningRequest` file on your desktop.

12. In the Key Pair Information panel, select 2048bits in the Key Size drop-down box.

13. Choose RSA for the Algorithm.

14. Click Continue to generate the certificate request.

15. In your web browser, go to the iOS Provisioning Portal section of the iOS Dev Center: https://developer.apple.com/ios/manage/overview/index.action.

Figure 19-3 shows the main page of the iOS Provisioning Portal.

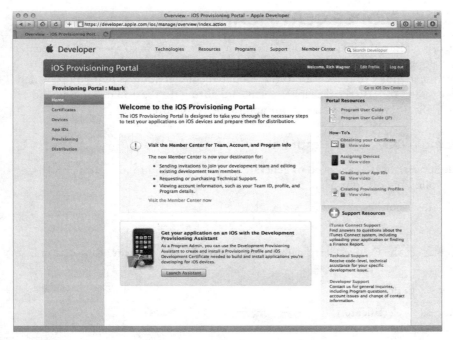

FIGURE 19-3

16. Click the Certificates link on the left.

17. Click the Request Certificate button.

18. Click the Choose File button on the Create iOS Development Certificate page and choose the `.certSigningRequest` file you just created on your desktop.

19. Click the Submit button.

How It Works

This process walks you through how to generate a certificate request and then submit it to Apple via the iOS Provisioning Portal online. The iOS Provisioning Portal location to which you will return to gets necessary credentials used to certify your app for iOS device installation. From here you can also manage members of your dev team, register devices used in testing, and create Provisioning Profiles used to code sign your app.

After your certificate request is submitted to Apple you receive an email notifying you that your request has been approved or denied. When your request is approved, you are able to download your developer certificate.

RETRIEVING THE DEVELOPER CERTIFICATE

When you receive an approval email you can go to the Program Portal to download the certificate. You download the developer certificate file (which is named `developer_identity.cer`) from Apple's iOS Provisioning Portal at `https://developer.apple.com/ios/manage/overview/index.action`.

Click the Certificates link to display the Current Development Certificates list. A certificate is shown in the list (see Figure 19-4). Click the Download button to retrieve the `developer_identity.cer` file.

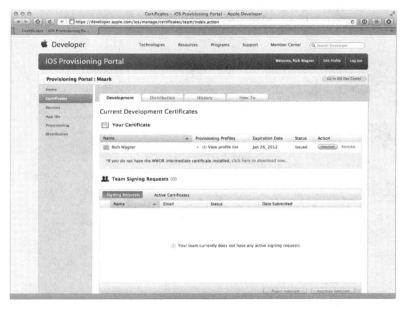

FIGURE 19-4

After you download the certificate, all you need to do is double-click the `developer_identity.cer` file to add it to the Keychain Access utility.

ADDING A DEVICE FOR TESTING

During the testing process, you should register your iOS device with the iOS Provisioning Portal to enable you to install apps you create onto the device for testing. Complete the following steps to register a device:

1. Connect your iOS device to your Mac using the USB cord.

2. Launch iTunes.

3. Display the Summary page for your iOS device.

4. Click the Serial Number displayed at the top to display the Unique Device Identifier (UDID).

5. Copy the UDID number to the Clipboard.

6. Go to the iOS Provisioning Portal at `https://developer.apple.com/ios/manage/overview/index.action`.

7. Click the Devices link and then click the Add Device button.

8. Type a descriptive name for the device in the space provided. From experience, I recommend making sure it is the name of the person and the type of device. That makes it much easier to manage than a name such as Amazing Phone of Wonder.

9. Paste the UDID of your device into the Device ID box.

10. Click Submit to add your device. The device is displayed in the list, as shown in Figure 19-5.

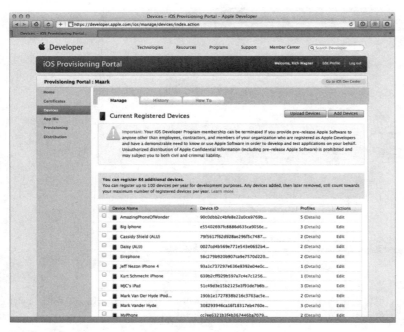

FIGURE 19-5

You can enter up to 100 devices annually for development and testing purposes.

CREATING AN APP ID

An App ID is used to uniquely identify your app as part of the provisioning and authentication process. It has two parts:

➤ The *Bundle Seed ID* is a 10-character prefix generated by Apple.

➤ The *Bundle Identifier* is a reverse-domain style string that you determine. It can contain standard alphanumeric characters (A–A, 0–9), periods, and hyphens.

For example, a typical App ID might look something like the following:

```
2MDCRUBLFG.com.richwagner.myamazingwebapp
```

To create an App ID for your app:

1. Go to the iOS Provisioning Portal at `https://developer.apple.com/ios/manage/ overview/index.action`.

2. Click the App IDs link.

3. Click the New App ID button to display the Create App ID page (see Figure 19-6).

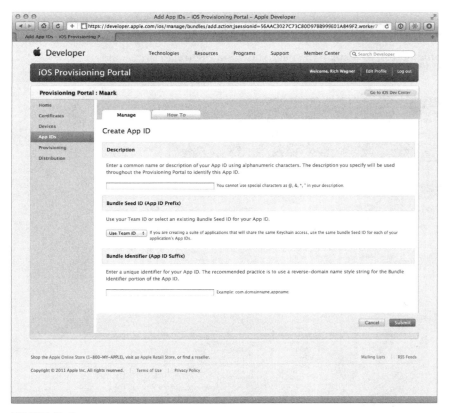

FIGURE 19-6

4. In the Description input box, enter a name or description of your app.

5. In the Bundle Seed ID drop-down box, select Use Team ID (the default item).

6. In the Bundle Identifier box, enter a reverse-domain name style string.

7. Click Submit to add the App ID.

CREATING A PROVISIONING PROFILE

If you have proceeded in order through the chapter, you have submitted and obtained a developer certificate, registered your iOS device for testing, and created an App ID. Now, you are ready to create the final and most important credential needed to install, run, and test your app on an iOS device — a Development Provisioning Profile.

TRY IT OUT: Obtaining a Development Provisioning Profile

To create a Development Provisioning Profile, follow these steps:

1. Go to the iOS Provisioning Portal at `https://developer.apple.com/ios/manage/overview/index.action`.

2. Click the Provisioning link.

3. Click the New Profile button to display the page shown in Figure 19-7.

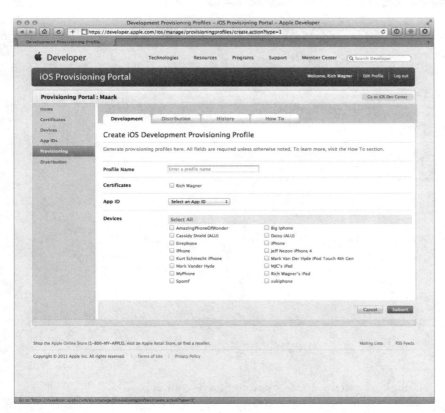

FIGURE 19-7

4. Type the name of the profile in the Profile Name box.

5. The name of your developer certificate (which you created earlier in the chapter) displays next to the Certificates label. Click the checkbox to assign your developer certificate to this profile.

6. Choose the App ID you created earlier in the App ID drop-down box.

7. Check all of the devices on which you want to be able to install your app for development and testing purposes.

8. Click the Submit button to create the Development Provisioning Profile.

9. Click the Download button next to the provisioning profile you just created to download the .mobileprovision file to your desktop. (You may have to wait a few seconds and refresh the page to see the Download button.)

How It Works

This exercise walks you through the process of creating a Development Provisioning Profile. A Development Provisioning Profile is used to tie together a developer certificate, a specific application, and a set of devices. You need to have a Development Provisioning Profile installed on each iOS device that runs your app. And you need to have a unique Development Provisioning Profile for every app you create.

INSTALLING THE DEVELOPMENT PROVISIONING PROFILE

As I stated earlier, a Development Provisioning Profile is a collection of digital credentials that ties an application and a testing device to a registered iOS developer. After you have the .mobileprovision file downloaded to your desktop, you need to install it in Xcode so it is ready to go when you need it.

Installing it is a quick, four-step process that doesn't require you to learn what pointers are or to make sense of Objective-C's strange programming syntax.

1. Launch Xcode. If this is the first time, you see a Welcome to Xcode window.

2. From the Window menu, choose Organizer.

3. Click the Devices button.

4. Drop the .mobileprovision file into the Library's Provisioning Profiles at the top left of the window (see Figure 19-8).

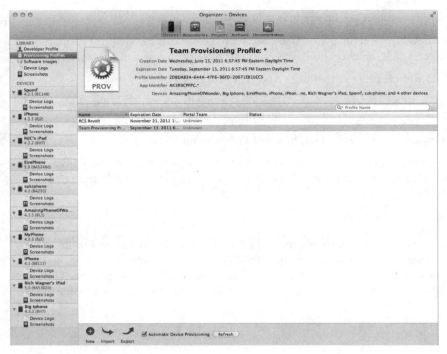

FIGURE 19-8

That's it! You have now gotten all of the busy work out of the way, so as you continue with Chapter 20, you can get back to wrapping your web app inside a native iOS shell.

EXERCISES

1.   What software is needed to create native iOS apps?

2.   Which is most important for installing your app onto your own iOS device for testing: a developer certificate, an App ID, device registration, or a Development Provisioning Profile?

3.   Can you use a Windows computer to create a native iOS app?

Answers to the Exercises can be found in Appendix A.

► **WHAT YOU LEARNED IN THIS CHAPTER**

TOPIC	KEY CONCEPTS
Joining the iOS Developer Program	Membership into the iOS Developer Program is required for installing, testing, and distributing native iOS apps.
Obtaining a Developer Certificate	A developer certificate ties your identity to a validated contact address that was provided to Apple when you registered.
Creating a Development Provisioning Profile	A Development Provisioning Profile is used to bind together a developer certificate, an app, and an iOS device (or devices). You need to have a Development Provisioning Profile installed on each iOS device that runs your app during testing.

20

PhoneGap: Native Apps from Your HTML, CSS, and JavaScript

WHAT YOU WILL LEARN IN THIS CHAPTER:

➤ Creating a PhoneGap project in Xcode

➤ Adding your web app code into PhoneGap

➤ Tweaking the project to fit your needs

Worlds collide. At least that's what happens when you use a tool like PhoneGap or one of its competing tools to combine native and web technologies. The solution is actually a quite ingenious solution for web developers: Get around the greatest limitations of an iOS web app by wrapping it in a native shell. The native wrapper enables you to make your app available on the App Store, enables users to install it on an iOS device's home screen, yet still enables you to keep the application UI and logic in the technology you want to utilize: HTML, CSS, and JavaScript.

In this chapter, I walk you through the steps to transform an iOS web app into a native app using PhoneGap. You don't have to know any Objective-C to pull it off, though you need to dive into the Xcode IDE to do everything you want to do.

INSTALLING PHONEGAP

If you worked through Chapter 19 already, you have already installed Xcode onto your development computer. If you haven't, be certain you do that before proceeding because the PhoneGap installer adds an application template to Xcode. Follow these steps:

1. Go to www.phonegap.com and download the latest release of PhoneGap.

2. Extract the contents of the zip file and then navigate to the iOS subdirectory to locate the iOS installer .dmg file.

3. Extract the `.dmg` file and then double-click the PhoneGap `.pkg` file launch the Installer.

4. Navigate through the steps in the Installer to install the tool onto your computer.

CREATING A NEW PHONEGAP PROJECT IN XCODE

With PhoneGap installed, you are ready to create a new project in Xcode.

TRY IT OUT **Creating a PhoneGap Project**

I walk you through how to take the Top Filmz app that you created in Chapter 4 and package it as a native iPhone app. Follow these steps:

1. Launch Xcode.

2. Choose File ➪ New Project from the menu.

3. In the template selection dialog box, click the PhoneGap-based Application (see Figure 20-1).

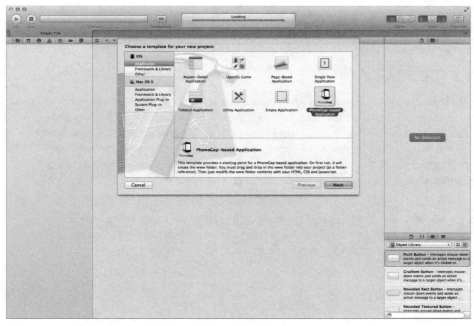

FIGURE 20-1

4. Click Next.

5. In the next dialog box (see Figure 20-2), enter the name of your project in the Product Name field. I am calling mine Top Filmz.

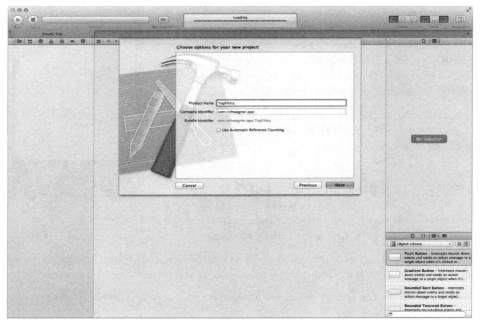

FIGURE 20-2

6. Enter a unique company id in a "reverse domain" syntax. I am using com.richwagner.app.

7. Uncheck the Use Automatic Reference Counting box. This is an important step with the current version of PhoneGap.

8. Click Next.

9. Choose a directory for your project.

10. Xcode creates your PhoneGap project and takes you to the IDE.

How It Works

When creating an iOS project using PhoneGap, you use the PhoneGap template to create all of the Objective-C "plumbing" you need to run your web app inside the native shell. In these steps, I showed you how to do that inside of Xcode.

RUNNING THE BASE PROJECT

Before continuing, you need to confirm that the Xcode part of your app is compiling and functioning correctly by running it inside of the iOS Simulator. Check out the Scheme combo box that lists your project name (e.g., Top Filmz) next to the targets on which to run the app on. Click the right-side of the Scheme combo box to display a list of deployment targets, including iPhone Simulators, iPad Simulators, and iOS devices. Select iPhone 5.0 Simulator or the latest iPhone version shown in the list. Click the Run button and the app is launched in the iOS Simulator (see Figure 20-3).

You'll receive an error message in the browser saying "Start page at 'www/index.html' was not found". That's to be expected, as you have not added the web files into the core app.

ADDING WEB FILES TO THE XCODE PROJECT

After you have the basic Xcode project running successfully, you are ready to add the web app to it by performing the following steps:

FIGURE 20-3

1. Go to Finder and locate the www folder in your project directory. This folder and its contents are included as part of the PhoneGap template that you used to create the Xcode project.

2. Drag the www folder from the Finder window onto the TopFilmz project in the Project Navigator pane in Xcode.

3. In the dialog that is displayed (see Figure 20-4), select the Create Folder References for Any Added Folders option.

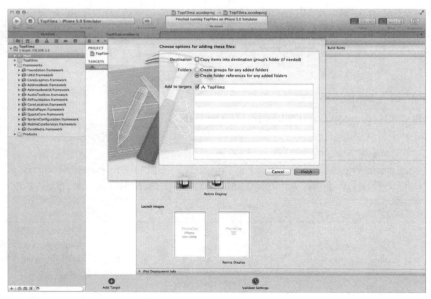

FIGURE 20-4

4. Make sure that the Copy Items into Destination Group's Folder box is unchecked.

5. Click Finish.

As shown in Figure 20-5, the Xcode project now has a direct link with the www folder.

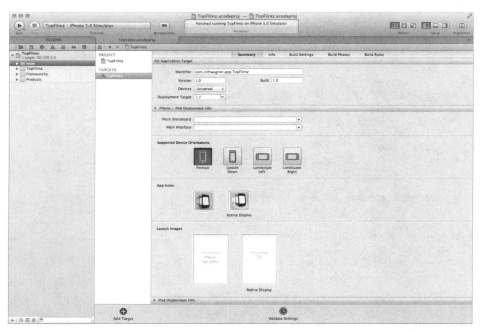

FIGURE 20-5

Click the Run button to run the app again in the iOS Simulator. Now that you have a connection with the www folder in the app, the Top Filmz app loads the dummy index.html file that is located in the directory and displays an alert box indicating success (see Figure 20-6).

MERGING YOUR WEB APP CODE

Now that you have the Xcode part of the puzzle working, you may be tempted to directly overwrite the default index.html file that is contained in the www folder with your own file and recompile. However, don't do that. The PhoneGap template index.html file contains essential HTML/JavaScript parts of a PhoneGap app, such as a reference to a PhoneGap JavaScript library file, default event handlers used to allow your app to work within the PhoneGap environment, and advanced event

FIGURE 20-6

handlers that you can uncomment if you want to utilize them in your app. The template `index.html` file is shown here:

```html
<!DOCTYPE html>
<html>
  <head>
  <title></title>

    <meta name="viewport" content="width=device-width,
      initial-scale=1.0, maximum-scale=1.0, user-scalable=no;" />
    <meta charset="utf-8">


    <!-- iPad/iPhone specific css below, add after your main css >
    <link rel="stylesheet"
      media="only screen and (max-device-width: 1024px)"
      href="ipad.css" type="text/css" />
    <link rel="stylesheet"
      media="only screen and (max-device-width: 480px)"
      href="iphone.css" type="text/css" />
    -->
    <!-- If your application is targeting iOS BEFORE 4.0 you MUST put json2.js
     from http://www.JSON.org/json2.js into your www directory and include
     it here -->
    <script type="text/javascript" charset="utf-8" src="phonegap-1.1.0.js">
    </script>
    <script type="text/javascript">


    // If you want to prevent dragging, uncomment this section
    /*
    function preventBehavior(e)
    {
      e.preventDefault();
    };
    document.addEventListener("touchmove", preventBehavior, false);
    */
        /* If you are supporting your own protocol, the var invokeString will
           contain any arguments to the app launch. See
           http://iphonedevelopertips.com/cocoa/launching-your-own-
           application-via-a-custom-url-scheme.html
           for more details -jm */
    /*
    function handleOpenURL(url)
    {
        // TODO: do something with the url passed in.
    }
    */

    function onBodyLoad()
    {
        document.addEventListener("deviceready", onDeviceReady, false);
    }

    /* When this function is called, PhoneGap has been initialized and is
```

```
       ready to roll */
    /* If you are supporting your own protocol, the var invokeString will
     contain any arguments to the app launch.
    see http://iphonedevelopertips.com/cocoa/launching-your-own-application-
    via-a-custom-url-scheme.html
    for more details -jm */
    function onDeviceReady()
    {
        // do your thing!
        navigator.notification.alert("PhoneGap is working")
    }

    </script>
</head>
<body onload="onBodyLoad()">
    <h1>Hey, it's PhoneGap!</h1>
    <p>Don't know how to get started? Check out <em><a target="_blank"
        href="http://www.phonegap.com/start#ios-x4">PhoneGap Start</a></em>
    <br />
    <ol>
        <li>Check your console log for any white-list rejection errors.</li>
        <li>Add your allowed hosts in PhoneGap.plist/ExternalHosts (wildcards OK)
        </li>
    </ol>
</body>
</html>
```

TRY IT OUT   **Migrating Your Web App to PhoneGap**

Follow the steps in this section to insert the essential parts of the Top Filmz `index.html` into the existing PhoneGap `index.html` file.

1. In Xcode (or your favorite editor), open the `index.html` file in your www folder.

2. Insert the header declarations from the Top Filmz file into the `index.html` file:

```
<!DOCTYPE html>
    <link rel="stylesheet"
        href="http://code.jquery.com/mobile/1.0b3/jquery.mobile-1.0b3.min.css" />
    <script type="text/javascript"
        src="http://code.jquery.com/jquery-1.6.3.min.js"></script>
    <script type="text/javascript"
        src="http://code.jquery.com/mobile/1.0b3/jquery.mobile-1.0b3.min.js"/>
    <style>
    img.poster
    {
        display: block;
        margin-left: auto;
        margin-right: auto;
    }
    </style>
```

Code snippet BIDHJ-Ch20-Ex1.html

3. Replace the existing boilerplate text in the body with the body code in the Top Filmz file.

4. Save the updated file.

5. Top Filmz app doesn't have any supporting CSS, JS, or image files, but if your app had them you would copy them into www folder now.

How It Works

In this exercise, you added the web app code into the PhoneGap template. Although you want to replace the body content in the PhoneGap template, you want to keep the header code intact to ensure that the app functions properly in the PhoneGap project. The full source code is shown below.

```
<!DOCTYPE html>
<!DOCTYPE html>
<html>
  <head>
  <title>Top Filmz</title>

    <meta name="viewport"
    content="width=device-width, initial-scale=1.0, maximum-scale=1.0,
    user-scalable=no;" />
    <!--meta charset="utf-8"-->

    <link href="http://code.jquery.com/mobile/latest/jquery.mobile.min.css"
       rel="stylesheet" type="text/css" />
    <script src="http://code.jquery.com/jquery-1.6.2.min.js"></script>
    <script src="http://code.jquery.com/mobile/latest/jquery.mobile.min.js">
     </script>


    <style>
    img.poster
    {
        display: block;
        margin-left: auto;
        margin-right: auto
    }
    </style>

    <!-- iPad/iPhone specific css below, add after your main css >
    <link rel="stylesheet" media="only screen and (max-device-width: 1024px)"
     href="ipad.css" type="text/css" />
    <link rel="stylesheet" media="only screen and (max-device-width: 480px)"
     href="iphone.css" type="text/css" />
    -->
    <!-- If your application is targeting iOS BEFORE 4.0 you MUST put json2.js
      from http://www.JSON.org/json2.js into your www directory and include it
      here -->
    <script type="text/javascript" charset="utf-8" src="phonegap-1.1.0.js">
    </script>
    <script type="text/javascript">

    // If you want to prevent dragging, uncomment this section
    /*
```

```
    function preventBehavior(e)
    {
      e.preventDefault();
    };
    document.addEventListener("touchmove", preventBehavior, false);
    */

    /* If you are supporting your own protocol, the var invokeString will
    contain any arguments to the app launch.
    see http://iphonedevelopertips.com/cocoa/launching-your-own-application-via-a-
    custom-url-scheme.html for more details -jm */
    /*
    function handleOpenURL(url)
    {
        // TODO: do something with the url passed in.
    }
    */

    function onBodyLoad()
    {
        document.addEventListener("deviceready", onDeviceReady, false);
    }

    /* When this function is called, PhoneGap has been initialized and is ready
       to roll */
    /* If you are supporting your own protocol, the var invokeString will
       contain any arguments to the app launch.
       see http://iphonedevelopertips.com/cocoa/launching-your-own-application-via-
       a-custom-url-scheme.html for more details -jm */
    function onDeviceReady()
    {
        // do your thing!
        //navigator.notification.alert("PhoneGap is working")
    }

    </script>



  </head>
  <body onload="onBodyLoad()">

<!-- Page -->
<div data-role="page" id="home">
    <div data-role="header">
        <h1>Top Filmz</h1>
    </div>

    <div data-role="content">
        <ul data-role="listview" data-theme="b">
            <li><a href="#theShawshankRemption">The Shawshank Redemption</a></li>
            <li><a href="#casablanca">Casablanca</a></li>
```

```
            <li><a href="#larsAndTheRealGirl">Lars and the Real Girl</a></li>
            <li><a href="#babettesFeast">Babette's Feast</a></li>
            <li><a href="#groundhogDay">Groundhog Day</a></li>
            <li><a href="#lesMiserables">Les Miserables</a></li>
            <li><a href="#thePrincessBride">The Princess Bride</a></li>
            <li><a href="#chariotsOfFire">Chariots of Fire</a></li>
            <li><a href="#signs">Signs</a></li>
            <li><a href="#vertigo">Vertigo</a></li>
        </ul>
    </div>

    <div data-role="footer">
        <h5>Hello World Apps</h5>
    </div>
</div>


<!-- Subpages -->

<div data-role="page" id="theShawshankRemption">
    <div data-role="header">
        <h1>The Shawshank Redemption</h1>
    </div>
    <div data-role="content" style="background-color:#ffffff">
        <img class="poster"
          src="http://ecx.images-amazon.com/images/I/
          519NBNHX5BL._SL500_AA300_.jpg"/>
        <a href="http://www.imdb.com/title/tt0111161/"
          data-role="button">Go to IMDB Page</a>
        <a href="#home" data-role="button" data-icon="home">Return to List</a>
    </div>
    <div data-role="footer">
        <h5>Hello World Apps</h5>
    </div>
</div>

<div data-role="page" id="casablanca">
    <div data-role="header">
        <h1>Casablanca</h1>
    </div>
    <div data-role="content" style="background-color:#ffffff">
        <img class="poster"
          src="http://ecx.images-amazon.com/images/I/
          51Mg3kdJ5KL._SL500_AA300_.jpg"/>
        <a href="http://www.imdb.com/title/tt0034583/"
          data-role="button">Go to IMDB Page</a>
        <a href="#home" data-role="button" data-icon="home">Return to List</a>
    </div>
    <div data-role="footer">
        <h5>Hello World Apps</h5>
    </div>
</div>

<div data-role="page" id="larsAndTheRealGirl">
```

```
        <div data-role="header">
            <h1>Lars and the Real Girl</h1>
        </div>
        <div data-role="content" style="background-color:#ffffff">
            <img class="poster"
             src="http://ecx.images-amazon.com/images/I/
             51Sn3wcuNGL._SL500_AA300_.jpg"/>
            <a href="http://www.imdb.com/title/tt0805564/"
               data-role="button">Go to IMDB Page</a>
            <a href="#home" data-role="button" data-icon="home">Return to List</a>
        </div>
        <div data-role="footer">
            <h5>Hello World Apps</h5>
        </div>
</div>

<div data-role="page" id="babettesFeast">
    <div data-role="header">
        <h1>Babette's Feast</h1>
    </div>
    <div data-role="content" style="background-color:#ffffff">
        <img class="poster"
         src="http://ecx.images-amazon.com/images/I/
         51A2BJ1WTML._SL500_AA300_.jpg"/>
        <a href="http://www.imdb.com/title/tt0092603/"
         data-role="button">Go to IMDB Page</a>
        <a href="#home" data-role="button" data-icon="home">Return to List</a>
    </div>
    <div data-role="footer">
        <h5>Hello World Apps</h5>
    </div>
</div>


<div data-role="page" id="groundhogDay">
    <div data-role="header">
        <h1>Groundhog Day</h1>
    </div>
    <div data-role="content" style="background-color:#ffffff">
        <img class="poster"
          src="http://ecx.images-amazon.com/images/I/
          51EVxBEKg6L._SL500_AA300_.jpg"/>
        <a href="http://www.imdb.com/title/tt0107048/"
          data-role="button">Go to IMDB Page</a>
        <a href="#home" data-role="button" data-icon="home">Return to List</a>
    </div>
    <div data-role="footer">
        <h5>Hello World Apps</h5>
    </div>
</div>

<div data-role="page" id="lesMiserables">
    <div data-role="header">
        <h1>Les Miserables</h1>
```

```
        </div>
    <div data-role="content" style="background-color:#ffffff">
        <img class="poster"
          src="http://ecx.images-amazon.com/images/I/
          51MeImdd92L._SL500_AA300_.jpg"/>
        <a href="http://www.imdb.com/title/tt0119683/"
          data-role="button">Go to IMDB Page</a>
        <a href="#home" data-role="button" data-icon="home">Return to List</a>
    </div>
    <div data-role="footer">
        <h5>Hello World Apps</h5>
    </div>
</div>

<div data-role="page" id="thePrincessBride">
    <div data-role="header">
        <h1>The Princess Bride</h1>
    </div>
    <div data-role="content" style="background-color:#ffffff">
        <img class="poster"
         src="http://ecx.images-amazon.com/images/I/
         51%2BOCP1DUSL._SL500_AA300_.jpg"/>
        <a href="http://www.imdb.com/title/tt0093779/"
         data-role="button">Go to IMDB Page</a>
        <a href="#home" data-role="button" data-icon="home">Return to List</a>
    </div>
    <div data-role="footer">
        <h5>Hello World Apps</h5>
    </div>
</div>


<div data-role="page" id="chariotsOfFire">
    <div data-role="header">
        <h1>Chariots of Fire</h1>
    </div>
    <div data-role="content" style="background-color:#ffffff">
        <img class="poster"
          src="http://ecx.images-amazon.com/images/I/
          51PyP5bti7L._SL500_AA300_.jpg"/>
        <a href="http://www.imdb.com/title/tt0082158/"
          data-role="button">Go to IMDB Page</a>
        <a href="#home" data-role="button" data-icon="home">Return to List</a>
    </div>
    <div data-role="footer">
        <h5>Hello World Apps</h5>
    </div>
</div>

<div data-role="page" id="signs">
    <div data-role="header">
        <h1>Signs</h1>
    </div>
    <div data-role="content" style="background-color:#ffffff">
```

```
        <img class="poster"
          src="http://ecx.images-amazon.com/images/I/
          51c02AOAyCL._SL500_AA300_.jpg"/>
        <a href="http://www.imdb.com/title/tt0286106/"
         data-role="button">Go to IMDB Page</a>
        <a href="#home" data-role="button" data-icon="home">Return to List</a>
    </div>
    <div data-role="footer">
        <h5>Hello World Apps</h5>
    </div>
</div>

<div data-role="page" id="vertigo">
    <div data-role="header">
        <h1>Vertigo</h1>
    </div>
    <div data-role="content" style="background-color:#ffffff">
        <img class="poster"
          src="http://ecx.images-amazon.com/images/I/
          51JF1C6DF5L._SL500_AA300_.jpg"/>
        <a href="http://www.imdb.com/title/tt0052357/"
          data-role="button">Go to IMDB Page</a>
        <a href="#home" data-role="button" data-icon="home">Return to List</a>
    </div>
    <div data-role="footer">
        <h5>Hello World Apps</h5>
    </div>
</div>

    </body>
</html>
```

Code snippet BIDHJ-Ch20-Ex1.html

TWEAKING THE XCODE PROJECT

Although you could compile the Xcode project and run it in the iOS Simulator, you would find that the app would neither function nor look as you expect. That's because you need to make some additional tweaks and adjustments in the PhoneGap project in Xcode.

Allowing External References

Recall from Chapter 4 that Top Filmz uses jQuery Mobile as its UI framework, which is integrated into the app through three external links — one CSS style sheet and two JS files. It also references movie poster images located on an external server. However, in order for PhoneGap to allow an external domain, you need to explicitly add it to the PhoneGap white list by doing the following:

1. In the Xcode Project Navigator, locate the `PhoneGap.plist` file in the TopFilmz ⇨ Supporting Files folder.

2. In the key-value pairs displayed in Xcode, locate the External Hosts key.

3. Click the + button next to the External Hosts key and enter `*.jquery.com` in the value field.

4. Click the + button again next to the External Hosts key and enter `*.images-amazon.com` in the value field.

5. Choose File ⇨ Save to save results.

Figure 20-7 shows the added domains.

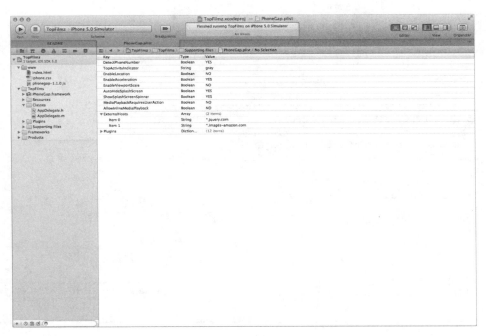

FIGURE 20-7

Opening External Links in Safari

Each of the movie detail pages of the Top Filmz app contains a button to jump to the film's IMDb page listing. However, within an app environment, suppose I'd prefer to jump to Safari on iOS for those external links rather than being inside the app itself. I can make a second tweak to examine the web links that are clicked and route it to the appropriate app. For internal app links I keep within the PhoneGap app. For external links, I call Safari to display them.

In order to do this, you need to modify an Objective-C method. However, you only need to copy and paste the code. Here's how to do this:

1. In the Xcode Project Navigator, locate the `AppDelegate.m` file inside of the TopFilmz ⇨ Classes folder.

2. Locate the `shouldStartLoadWithRequest` method:

```
(BOOL)webView:(UIWebView *)theWebView
    shouldStartLoadWithRequest:(NSURLRequest *)request
            navigationType:(UIWebViewNavigationType)navigationType
```

3. Replace the existing method code with the following updated source code:

```
(BOOL)webView:(UIWebView *)theWebView
    shouldStartLoadWithRequest:(NSURLRequest *)request
            navigationType:(UIWebViewNavigationType)navigationType
{
  NSURL *url = [request URL];

  // If external URL, use Safari
  if ([[url scheme] isEqualToString:@"http"] ||
   [[url scheme] isEqualToString:@"https"])
  {
    [[UIApplication sharedApplication] openURL:url];
    return NO;
  }
  // Otherwise, treat as internal link
  else
  {
    return [ super webView:theWebView
    shouldStartLoadWithRequest:request navigationType:navigationType ];
  }

}
```

4. Save the file.

Adding an Icon and Launch Image

Your final step is to create an app icon and launch image. The icon is obviously used for the home screen, and the launch image is displayed when the app loads. Because you need to provide support for both Retina Display (4 and higher) and standard (3GS and lower), the files should be according the following specifications:

➤ Standard icon 57 × 57, named `Icon.png`

➤ Retina Display icon 114 × 114, named `Icon@2x.png`

➤ Standard launch image 320 × 480, named `Default.png`

➤ Retina Display launch image 640 × 960, named `Default@2x.png`

After you have these created according these standard size and naming conventions, replace the canned files that PhoneGap already added by overwriting them in your project folder. Figure 20-8 shows the Summary page with the updated images.

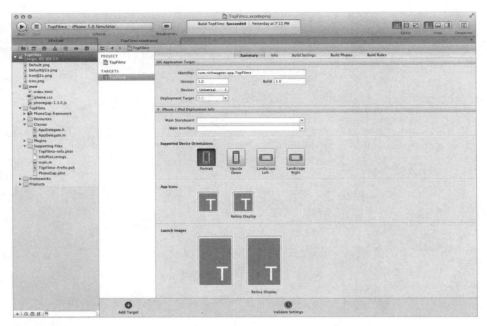

FIGURE 20-8

RUNNING THE FINISHED APP

When you have made all of the final adjustments, you are ready to test your finished app. Click the Run button in Xcode and run the app in iOS Simulator. Figure 20-9 shows the app when it loads, and Figure 20-10 shows the app running.

FIGURE 20-9   **FIGURE 20-10**

EXERCISES

1. True/False. When adding your web app code to the PhoneGap project, you should overwrite the existing `index.html` file that is supplied by PhoneGap.

2. Why won't a PhoneGap web app access an external resource by default?

3. What are the naming conventions and the dimensions of the icon and launch images used for your app?

Answers to the Exercises can be found in Appendix A.

▶ **WHAT YOU LEARNED IN THIS CHAPTER**

TOPIC	KEY CONCEPTS
Installing PhoneGap	Download and install PhoneGap *after* you have installed Xcode
Create a PhoneGap project	Use the PhoneGap-based Application template when you create a new Xcode project
Merging your web app code	Insert your code into the PhoneGap boilerplate `index.html` file

21

Submitting Your App to the App Store

WHAT YOU WILL LEARN IN THIS CHAPTER:

➤ Getting a distribution certificate

➤ Obtaining a distribution provisioning profile

➤ Publishing your app to the App Store

If you have made it this far, you've designed, coded, and tested your web app, and you've wrapped it in PhoneGap or Titanium for native distribution. As a final step, you're ready to distribute your app to others by publishing it to the App Store. In this chapter, I show you how to do that.

However, before you submit your app to the App Store, you need to check out the App Store Review Guidelines, which tells you what Apple considers when determining whether or not to approve an app. Sign in with your Apple ID, and then find the guidelines at `https://developer.apple.com/appstore/resources/approval/guidelines.html`. When you are satisfied that your app meets the guidelines you're ready to begin the four-step submission process described in this chapter.

 NOTE *Be sure to read Chapters 19 and 20 before you work through this chapter.*

STEP 1: GETTING A DISTRIBUTION CERTIFICATE

iOS apps must be signed by a valid certificate before they can be run on an iPhone, iPad, or iPod touch. Similar to what you did when you obtained a developer certificate to develop and install your apps on your own device for testing, you need to get a distribution certificate that is used when building the app for your published release.

TRY IT OUT Obtaining a Distribution Certificate

The following steps outline how to get a distribution certificate from the iOS Dev Center.

1. Log in to the iOS Dev Center at `http://developer.apple.com`.

2. Click the iOS Provisioning Portal link. The iOS Provisioning Portal page is displayed, as shown in Figure 21-1.

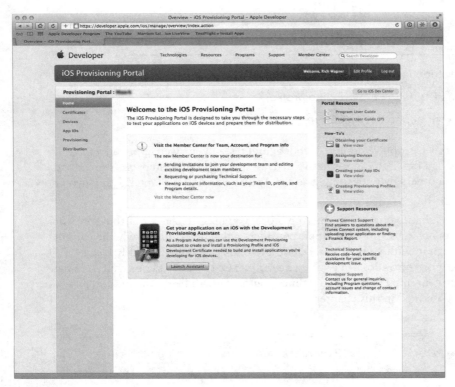

FIGURE 21-1

3. Click the Certificates link on the left sidebar.

4. Click the Distribution tab. A list of existing certificates is displayed (see Figure 21-2).

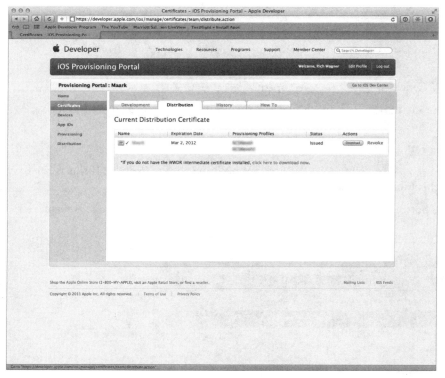

FIGURE 21-2

5. If you have a certificate ready, click the Download button. If you don't, follow the instructions to create one. After it is created, then you can download the `developer_identity.cer` file and continue.

6. When you have downloaded it, double-click the `developer_identity.cer` file to add it to your Mac OS X keychain.

How It Works

You obtain the distribution certificate directly from the iOS Dev Center through its Provisioning Portal. After you download it, you need to make it available by adding it to your Mac OS X keychain. When you've done that, you can use the distribution certificate for code signing when you publish your app.

STEP 2: CREATING A DISTRIBUTION PROVISIONING PROFILE

After you have added the certificate to your keychain, you are ready to obtain a Distribution Provisioning Profile. A Distribution Provisioning Profile is a collection of digital entities that uniquely ties an application to a registered iOS developer. Although a Developer Provisioning Profile includes actual device GUIDs for testing, the Distribution Provisioning Profile does not include device info.

Obtaining a Distribution Provisioning Profile

A Distribution Provisioning Profile is much like your app's passport and is required for entry into the App Store. Here's how to download your own Distribution Provisioning Profile from the iOS Dev Center.

1. Log in to the iOS Dev Center at `http://developer.apple.com`.

2. Click the iOS Provisioning Portal link. The iOS Provisioning Portal page is displayed (refer to Figure 21-1).

3. Click the Provisioning link on the left sidebar.

4. Click the Distribution tab to display the list of Distribution Provisioning Profiles. If this is the first time you've selected this tab, you'll find this area blank.

5. Click the New Profile button. The Create iOS Distribution Provisioning Profile page is displayed. (See Figure 21-3.)

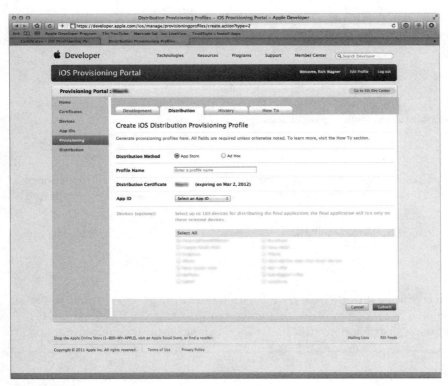

FIGURE 21-3

6. Fill out the profile form for the app you want to submit and click the Submit button when you are done. The Provisioning Profile is added to your list with a Pending status.

7. Give Apple a few moments to process your request and then refresh the browser to see the profile status changed to Active.

8. Click the Download button to download the `.mobileprovision` file.

9. Save this file to your hard drive.

10. Launch Xcode and display the Organizer window.

11. Drop the `.mobileprovision` file into the Library's Provisioning Profiles (see Figure 21-4).

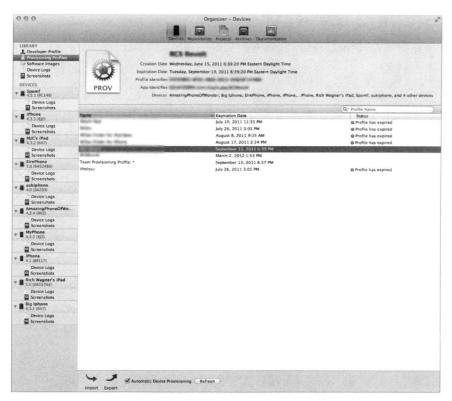

FIGURE 21-4

How It Works

The Provisioning Profile is used by Xcode when you build your app for code signing. In order to publish to the App Store, the `.ipa` file you build needs have a Distribution Provisioning Profile, which is obtained from the iOS Dev Center. After you've downloaded and dropped the file into Xcode you can use it to code sign your app's `.ipa` file.

STEP 3: BUILDING A DISTRIBUTION RELEASE OF YOUR APP

Now that you have all the preliminaries completed and your credentials in order, you are ready to publish the final distribution release of your native iOS app.

TRY IT OUT   Publishing a Distribution Release

Use the following steps to build an archive that will be submitted to the App Store.

1. Open your app's project in Xcode. (You created this in Chapter 20.)

2. Click the project in the Project Navigator.

3. Click the Project item in the list to display the project settings (see Figure 21-5).

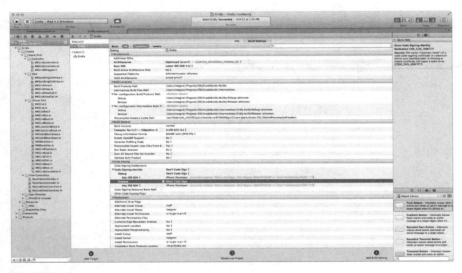

FIGURE 21-5

4. In the Code Signing section, click the Release drop-down box and then select your Distribution Provisioning Profile from the list.

5. From the Product menu, choose the Archive menu item. (If Archive is disabled, make sure that your configuration is set to iOS Device, not a simulator.)

6. The Organizer is displayed showing the Archives section. (See Figure 21-6.)

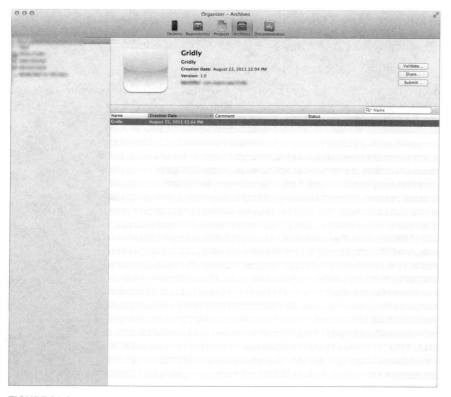

FIGURE 21-6

How It Works

When you perform these actions, you build an archive file. In the next section, you take this archive file and submit it to the App Store.

STEP 4: SUBMITTING YOUR APP TO THE APP STORE

After you have your app compiled and ready to go, it is time for the Big Finish: submitting your app to the App Store. Once reviewed and approved by Apple, anyone will be able to download your app through the App Store.

TRY IT OUT Submitting to the App Store

Follow these steps to submit your app to the Apple App Store.

1. Log in to the iOS Dev Center at `http://developer.apple.com`.

2. Click the iTunes Connect link. You are taken to the iTunes Connect website, as shown in Figure 21-7. This is the website that you use for managing your store content.

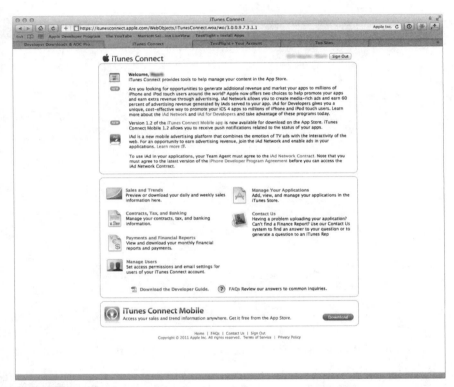

FIGURE 21-7

You can also go directly there at `https://itunesconnect.apple.com`.

3. Click the Manage Your Applications link.

4. Click the Add a New App link.

5. Add info about your app on the App Information page.

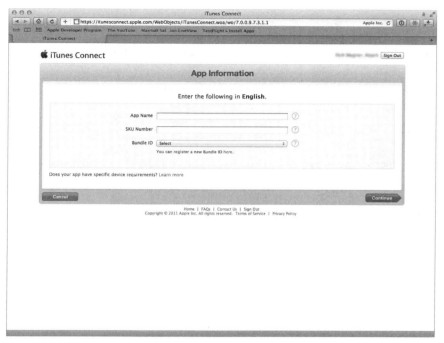

FIGURE 21-8

6. Enter the name of your app in the App Name box.

7. Enter a unique number to identify your app. This value isn't a version number; it's a way to differentiate between multiple apps you submit.

8. Select your provisioning profile from the list and then click Continue.

9. Enter additional details about the app, including availability date, price, and so on. Click Continue.

10. Enter meta data about the app in the next page. As part of this process, you will need to assign a content rating for your app.

11. In the Uploads section, provide a 512 × 512 icon and at least one screenshot.

12. Click Save.

13. Return to Xcode and go to the Organizer window.

14. Select your archive and click the Validate button. This feature is sort of a presubmission check for you to ensure that your app passes basic tests that Apple puts your app through.

15. Follow the steps in the dialog box to validate your app. If you are not successful then modify your app based on the test results. If you are successful then continue.

16. Click the Submit button to submit your app to the App Store.

17. Follow the instructions for uploading and submitting your app to the App Store.

How It Works

You just walked through the final, critical stage of submitting your app to the App Store. That's it! You now just have to wait for Apple to review your app over the next week or weeks before it is officially available.

1. Do you need a different certificate and Provisioning Profile for distribution when you already have one for testing?

2. What is a release build of your project called in Xcode?

3. When you submit your app to the App Store, is it available right away for the public?

Answers to the Exercises can be found in Appendix A.

▶ **WHAT YOU LEARNED IN THIS CHAPTER**

TOPIC	KEY CONCEPTS
Distribution Certificate	iOS apps must be signed by a valid certificate before they can be run on an Apple device.
Distribution Provisioning Profile	A Provisioning Profile is a collection of digital entities that uniquely ties an application to a registered iOS developer.

APPENDIX

Exercise Answers

CHAPTER 1

1. A native app runs executable code on the device and is installable through the App Store. A web app runs inside of Safari on iOS and requires no installation onto the device. A native app is written in Objective-C whereas a web app is written using HTML, CSS, JavaScript, and AJAX.

2. Yes. A user can add a web app to the Home screen through the Safari menu.

3. A finger can emulate normal mouse actions — a click, scroll, and mouse move. However, it also has additional touch-related actions that have no mouse equivalent, including a tap, flick, drag, and pinch.

CHAPTER 2

1. Use `var` to declare a keyword, such as `var index = 0;`.

2. A local variable is accessible only inside a JavaScript function, whereas a global variable is accessible anywhere in the document.

3. The `=` assigns a value whereas the `==` operator is used to compare whether two values are equal.

4. `!=`

5. The basic structure of a `for` loop looks something like:

```
for (var i=0;i<10;i++)
{
    // Do something here
}
```

6. Use `arguments.length` to determine to the total number of parameters passed to a function.

7. No. JavaScript treats an empty string as a different value than `null`.

CHAPTER 3

1. The *node* is the basic component of the DOM.

2. False. A DOM hierarchy is not exactly the same as the element hierarchy that is shown in an HTML document. For example, attributes and text content of an element are child nodes of that element rather than being a descriptor of it.

3. A NodeList is a collection of nodes.

4. A *document fragment* is a temporary "off-line" document that you can use to create and modify part of a tree before you add the fragment to the actual DOM tree.

CHAPTER 4

1. The advantage of using a mobile framework like jQuery Mobile is that it automates many of styling and scripting parts of your mobile app. You can even optimized it for both iPhone and iPad devices without any changes on your part.

2. No, you can store them in separate `div` elements in the same page, demarking them with a `data-role="page"` attribute.

3. You can link to another virtual page by referencing the destination page's unique id in an `href` attribute, prefixed with a # symbol (`href="#mypage"`).

CHAPTER 5

1. No, iOS devices do not support Adobe Flash.

2. A *viewport* is a rectangular area of screen space within which a web page is displayed. It determines how content is displayed and scaled to fit onto the iPhone or iPad.

3. The `device-width` constant is treated as 320px on an iPhone and 1024px on an iPad.

4. Columns make your page readable like a newspaper and help you avoid wide blocks of text that cause users to horizontally scroll left and right to read.

5. It is recommended that your iPad media query look like the following:

```
<link
  media="only screen and (min-device-width: 768px) and (max-device-width: 1024px)"
  type="text/css" rel="stylesheet" href="iPad.css" />
```

CHAPTER 6

1. Edge-to-edge navigation lists are the standard way to present list or hierarchical information.

2. It is generally recommended that you size your UI element by 40 pixels or more for ease of touch.

3. False. You won't find it on an iOS device.

4. False. Web apps have no control over screen orientation. Therefore, your design must accommodate both portrait and landscape orientations.

CHAPTER 7

1. False. Your iPad web app should include a `viewport` meta tag.

2. Trick question. They are equally important in nearly every case, so your design should account for both.

3. You can use iScroll library or other similar open-source solutions to overcome this Safari on iOS limitation.

CHAPTER 8

1. Safari on iOS supports most of the properties that are prefixed with `-webkit-` before their names.

2. For a normal website, `-webkit-text-size-adjust: auto` is recommended for improving the readability of text. However, if you are developing an application, you almost always want to use `-webkit-text-size-adjust: none`.

3. Use the `-webkit-border-image` property.

CHAPTER 9

1. You can link to a `div`, `ul`, or `form` container in the same page by referencing its `id` as an anchor (for example, `#mylist`).

2. You can create a link and add `target="_replace"` as an attribute. iUI loads the items from the URL replacing the current link.

3. The answer ultimately depends on your target audience, but generally speaking, you need to design your app using a framework that is compatible for both iPhone and iPad — and, depending on your audience, Android as well.

CHAPTER 10

1. Mouse emulation, touch, and gesture events.

2. No, there are several touch interactions that are handled for you by default by Safari on iOS. These include flick-scrolling, zoom pinching and unpinching, and one-finger panning (or scrolling).

3. The `body` element's `onorientationchange` event.

CHAPTER 11

1. The `context` object, obtained from the `canvas` object's `getContext()` method.

2. To create a reflection, use the `-webkit-box-reflect` property.

3. The `save()` method saves a snapshot of the canvas, which can then be retrieved using the `restore()` method. The `save()` and `restore()` methods enable you to return to a default drawing state with minimal additional code and without needing to painstakingly re-create every setting.

CHAPTER 12

1. Because different iOS devices have different hardware capabilities (e.g., phone, GPS, camera), you should identify the device type when you are trying to access an iOS service to ensure that the device can support the request.

2. You should use the following URL protocols:

Phone number: `tel:`

Email message: `mailto:`

SMS: `sms:`

3. Yes. On iPhone, the `maps.google.com` link takes you to the native Maps app. On iPod touch, the same link takes you to web-based Google site in Safari.

CHAPTER 13

1. A bookmarklet uses the `javascript:` protocol followed by script code.

2. The `data:` protocol enables you to encode an entire page's content — HTML, CSS, JavaScript, and images — inside a single URL.

3. If you are going to use images in a data URL then you need to encode them first.

CHAPTER 14

1. The user agent string of an iPad has the text `iPad` in its platform string portion.

2. *Stroking* refers to drawing a line on a path, whereas *filling* is the painting of an area inside a path.

3. A path is composed of a series of subpaths, such as a straight line or an arc, that together form a shape.

4. You can draw an encoded image to eliminate the need for an external image file for canvas drawing.

CHAPTER 15

1. A manifest file is a text file used to list the files you want to store in an offline cache.

2. Yes, make sure your server assigns the MIME type `text/cache-manifest` to the `manifest` extension.

3. Although cookies are sent back to the server, saved key-value data is not unless you explicitly do so through JavaScript. You also have greater control over the data persistence and window access to that data using key-value storage.

CHAPTER 16

1. The more important cross-platform is to you, the less you are typically able to provide a native iOS-like experience. jQuery Mobile is cross-platform whereas iWebKit is focused on iOS-specific look and feel.

2. jQuery Mobile.

CHAPTER 17

1. Yes. Loading additional files take 60% to 90% of the total load time an HTML page.

2. The longer your identifiers are, the more space your files take. Don't go to extremes, though, and make them so short that they become hard to work with.

3. `getElementById()` is more efficient than using dot notation.

CHAPTER 18

1. `alert()` debugging is the use of `alert()` dialog boxes to display the current state of your code. The problem is that it is not only inefficient, but it can also throw off the timing of your script, making it difficult or impossible to simulate real-world results.

2. You can enable the Develop menu in the Preferences dialog box of Safari.

3.   Enable the Debug Console through Settings ➪ Safari ➪ Developer. Once enabled, the Debug Console is displayed below the URL bar when an error occurs.

CHAPTER 19

1.   Xcode, which is available for free from the Mac App Store.

2.   All of the above. The Development Provisioning Profile is installed onto the iOS device itself, but it requires each of the other components.

3.   Sorry, Windows fans. For better or worse, Xcode only runs on Mac OS X.

CHAPTER 20

1.   False. Add your existing code to the `index.html` that comes with PhoneGap.

2.   If you want to access an external resource, you need to add it to the project's External Hosts white list in `PhoneGap.plist`.

3.   Icons: `Icon.png` (57 × 57), `Icon@2x.png` (114 × 114)

   Launch: `Default.png` (320 × 480), `Default@2x.png` (640 × 960)

CHAPTER 21

1.   Yes, you need to create a new certificate and Provisioning Profile for distribution.

2.   An archive.

3.   No. The review process by Apple can take days or even weeks.

INDEX